The Contemporary Superintendent

A volume in
Research on the Superintendency
Meredith Mountford and Leigh E. Wallace, *Series Editors*

The Contemporary Superintendent

(R)Evolutionary Leadership in an Era of Reform

edited by

Meredith Mountford

Florida Atlantic University

Leigh E. Wallace

University of Wisconsin-Milwaukee

INFORMATION AGE PUBLISHING, INC.
Charlotte, NC • www.infoagepub.com

Library of Congress Cataloging-in-Publication Data

Names: Mountford, Meredith, editor. | Wallace, Leigh (Leigh E.), editor.
Title: The contemporary superintendent : (r)evolutionary leadership in an era
  of reform / edited by Meredith Mountford, Leigh E. Wallace.
Description: Charlotte, NC : Information Age Publishing, Inc., [2019] |
  Series: Research on the superintendency | Includes bibliographical
  references.
Identifiers: LCCN 2019002037 (print) | LCCN 2019008544 (ebook) | ISBN
  9781641135269 (Ebook) | ISBN 9781641135252 (hardcover) | ISBN
  9781641135245 (pbk.)
Subjects: LCSH: School superintendents. | Educational leadership. |
  Educational change.
Classification: LCC LB2831.7 (ebook) | LCC LB2831.7 .C66 2019 (print) | DDC
  371.2/011–dc23
LC record available at https://lccn.loc.gov/2019002037

Printed in the United States of America

CONTENTS

ACKNOWLEDGMENTS

The series editors would like to thank all of the authors for their hard work and dedication to this book. Particularly, we would like to emphatically thank them for their patience with the series editors. It is truly appreciated as we struggled to meet our own timelines during a truly "r(e)volutionary" time both editors happened to be undergoing while this book was being written. This appreciation extends as well to George Johnson and Lisa Brown at Information Age Publishing (IAP) who were both understanding, patient, and extremely helpful throughout the entire process.

We would like to also thank our colleagues at Florida Atlantic University and University of Wisconsin–Milwaukee for their continual encouragement to publish research in an otherwise under researched area. We appreciate all of the encouragement and support from the University Council of Educational Administration (UCEA), the UCEA Joint Center for Research on the Superintendency and District Governance, and the American Educational Research Association (AERA) as well as the AERA Special Interest Group, Research on the Superintendency for providing platforms for us to share the research in this book and gain wise feedback from conference attendees. We cannot express enough gratitude to Cryss Brunner, Michelle D. Young, Margaret Grogan, Lars Bjork, Charol Shakeshaft, Tom Glass, Thomas Alsbury, and other foundational superintendency scholars who pioneered research on the superintendency and whose concepts and theories permeate many of the chapters of this book.

The Contemporary Superintendent, pages vii–viii
Copyright © 2019 by Information Age Publishing
All rights of reproduction in any form reserved.

Finally, we would like to thank our husbands, parents, and other family members who supported us throughout this project. We feel blessed to have an outlet like IAP press to continue the important work of superintendents across the country and their international counterparts.

CHAPTER 1

(R)EVOLUTIONARY LEADERSHIP

An Innovative Response to Rapid and Complex Change

Meredith Mountford
Florida Atlantic University

Leigh Ellen Wallace
University of Wisconsin–Milwaukee

Leadership matters. Few would refute this statement. In fact, scholars have found building and district leadership account for about 25% of total direct and indirect effects on student learning; second only to the teacher's influence in the classroom (Leithwood & Louis, 2010; Leithwood, Louis, Anderson, & Wahlstrom, 2004). Additionally, Waters and Marzano (2006) found a significant correlation (.24) between district-level leadership and student achievement. Over 20 years ago, Carter and Cunningham (1997) reported the results of research conducted by The Horace Mann League and laid out the "top ten destructive factors influencing education" (pp. 11–12). Many

The Contemporary Superintendent, pages 1–12
Copyright © 2019 by Information Age Publishing

of those factors are still problematic today. For example, negative news stories about public schools are much more prominent than success stories, a lack of federal and state funding, unfunded mandates, family structure breakdowns, inattention to social issues that impact schools and students, an expectation that all schools achieve the same results regardless of resources. They further stated,

> The real problems are rooted in economics, crime, violence, divorce, inadequate parenting, abuse, mobility, vulnerability, disabilities, destructive relationships, social and psychological dysfunction, general alienation, and greed. These are examples of the types of problems with which school superintendents must now contend... superintendents live in a permanent condition of turbulence and pressure. (p. 13)

Today's school leaders not only have to deal with all of the issues found 20 years ago, but now must also deal with new problems such as keeping up with the complexities of online learning and the challenge of staying current with technology, an increase in the number of board members serving for politically motivated reasons or elected board members; sometimes backed by wealthy partisan donors (Mountford, 2008), school safety, deteriorating facilities, charter school laws, and increasing segregation between White and students of color and low and high SES students, excessive mandated testing and reporting, and a stubborn achievement gap, (Björk, Kowalski, & Browne-Ferrigno, 2014; Mountford, 2012). What remains consistent over time is a continual decline in government spending on education and in some, intentional measures to defund public education in favor of funding private or charter schools instead (Björk & Browne-Ferrigno, 2014; Björk et. al, 2014).

School superintendents are hired to manage the complex task of leading a school district, spearheading initiatives that improve student learning, balancing ever tightening budgets and diminishing resources, and navigating the often perilous waters of political and social unrest. As the district's executive leader, the 21st century school superintendent must be prepared to tackle the social and economic challenges mentioned above, yet also embrace practices promoting justice and equity for every child as well as responding to myriad contextual and environmental factors. Increased accountability at the national, state, and local levels—as well as in the court of social media and public opinion—continue to create environments that make it increasingly difficult for superintendents to focus instructional outcomes and the well-being of the school community.

Public K–12 school district leaders must also address severe budget cuts, privatization and the proliferation of choice and charter schools, diminishing professional standards for teachers, and increased accountability for results. Barnett, Shoho, and Bowers (2013) remind us "...successful leaders must balance the need to create learning communities, manage the organizational climate, and encourage community involvement with the consequences testing has on teacher morale and public scrutiny" (p. 1). In the midst of this murky climate, superintendents must develop a forward focused vision, as well as an enhanced understanding of, and agile response to this diverse and incredibly challenging landscape.

Public education has become an easy and familiar target on which to focus empty political rhetoric. It is imperative that district leaders stand up to the criticism publicly and debunk quasi-research rhetorical propaganda. Failure to do so will only allow threats to the profession, the institution, and will remain unchallenged. Harvey, Cambron-McCabe, Cunningham, and Koff (2013) worked with approximately 300 superintendents over a 20-year period for a study intended to be a "... sweep of the state of education and public affairs in the United States" (p. 20) as part of the National Superintendents Roundtable and the Danforth Forum for the American School Superintendent. Their discussion considered leadership theory and challenges to the superintendency. The group determined commonplace issues critical to the role of a school district superintendent. Among those critical issues, the report found that superintendents must keep up with constantly evolving tools for learning and assessment, demonstrate the ability to engage with the wider community, develop and sustain authentic partnerships, and secure collaborative grants with state, federal, or private funders to offset the paucity of school funding in most states. Meanwhile, superintendents must also work with increasingly divided school boards and school board members who may be backed and funded by political interests that deprioritize just and fair teaching and learning practices and instead prioritize partisan politics (Mountford, 2012). While these issues are not new to the superintendency, they are certainly more complex and intense in the current era of accountability and diminishing teacher and leader autonomy and district funding (Alsbury & Mountford, 2015; Alsbury & Whitaker, 2007). Additional studies over time support the complexity and ever-changing nature of the work (Glass & Franceschini, 2007; Glass, Bjork, & Brunner, 2001; Kowalski, McCord, Peterson, Young, & Ellerson, 2011).

We recognize public schools are changing and require renewed focus, understanding, and a very different response to the myriad social and economic factors that impact student learning. Leaders must engage in practices that address the changing nature of schools and society, advocate for, and confront current and proposed practices that diminish the quality of student outcomes and experiences. Leading for social justice must also be a primary consideration when studying the role of superintendents and the impact of their leadership. Garza (2008) states, "Leading for social justice incites political unrest because the hegemonic culture will resist change that provides equity to all members of society" (p. 163). The contemporary school district leader must recognize and actively embrace the challenges, personal risk, and political upheaval inherent in this critical work.

WHAT IS (R)EVOLUTIONARY LEADERSHIP?
WHY DOES IT MATTER?

How can contemporary school district administrators, specifically superintendents, contend with so many difficult, and almost impossible competing commitments? They must often feel like Homer's Odysseus: trapped between the monstrous Scylla and the terrifying Charybdis. In spite of these seemingly overwhelming challenges, we recognize there are superintendents that not only survive, but thrive and innovate in these environments. Building on the definitions of revolution, revolutionary, evolution, and evolutionary, the notion of the *(r)evolutionary leadership* emerged while discussing the need for school district leaders to push back against the status quo while improving teacher and leadership practices, improving student learning outcomes, engaging with the community, and ensuring decision making processes that include check and balance systems that are just, fair, and equitable for all.

We critically reviewed each chapter proposal submitted for this book searching specifically for superintendents or research on superintendents in which these tenants were practiced; both in their ability to enact radical change by "overthrowing" the status quo—as well as evolutionary in their deliberate approach to viewing change as a process they can control over time. We found a plethora of research and accounts of (r)evolutionary and evolutionary leaders who were willing to confront and defy practices and policies that do not support student well-being and achievement, yet also know how to leverage what is to attain their desired result and future. The chapters chosen for inclusion in this volume are those which offered a glimpse of these revolutionary tenants in practice.

As we explored and wrestled with this fledging concept we considered what we already know about leadership theory. As educational leadership scholars and practitioners, we have learned a great deal over the years. Van Seters and Field (1990) provide a discussion of the evolution of leadership theory beginning with the personality era, or the "Great Man Period," focused on trait theory and ending with transformational leadership theory. The authors assert that in order for leadership theory to continue to evolve, scholars and practitioners alike must recognize that leadership

1. is a complex, interactive process with behavioral, relational, and situational elements;
2. is found not solely in the leaders but occurs at individual, dyadic, group, and organizational levels;
3. is promoted upward from lower organizational levels as much as it is promoted downwards from higher levels;

4. occurs internally within the leader-subordinate interactions, as well as externally in the situational environment; and

5. motivates people intrinsically by improving expectations, not just extrinsically by improving reward systems.

They also emphasize leaders must be visionary, willing to take risks, highly adaptable to change, able to delegate authority and engage in distributed leadership practices, empower others, and understand the environmental factors that influence and impact the organization (p. 39). These are the same traits and behaviors we believe we would see in a (r)evolutionary leader. As we made decisions about which chapters to include in this first book of the series, transformational leadership, transformative leadership, servant leadership, and authentic leadership as those most closely capturing the essence of what we envisioned as a part of (r)evolutionary leadership practices.

Transformational leaders are optimistic, fairly charismatic, and possess a strong moral and ethical center (Leithwood & Janzi, 2000; 2009). Transformative leaders also operate with a strong moral purpose but also focus on social justice and are willing to take a stand against inequities (Shields, 2013). Greenleaf's (1970) servant leadership theory resonates with superintendents who believe leadership is selfless, empathetic, engenders trust, and is focused on community building and the development of others (Spears, 2010). Similarly, authentic leadership builds on these leadership practices but is primarily driven by a strong sense of right and wrong, and is guided by the mission and purpose of the organization (Cooper, Scandura, & Schriesheim, 2005; George, 2003; George & Sims, 2007).

Evolutionary leadership theory (ELT) is not a new concept. We examined the extent of literature on ELT and considered the work of Kenney (2012), Van Vugt (2006), and Van Vugt and Ronay (2014). Our review of ELT expanded how we thought about (r)evolutionary leadership. Kenney's (2012) work on evolutionary leadership theory (ELT), asserts leadership emerges more quickly when the group is under threat and leaders are usually those already willing to take risks. They recognize the payoff is often the same whether they step up, or allow others to do so, yet see themselves in a position of power or authority. Van Vugt and Ronay's (2014) posited transformational leaders as more effective than simply dominant ones, shared or distributed leadership as a necessary component to thrive in uncertain environments, and confirmed the evolutionary bias that continues around leadership selection. The physically strong are still perceived as the most capable to lead.

The (r)evolutionary leader would certainly fit within any of these typologies and may share some common links to ELT, but we believe they are even more laser focused on the need and urgency for deliberate, decisive, substantive change. They are not afraid to be political and use their influence to advocate for their schools, districts, and communities. These leaders are not meant to be held up as "hero" leaders who accomplish extraordinary things (although they may), but as leaders willing to push back against policies, practices, or systems that do not benefit all students. These leaders recognize change is inevitable and will occur whether they harness its unwieldy power or simply let it happen. They are able to look forward to a future with a clear vision that puts the mission of serving students and communities first. Perhaps, though, and of great importance, (r)evolutionary leaders don't wield power in abusive, threatening, or in coercive ways. Instead, they let ethical frameworks lead their way and value input from those willing to make their voices heard.

This volume grew out of our ongoing discussions with colleagues, practitioners, and scholars. We shared our conceptual idea (and ideal) of (r)evolutionary leadership at professional conferences, in department meetings, and in conversations with practitioner superintendents in the field. Our description does not seek to support or define or delineate the characteristics of a (r)evolutionary leader or how one might enact (r)evolutionary leadership—but serves as a way to (re)think the way we view the vastly complex work of school district administrators, specifically the superintendent. (R)Evolutionary leadership may change our ways of thinking about the significant advocacy role a superintendent can play in influencing both practice and policy to enact the change necessary to move forward issues of justice, equity, and quality in PK–12 schools to improve educational and social outcomes for those we serve.

We ask that you consider this emerging concept as you explore the chapters of our book. You will find the (r)evolutionary leaders you meet in the chapters know how to evolve, not just to stay alive, but to ensure the organization (school) remains relevant and vital to society. These leaders use their positional power, social capital, and expertise to advocate for policies and practices that are in the best interest of the school community and they innovate in ways that challenge the status quo. You will also find practices that are (r)evolutionary and provide ways for leaders to innovate, collaborate, and simply take care of themselves and those around them. (R)Evolutionary superintendents know they must innovate and change, yet also recognize a need to push back and challenge inequities and practices or policies that limit opportunity and outcomes for all students—regardless of race, gender, sexual orientation or identity, class, learning (dis)ability or zip code. (R)Evolutionary superintendents recognize that the health and well being of their communities are often contingent upon the quality of their public schools—and these superintendents do not "stand down" or allow ineffective or inequitable practices or policies to perpetuate the status quo.

Heilbrunn (1996) reminds us that while leadership scholars have created numerous typologies, identified many important leadership traits, and made valuable contributions to our understanding of how leaders and followers interact, "... to grow as a discipline, it will have to cast a wider net. Doing so, it may discover that the most important things about leadership lie far beyond the capabilities of science to analyze" (p. 11). It is possible that (r)evolutionary leadership is a way to "cast a wider net" in our thinking about leadership response. It may not be a new typology or concept, but rather a different way for leaders to frame their responses and the manner in which they choose to lead their schools and communities into the uncertain future of accountability, reform ... and possibility.

We encourage readers, and particularly students aspiring to the superintendency, to read each chapter and identify the (r)evolutionary practices used by the superintendents highlighted in the following chapters. How have these practices influenced the personal lives of the superintendents featured in these chapters? In other words, what was the toll on the superintendent for being (r)evolutionary? What were the benefits in learning for teachers and students? Further we ask students and practitioners of the superintendency to discuss how the superintendents in these chapters evolved from evolutionary superintendents into (r)evolutionary superintendents. Finally, in some of the final chapters of this volume, our authors provide advice and support for those superintendents who strive to become (r)evolutionary leaders. We truly hope these chapters both inspire and lend courage to those willing to start a new kind of revolution in which democracy, social justice, and ethical decisions guide the work of the superintendent with laser precision focus.

THE CHAPTERS

The first four chapters of Volume I of Research on the Superintendency book series focuses on leaders learning from and with others nationally and internationally in an effort to revolutionize system processes in education in the United States, England, and Canada. Chapter 1 of our series begins with an overview of the theoretical underpinnings of evolutionary and revolutionary nascent theory as it relates to the superintendency. Following the first chapter, from Colorado, *Colorado School Superintendents: Meeting the Challenges of Leadership* illustrates how (r)evolutionary superintendents in Colorado manage a conflict of culture that emerged due to legislative changes, funding challenges, and personnel constraints; all of which have arisen throughout the state during the past 35 years. Others can learn from the efforts in Colorado to combat (revolt against) and cope with the immense federal and state intrusion and co-option of public education all over the United States and beyond as we see in later chapters.

In an effort to contextualize U.S. educational policy internationally, the third chapter, *Effective Systems' Leadership in a Rapidly Changing English Education Landscape: Ways Forward for U.S. Superintendents* traces the recent development in England's compulsory state education system and encourages comparisons between the English and U.S. systems at present. Similar to the experiences found in Colorado, Chapter 2 examines system leaders in England, who, like the United States, find themselves in an increasingly dynamic, unpredictable national and local education system. This chapter examines system leaders working in settings where accountability and autonomy are growing as well as where it is not. The chapter concludes by offering suggestions to superintendents regarding effective practices in England in preparing their schools, staff, and students for an increasingly globalised, challenging, uncertain and exciting world; a common goal of system leaders in England and the United States. Similarly, Chapter 4, *Superintendents Who Lead for Optimum Learning: Nine Insights* illuminates nine insights about the leadership practices employed in Alberta by superintendents whose resolute focus on educator and student learning which yielded positive results within their school systems.

The next few chapters innately appreciate the evolution occurring in the world of the superintendency from a fairly stable era and decisions controlled locally to a much more complex fast moving, highly technological era in which decisions are ceded to the state or federal levels. These chapters discuss the nature of research needed to help superintendents during a time when superintendents must make decisions or implement new district policies and practices amidst a tumultuous external environment. Chapters 5 and 6 demonstrate the need superintendents have for new research from the field couched in the necessity of preexisting stability in the district prior to implementation of new initiatives as well as an ethical and transparent environment if they wish to be successful revolutionizing new policies and practices. Chapter 5, *Succession Planning for Administrative Positions: Supporting Order During Tumultuous Transition* presents a framework that allows superintendents to begin the search for quality front line administrators before the need arises. Further, by allowing all stakeholders and constituents of the hiring decision an opportunity to participate and have their voices heard, the authors posit that some of the uneasiness and emotional reaction to a leaderless program can be minimized. Equally, Chapter 6, *Ethics and the Superintendency*, highlights recent research on the topic of ethics as it applies to the superintendency. More specifically, the chapter focuses on ethical leadership perspectives of state and district level superintendents, and how those perspectives vary according to state education/school district characteristics and state/district leader demographics.

We change pace a bit in Chapters 7, 8, and 9. While these chapters are reflective of earlier chapters by stating from the onset that the superintendency has become more complex as has its surrounding environment, the authors of these three chapters discuss the importance of superintendents empowering teams and professional learning communities to assist in implementing change or new policies. The authors of all three chapters emphasize the importance of a team approach and distributive empowerment. These chapters explain why superintendents cannot work in isolation in the current educational environment if they intend to revolutionize.

Chapter 7, *Inclusive Leadership: Breaking Down Isolated Practice and Developing a Culture of Inquiry to Increase Student and Adult Learning,* describes superintendents' innovative work to foster meaningful change across ten school districts. This chapter examines the commitments and practices of superintendents in districts identified for their work to close achievement gaps between students with disabilities and other students as part of district efforts intended to improve learning for all students. With good reason, the authors of this chapter describe the superintendents they studied as revolutionary. In Chapter 8, *Leading for Learning: District Leaders as Networked Change Agents,* the authors map out the work of a school district consortium and explain how an inquiry minded approach has enhanced innovation by focusing on student learning and student success at the district level. While Chapter 8 discusses change in very concrete and fundamental ways, Chapter 9, *Some "Central Issues" in Creating Professional Learning Communities: A Superintendent's Perspective,* proffers a way forward to sustain change. In this chapter, the authors demonstrate school improvement via professional learning communities and demonstrate how they require strong district support and active participation at different levels. The superintendent's perspective on how to be revolutionary around professional learning communities will serve to help guide other superintendents and superintendent preparation programs.

The final three chapters of this volume bring the issue of the superintendency down from a district level to an individual level in which gender, race, stress, and the well-being of superintendents are put under the microscope. We conclude the book with an inspirational chapter about the importance of mindfulness we hope all superintendents and other leaders who read this book take to heart in their everyday lives. Chapter 10, *X Chromosome in a Y-Dominant World: What Could Possibly Go Wrong?* examines some generally held positions of thought concerning women in the CEO (superintendent) position in schools. Voices of women who hold superintendent positions will speak through some selected qualitative research and the political role of the superintendent, regardless of sex, will be considered, with some application about how execution of the role may be approached differently by women. Similarly Chapter 11—*Like Father, Like Son: Superintendents*

Mentoring for Success Through Fictive Kinship Community—effectively teaches us a lot about what it takes to truly be a revolutionary change agent. Change agents often ruffle many feathers and Chapter 12, *The Superintendency: The Cost of Making a Difference—The Personal Toll*, specifically explores the nature and prevalence of the personal toll exacted upon superintendents and their families and how their experience demands a new kind of (r)evolutionary leadership; an approach that takes proactive steps to inject work-life/personal-life balance into the life of a superintendent.

Chapter 13, our final chapter in Volume I of the Research on the Superintendency series, *Evolving Practices for Dealing With Superintendent Stress: Mindfulness, Compassion, and Self-Compassion*, includes information about the contemporary life of superintendents, outlining how constructs of mindfulness, compassion, and self-compassion may offer research-related benefits to serve them in stressful moments, and offer practices to calm and sustain them. This chapter is written for superintendents, and the people who offer training and professional development targeted for their needs. In this chapter, the contemplative practices of finding stillness and quiet are explained as ways to reduce, cope with, and thrive, despite the stress that superintendents face. This chapter provides a blueprint for a journey of self-discovery and self-care. The messages in this writing invite busy superintendents to slow down their world to: *face the storm because it is there anyway; and embrace the quiet—it is there within.* Kabat-Zinn reminded us, "You can't stop the waves but you can learn to surf" (1994, p. 30). This chapter is about learning to surf...

We truly hope you enjoy Volume I on the Research on the Superintendency series.

REFERENCES

Alsbury, T., & Mountford, M. (2015, November). UCEA Center for Research on the Superintendency & District Governance Symposium. *Balanced board leadership.* A symposium presented at UCEA's 2015 annual conference. San Diego, CA.

Alsbury, T. L., & Whitaker, K. S. (2007). Superintendent perspectives and practice of accountability, democratic voice and social justice. *Journal of Educational Administration, 45*(2), 154–174.

Barnett, B., Shoho, A. R., & Bowers, A. J. (Eds). (2013). *School and district leadership in an era of accountability.* Charlotte, NC: Information Age.

Björk, L. G., & Browne-Ferrigno, T. (2014). Introduction: International perspectives on educational reform and superintendent leadership. *Leadership and Policy in Schools, 13*(4), 357–361.

Björk, L. G., Kowalski, T. J., & Browne-Ferrigno, T. (2014). The school district superintendent in the United States of America. *Educational Leadership Faculty Publications.* Paper 13. University of Dayton, Dayton, OH.

Carter, G. R., & Cunningham, W. G. (1997). *The American school superintendent: Leading in an age of pressure. The Jossey-Bass Education Series.* San Francisco, CA: Jossey-Bass.

Cooper, C. D., Scandura, T. A., & Schriesheim, C. A. (2005). Looking forward but learning from our past: Potential challenges to developing authentic leadership theory and authentic leaders. *The Leadership Quarterly, 16*(3), 475–493.

Garza Jr., E. (2008). Autoethnography of a first-time superintendent: Challenges to leadership for social justice. *Journal of Latinos and Education, 7*(2), 163–176.

George, B. (2003). *Authentic Leadership: Rediscovering the secrets to creating lasting value.* San Francisco, CA: Jossey Bass.

George, B., & Sims, P. (2007). *True north: Discover your authentic leadership.* San Francisco, CA: Jossey Bass.

Glass, T. E., Bjork, L., & Brunner, C. C. (2001). *The study of the American superintendency, 2000: A look at the superintendent of education in the new millennium.* New York, NY: Rowman & Littlefield Education.

Glass, T. E., & Francschini, L. A. (2007). *The state of the American school superintendency: A mid-decade study.* New York, NY: Rowman & Littlefield Education.

Greenleaf, R. K. (1970). *The servant as leader.* Westfield, IN: Greenleaf Center for Servant Leadership.

Harvey, J., Cambron-McCabe, N., Cunningham, L. L., & Koff, R. H. (2013). *The superintendent's fieldbook* (2nd ed.). Thousand Oaks, CA: Corwin.

Heilbrunn, J. (1996). Can leadership be studied? In P. S. Temes (Ed.), *Teaching leadership: Essays in theory and practice* (pp. 1–11). New York, NY: Peter Lang.

Kabat-Zinn, J. (1994). *Wherever you go, there you are: Mindfulness meditation in everday life.* New York, NY: Hachette Book Group.

Kenney, M. T. (2012). Evolutionary leadership theory. *Journal of Leadership Studies, 6*(1), 85–89.

Kowalski, T. J., McCord, R. S., Peterson, G. J., Young, P. I., & Ellerson, N. M. (2011). *The American school superintendent: 2010 decennial study.* New York, NY: Rowman & Littlefield Education.

Leithwood, K., & Jantzi, D. (2000). The effects of transformational leadership on organizational conditions and student engagement with school [Electronic version]. *Journal of Educational Administration, 38*(2), 112–129.

Leithwood, K., & Jantzi, D. (2009). Transformational leadership. In B. Davies (Ed.), *The essentials of school leadership* (pp. 31–43). Thousand Oaks, CA: SAGE.

Leithwood, K., & Louis, K. S. (2010). *Linking leadership to student learning.* San Franciso, CA: Jossey-Bass.

Leithwood, K., Louis, K. S., Anderson, S., & Wahlstrom, K. (2004). How leadership influences student learning. *Center for Applied Research and Educational Improvement, University of Minnesota,* 289–342.

Mountford, M. (2008). Historical and current tensions among board/superintendent teams: Symptoms or cause? In T. Alsbury (Ed.), *Relevancy and revelation: The future of school board governance* (pp. 81–114). Lanham, MD: Rowman & Littlefield.

Mountford, M. (2012). Are school boards necessary in today's public schools? Yes, unequivocally. In R. Hunter, F. Brown, & S. Donahoo (Eds.), *School Governance* (Vol. 7, pp. 111–121). Thousand Oaks, CA: SAGE.

Shields, C. M. (2013). *Transformative leadership in education: Equitable change in an uncertain and complex world.* New York, NY: Routledge.

Spears, L. C. (2010) Servant leadership and Robert K. Greenleaf's legacy. In D. Van Dierendonck & K. Patterson (Eds.), *Servant leadership: Developments in theory and research* (pp. 11–24). New York, NY: Macmillan.

Van Seters, D. A., & Field, R. H. (1990). The evolution of leadership theory. *Journal of organizational change management, 3*(3), 29–45.

Van Vugt, M. (2006). Evolutionary origins of leadership and followership. *Personality and Social Psychology Review, 10*(4), 354–371.

Vugt, M. V., & Ronay, R. (2014). The evolutionary psychology of leadership: Theory, review, and roadmap. *Organizational Psychology Review, 4*(1), 74–95.

Waters, T. J., & Marzano, R. J. (2006). *School district leadership that works: The effect of superintendent leadership on student achievement.* Denver, CO: McRel.

CHAPTER 2

COLORADO SCHOOL SUPERINTENDENTS

Meeting the Challenges of Leadership

Wendy A. Clouse
University of Colorado

Patrick Radigan
Colorado State University

Al Ramirez
University of Colorado

William Dallas
University of Colorado

Dallas Strawn
University of Colorado

Kevin Brooks
University of Colorado

Pat Green
University of Colorado

This chapter presents an analysis of how superintendents in Colorado lead their school districts in the face of challenges they must overcome on an ongoing basis. Sources for the chapter come from data collected directly from superintendents across the state (Ramirez, Strawn, Clouse, & Radigan, 2015)

The Contemporary Superintendent, pages 13–36
Copyright © 2019 by Information Age Publishing
All rights of reproduction in any form reserved.

and existing public access databases. These data were compiled through surveys, focus groups, and interviews. The chapter lays out the systemic issues to which school superintendents must adapt in order to deliver quality education to all students. Four major themes, derived from the data, are the focus of the chapter: (a) serving students well in an environment of declining resources; (b) attracting, retaining, and supporting quality personnel; (c) managing the crush of policy initiatives from the state and federal levels; and (d) finding a balance between work and family life.

The theoretical framework for the chapter is built from extant literature on leadership theory in the superintendency as related to the four major themes listed above. For example, the following concepts are incorporated within the chapter: policy overload (Arnold, 2000; Johnson & Howley, 2015), turnover in the superintendency (Tekniepe, 2015), and teacher quality (Ellis, 2008). In addition, special emphasis will draw attention to the unique plight of small school district superintendents. The research-based theories about leadership in the superintendency will serve as an underpinning for the analysis of data taken from focus groups, questionnaires, and personal narratives that were part of the *Colorado Superintendent Study* and data on state school finance, school personnel, and other state sources of interest to the chapter.

A summary and conclusion section will provide recommendations for leadership in the superintendency in consideration of the successes achieved by working Colorado superintendents in meeting the major challenges of their job. Moreover, it will demonstrate the conflict of culture that has emerged due to legislative changes within the last decade. Because respondents throughout the data collection cycle articulated so many difficulties and negative aspects associated with the school superintendency, it is essential to study and understand how successful school superintendents face the difficulties of the position and provide positive, controlled, and optimistic leadership for their school district and the school community.

UNDERSTANDING THE COLORADO CONTEXT

Colorado has 178 school districts spread across a very diverse geography. While the common image of the state is one of alpine forests and towering mountain peaks, consider that half the state's land mass is comprised of open plains and semi-arid, high desert. Most of the state's 5.5 million population lives along the "Front Range," a corridor just east of the Rocky Mountains, that hugs U.S. Interstate 25. At the hub of this population mass is the Denver area megalopolis. This array of geography is reflected in the distribution and configuration of school districts throughout the state.

In the 2015–2016 academic year, the State of Colorado reported that approximately 900,000 students were served by 38,000 teachers in 1,800 schools. School district enrollments range from 90,000 in the Denver County 1 District to enrollments of less than 100 per district in twelve outlying town and remote districts within the state. According to the Colorado Department of Education (CDE, 2016a), over the past 20 years the state pupil enrollment mean growth rate is 1.4%, and the state has not seen a decrease in enrollment since 1988. The largest 15 districts enroll a total of 607,254, which represents 68% of the total statewide enrollment. The remaining 32% of student enrollment is distributed among 163 school districts. More than 100 of these school districts have enrollment of less than 1,000 students. The racial and ethnic composition of the student population is equally varied (Table 2.1). While these racial and ethnic groups are widely found among Colorado school districts, selected urban, suburban, and rural school districts have larger concentrations of students of color than other districts.

Financial resources follow a similar pattern to enrollment size. The 20 largest school districts garnered almost five billion dollars in state's school aid during the 2015–2016 academic year. This contrasts with the 20 smallest school districts that will see 24 million divided among them. This variation is no surprise, considering that state aid is driven by enrollment, but as will be shown later in the chapter, financial resources are a major challenge for superintendents across the state.

The superintendents who lead these school districts are a more homogeneous group than the students they serve: approximately 75% are male, their median age is 54, and 95% are White. Most hold a master's degree (60%) and the remainder have education specialist, EdD, or PhD degrees. Eighty-nine percent of these individuals took a traditional path to the superintendency (i.e., served as teachers and school administrators), while 11% followed a nontraditional route. On average, Colorado superintendents have 7 years'

TABLE 2.1 Radical and Ethnic Composition of Students in Colorado School Districts	
Racial/Ethnic Group	**2015**
American Indian or Alaska Native	0.7%
Asian	3.1%
Black or African American	4.6%
Hispanic/Latino	33.4%
White	54.1%
Native Hawaiian or Other Pacific Islander	0.2%
Two or More Races	3.8%

Source: Colorado Deptartment of Education: http://www.cde
.state.co.us/cdereval/pupilcurrentstate

experience in the job and have held such positions in fewer than two school districts. Overwhelmingly, the majority (89%), of these leaders feel they were prepared or well prepared for their role. Most of the superintendents expect to retire or leave the job in the next 7 years, which is not surprising given their average age. They assert a high level of satisfaction with their job and slightly less satisfaction with their compensation and the balance between work and life. Half of the superintendents signified they work 60 hours per week.[1]

CHALLENGE 1: SERVING STUDENTS WELL IN AN ENVIRONMENT OF DECLINING RESOURCES

Like many states, Colorado has a complex and obscure school funding system with multiple formulas and sub formulas. Basically, the system is enrollment driven; more students equals more money for each district. There is also an equalization mechanism, which assists school districts that cannot reach the state set minimum guarantee level of support per student. The state aid formula has been tested in court several times and been determined to be constitutionally sound (National Education Access Network, 2015).

Although the funding formula has been challenged in court, the soundness of the formula is disputed by many school district superintendents from big and small school districts alike. The major complaint about the formula from district personnel is that the funding per pupil is inadequate for the job they are asked to do. One reason for this is that Colorado has a voter initiative process, which has made it relatively easy to promote referenda and constitutional amendments that bypass the legislature. This form of direct democracy has created a school funding Gordian knot that has been impossible to fix. Given the limited space for this chapter, we have included Figure 2.1, which capsulizes the problem and its results over time. We will briefly describe what it reports.

The horizontal zero dollar line represents the average per student spending across the United States over time. The red trend line shows Colorado's per pupil funding compared to the national average, which by the mid-1980s has been in a nose dive. The vertical lines show three voter approved ballot measures: the Gallagher Amendment, the Taxpayer Bill of Rights, and Amendment 23. The Gallagher Amendment fostered a major shift away from local residential property tax, the result of which has been to shift costs for the source of revenue for school aid, so that now on average over 65% comes from the state and less than 35% is raised locally. The TABOR Amendment (Taxpayer Bill of Rights) constrains government budget growth. It restrains budget growth for all Colorado public entities including school districts to the rate of inflation plus the percent of population growth, which for school districts is enrollment growth. The TABOR mechanism is in force regardless

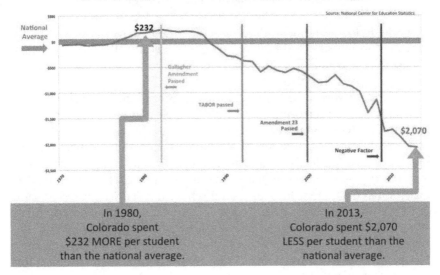

K-12 Per Pupil Funding:
Colorado versus National Average

Figure 2.1 School funding trends in Colorado 1970–2011. *Source:* Great Education Colorado. Used with permission

of the amount of revenue collected. Amendment 23, a constitutional change passed in 2000, was an effort to add more funding for schools and reverse the downward trend realized through both the Gallagher Amendment and TABOR, but as can be seen in Figure 2.1, it has not worked due to a reinterpretation of the constitutional amendment by the state legislature in 2009.

To make matters worse, in response to the Great Recession of 2008 the Colorado legislature enacted a work around to Amendment 23 and added the "Negative Factor" to the state aid formula as a means to claw back funds that should go to schools as per Amendment 23. Remarkably, the Colorado Supreme Court ruled the Negative Factor did not violate the state constitution and Amendment 23, which mandates increases at least equal to the rate of inflation. The implications of this failure, as reported by school superintendents across the state are listed here below.

When asked if they felt their school district had sufficient resources to meet an assortment of challenges they responded as follows:

- *Meet new academic standards*—Barely one quarter thought they did.
- *Ability to maintain school facilities*—Over 80% said no.

- *Funding to build new schools or expand existing facilities*—83% were doubtful.
- *Attract high quality personnel*—83% expressed concern.
- *Retain high quality personnel*—78% had apprehensions.

Only one in four Colorado school superintendents surveyed perceived the state aid formula as distributing funding on an equitable basis. Therefore, adequate and equitable funding are seen as two constant challenges for school leaders in the state.

As the state worked its way out of the recession, superintendents placed a big emphasis on restoring salaries for teachers and other school personnel, who in many cases saw no annual raises and even salary reductions for several years. Many of the local school boards went to their community to ask for mill levy increases to supplement operating budgets, often with the explanation that much of the money would be used for teacher salaries. Unfortunately, for small rural school districts, the assessed value in the community from which to draw additional revenue can be so small, it has little to no meaning. Regardless of the size of the district, potential revenue through mill levy overrides (MLO), only 65% of school districts in Colorado have a successful MLO contributing to the district revenue stream (Colorado School Finance Project, 2015). However, common practice among Colorado superintendents is to just "tighten the belt" and work hard to keep the cuts away from the classroom.

CHALLENGE 2: ATTRACTING, RETAINING, AND SUPPORTING QUALITY PERSONNEL

Colorado education leaders are well aware that student learning takes place in classrooms, and that high performing schools are strongly correlated to high performing teachers and staff. The state has been fortunate to draw many good Colorado students to its colleges of education. It also relies heavily on hiring many educators from other states. The recession, which hit many other states harder than Colorado helped in this regard. But new developments are confronting Colorado superintendents in the area of recruitment and retention of staff. A nation-wide teacher shortage is mounting (Moller, Moller, & Schmidt, 2015) and according to the Colorado Department of Education's 2016 Legislative Report for Educator Preparation, enrollments in Colorado colleges of education are well below average (CDHE, p. 14, 2016b).

School leaders speculate that the cause of this is primarily fourfold: the constant drum beat in the media about the failing public schools, the onerous accountability practices that scapegoat teachers for social conditions that are a drag on student achievement, low teacher salaries combined with the cost of higher education, and the high cost of housing in resort mountain towns and Denver metropolitan school districts. Such factors make teaching a less desirable profession. Data derived from our statewide superintendent survey clearly underscores the challenge.

When asked if their schools can attract quality personnel to teaching and instructional support positions they report major problem, particularly in certain areas.

- *Mathematics*—78% say they have big shortages.
- *Foreign language*—65% have a problem.
- *Special education*—65% report deficits.
- *Special education support services*—72% short fall.
- *Teachers for English language learners*—60% are in need.
- *Science*—68% say they are lacking.

Yet, contrasted with these shortages the superintendents indicate that, generally, they believe that the education professionals they have perform fairly well. They are most sanguine about school-level leaders, central office administrators and other central office professionals. As a group, these categories are mostly rated as performing satisfactorily, garnering survey satisfaction scores from the mid 60% to mid 70%. Many school districts have adapted to these personnel shortages by entering into partnerships with local colleges and intermediate education agencies to develop alternative licensure programs in an effort to "grow their own." Unfortunately, many small rural school districts are disadvantaged if they are located considerable distances from the few major city hubs available, and in some cases, the topography of Colorado contributes to this challenge. In addition, common practice is to provide extensive support to novice and veteran educators alike to continuously improve instruction in their schools.

Particularly hard hit by these shortages are schools and school districts in high poverty areas, remote locations and inner cities. Personnel retention is a major issue in such settings, because turnover is higher as teachers and other professional staff move on to what they perceive as more desirable schools and school districts. As one superintendent put it, "in the past we would go to the teacher fairs and have a few teachers sign up after the suburban and ski-towns filled their quotas. Now we don't even get the leftovers." A common scenario among these school districts is to hire a teacher who will stay for a year or two until they can find employment in one of the more desirable school districts or schools. We call it the "Colorado two-step."

Another source of recruitment for all school districts are the charter schools in the state, which tend to hire unlicensed personnel. Many charter school teachers migrate to regular public schools after they gain licensure. The usual reasons are better pay and benefits. But the shortages of teachers and other school personnel remains an extant and growing challenge for Colorado school district superintendent. And this is a major challenge for superintendents in the small school districts scattered throughout the state.

CHALLENGE 3: MANAGING THE CRUSH OF POLICY INITIATIVES FROM THE STATE AND FEDERAL LEVELS

Most of the Colorado superintendents have progressed in their careers in the era of rigorous accountability policies. Generally, they find many of these policies to be unproductive and sometimes even onerous in advancing student achievement. They believe that in too many cases policy makers are uninformed about the needs and challenges of delivering a quality education for all students. Furthermore, the superintendents we studied expressed frustration that they do not have a voice in the policy-making process. This is particularly the case when they criticize "one size fits all" policies that ignore the realities of individual school districts and their unique circumstances. Ironically, Colorado superintendents support strong accountability measures and are enthusiastic about demonstrating how their school districts serve their communities, but they perceive many of the current accountability policies are casting their school districts in an unfair light. Specifically, blaming schools for the impact on learning of social and economic conditions over which they have minimal influence.

Two examples underscore this frustration: the student testing regime demanded by the federal No Child Left Behind Law (NCLB, Public Law PL 107-110, the No Child Left Behind Act of 2001) and the Colorado legislation for teacher evaluation (SB10-191, Concerning Ensuring Quality Instruction Through Educator Effectiveness [EQUITEE]) inspired by the federal government's "Race to the Top" grant program. On the whole, Colorado superintendents saw these two policies as costly unfunded mandates. In their efforts to implement these policy initiatives they found them to be of modest value in consideration of the time, personnel effort, and resources they were required to devote to them. Furthermore, the superintendents also recounted that both policies provide limited return in student achievement to the school district for the investments needed to meet the mandates.

Here are some examples of the level of dissatisfaction with the policy crush they must manage:

- 98% expressed a range of dissatisfaction about having sufficient resources to manage state mandates.

- 90% expressed dissatisfaction regarding ample time to implement state mandates.
- 83% reported that multiple and layered state mandates were adversely affecting their school district.
- 66% indicated a range of dissatisfaction with the mandated teacher evaluation system (SB10-191).
- The group was split 50/50 on whether the teacher evaluation policy, overall, was having a positive or negative impact on their school district.
- 73% felt they do not get student testing data results in a timely manner for school district level planning.
- Similarly, 87% considered the receipt of timely test data a problem for school level planning.

Figure 2.2 represents an analysis of comments from superintendents when asked for responses to Colorado's current teacher evaluation policies.

CHALLENGE 4: FINDING A BALANCE BETWEEN WORK AND FAMILY LIFE

In this fourth area of obstacles faced by Colorado superintendents, we find a more complex and nuanced set of issues. Multiple aspects of the job converge on the school leader as an individual and often take a personal toll.

Figure 2.2 Summary of frequently used words in open ended survey question to describe reactions to Colorado's teacher evaluation policy.

These issues are wide-ranging: from the time demands of the job, to portrayal in the media, to relations with their school board, to support from colleagues and professional organizations. The message that comes across from these school leaders is that despite the personal sacrifices made by them, and often their families, they see their work as valuable.

Here are examples of what they say about the many issues that affect them at a personal level:

- More than half the superintendents acknowledged that they were on a spectrum from somewhat likely to very likely of experiencing "burn-out."
- Almost three-fourths of the group do not contemplate moving out of the superintendency in the near future despite experiencing high levels of "burn-out."
- Over half have a rolling contract and buyout provisions.
- They rate their autonomy for decision-making as a five on a six point scale, indicating a high degree freedom to carry out their duties.
- As a group, Colorado superintendents report that they have support systems comprised of colleagues, professional organizations, and opportunities for professional development.
- 90% of the respondents reported their school districts do not have a union or teacher bargaining unit.
- On average, their school districts have had 2.82 superintendents over the past 10 years.
- 77% said they have employees or relative of employees on their school board; moreover, almost 70% feel that having an employee or relative of an employee on the school board creates a conflict of interest.
- The group rated their school board members' preparation for meetings average (three on a six point scale).
- The average length of school board meetings is 2.33 hours and meetings occur at a rate two per month.
- 80% felt that responsibilities between their board and themselves were clearly delineated.
- The superintendents reported spending 5.3 hours per week on average attending to board members individual requests.
- When asked about whether policies promoted by board members were based on political ideology, 48% said never or rarely. They also said (89%) their boards often, very often or always promoted policies in the best interest of students.
- 35% question the relevance of school boards today given the amount of policy direction coming from the state and federal levels.

Yet, 88% thought hiring and firing the superintendent was an important board role and 80% saw financial oversight as an essential board role.

- With regard to support for the school district: 83% saw parents as supportive; 78% saw the local media as supportive, while they view the national media (35%) as less so. A large majority perceived the school boards association and school administrators association as constructive sources of support. However, Colorado state government scored the lowest, as only 33% of superintendents viewed the state as supportive.

- The superintendents missed, on average, 4.5 family functions or personal social functions in the month preceding the survey because of work.

- Lastly, Colorado superintendents reported their level of stress was average (4.5 on a 10-point scale).

Despite these findings, Colorado school superintendents maintain a vision of schooling in which the public schools they lead are a foundational institution for their community, the state, and the country. They are clear about their mission to educate a new generation of Americans, irrespective of their students' family background. They are focused on ensuring that children and youth who pass through their schools experience success in school, are ready for employment as adults, prepared for post-secondary education, and able to engage in the civic life of our democracy. Despite the many challenges they face, Colorado superintendents remain resolute in their mission.

FACING ADVERSITY: LEADERSHIP THEORY

In late 2015, the National Policy Board for Educational Administration (NPBEA) approved new professional standards for educational leaders. The purpose of this initiative was to create a set of professional standards that incorporate clear principles of leadership that are focused on students and student learning. Table 2.2 provides an overview on the 2015 standards as published by the Council of Chief States School Officers and NPBEA as well as an overview of the existing management strengths and opportunities for improvement related to these new criteria. What we found among our study population was that Colorado superintendents are already using premises found in diverse models of leadership theory, specifically transformational leadership, to manage their districts according to the new NPBEA standards.

How do superintendents face adversity? For a school superintendent to be successful in her or his position, they must evaluate if the position is the correct job for them to pursue. Specific cost and benefits associated with

TABLE 2.2 Professional Standards: Opportunities and Strengths, Adapted from NPBEA 2015	
Professional Standards for Educational Leaders 2015 and Colorado Strengths & Opportunities	
Standard 1: Mission, Vision, and Core Values	
"Effective educational leaders develop, advocate, and enact a shared mission, vision, and core values of high quality education and academic success and well-being of each student."	**Strength:** Superintendents are looking for ways to market their district through the use of mission, vision, and core values to attract and retain higher pupil counts. This seems to be as much about free-market enterprise, as it is about developing a purpose for the school district to stand behind. However regardless to the intent, superintendents use these philosophies as the backbone of their decisions, and the method to which they govern their districts.
Standard 2: Ethics and Professional Norms	
"Effective educational leaders act ethically and according to professional norms to promote each student's academic success and well-being."	**Strength:** Colorado superintendents are working together to develop professional norms and standards across districts. Respondents in our data collection reported a growing sense of unity among districts and district personnel as they try to understand and implement the plethora of new initiatives that have been mandated by the state in the last 6 years.
Standard 3: Equity and Cultural Responsiveness	
"Effective educational leaders strive for equity of educational opportunity and culturally responsive practices to promote each student's academic success and well-being."	**Strength & Opportunity for Improvement:** Colorado superintendents have reported positive student growth and attainment; however, they also see the need for more support. They understand the equity and responsiveness issues related to a constrained applicant pool and lack of district resources.
Standard 4: Curriculum, Instruction, and Assessment	
"Effective educational leaders develop and support intellectually rigorous and coherent systems of curriculum, instruction, and assessment to promote each student's academic success and well-being."	**Strength:** Exploring new opportunities to attract and regain pupil counts. In many cases superintendents are willing to take temporary losses in funding if they believe the program has the potential for growth to at least stabilize the enrollment, if not to increase it. Many of these initiatives result in better or new opportunities for students as well, however if they do not reach a level of financial stabilization they are often replaced or removed all together.
Standard 5: Community of Care and Support for Students	
"Effective educational leaders cultivate an inclusive, caring, and supportive school community that promotes the academic success and well-being of each student."	**Opportunity for Improvement:** 49% of Colorado superintendents surveyed report that their community provides an appropriate level of support for their district and 47% of superintendents we surveyed report that parents provide an appropriate level of support for their district. There is a clear opportunity to increase community and parental support within the state.

(continued)

TABLE 2.2   Professional Standards: Opportunities and Strengths, Adapted from NPBEA 2015 (continued)

Professional Standards for Educational Leaders 2015 and Colorado Strengths & Opportunities

Standard 6: Professional Capacity of School Personnel

"Effective educational leaders develop the professional capacity and practice of school personnel to promote each student's academic success and well-being."	**Opportunity for Improvement:** Superintendents are forced to be more reliant in growing the capacity for school and district leadership personnel as a result of trickle down policy crush reported by superintendents. Many of the school and district leaders are required to implement the onslaught of mandates. Coupled with limited financial capacity for competitive national salaries, Colorado superintendents are forced to look more within their organizations for potential talent pools.

Standard 7: Professional Community for Teachers and Staff

"Effective educational leaders foster a professional community of teachers and other professional staff to promote each student's academic success and well-being."	**Opportunity for Improvement:** Many superintendents are looking for ways to attract and retain staff in their districts, often playing more on the sense of community and organizational loyalty. In these cases, superintendents are placing higher emphasis on staff culture and climate surveys to ensure that individuals are happiest with their positions. This is a positive approach to leadership, however as personal financial resources shrink, there is only so much that can be done to attract and retain employees, and as other districts incentivize moving from one district to another, a sort of staff shuffle begins to take place. An example of this is when an employee, who has seen multiple years of pay freezes, can recoup those lost years by moving to another school district.

Standard 8: Meaningful Engagement of Families and Community

"Effective educational leaders engage families and the community in meaningful, reciprocal, and mutually beneficial ways to promote each student's academic success and well-being."	**Strength & Opportunity for Improvement:** This particular area of leadership has seen great expansion as a result of financial constraints. In many cases, superintendents are forced to look for the most favorable way to solve their shrinking revenue issue locally through bond issues and MLOs. Engaging with the families and communities who will decide the outcomes of any potential ballot measure has become an essential component of the superintendent's responsibilities and duties.

Standard 9: Operations and Management

"Effective educational leaders manage school operations and resources to promote each student's academic success and well-being."	**Strength:** Superintendents are constantly looking for ways to squeeze every last penny out of operations and management. This has resulted in reshuffling of positions, restructuring of district personnel, and a net negative impact to the infrastructure of our schools. In many cases school districts are lengthening the life span of facilities, resources, and technology far beyond the planned replacement window. This will eventually result in a compounding problem as outdated facilities and resources begin to pile up, eventually costing more to meet the needs of students.

(continued)

TABLE 2.2 Professional Standards: Opportunities and Strengths, Adapted from NPBEA 2015 (continued)	
Professional Standards for Educational Leaders 2015 and Colorado Strengths & Opportunities	
Standard 10: School Improvement	
"Effective educational leaders act as agents of continuous improvement to promote each student's academic success and well-being."	**Opportunity for Improvement:** 53% of superintendents surveyed within the state of Colorado reported that they are satisfied with their ability to seek professional development for emerging issues within the field while only 29% reported they are satisfied with professional support provided by the Colorado Department of Education. This indicates that superintendents are willing to seek improvement to promote student welfare; however, help may not always be available.

the superintendency have been provided by Lee and King (2001). Costs and benefits have been identified as a leader's ability to understand and personally evaluate the following:

- *Visibility*—A superintendent must accept that the role is not isolated within their district, but their entire community and state.
- *Public Duties*—The more one achieves higher leadership positions, there are obligations outside the organization one must attend. Political acumen becomes front and center in most decisions one would make in the position.
- *Separation*—The superintendent position is often lonely and a focus on developing colleague support from others is necessary to avoid isolation.
- *Caretaking*—Not only does the superintendency require a major focus on successful operation of the educational enterprise, part of the job also requires attention to supporting and maintaining emotional stability of all the parts of the organization.
- *Stamina*—The superintendent of a school district must not only take care of others, but also herself or himself. On occasion, the requirements of the job will be all-consuming, and issues of unhealthy stress, loss of family time and recreational activities will be lost. If a superintendent is not healthy and taking care of his or her personal needs, they will not have the energy and stamina to provide meaningful assistance to others.
- *Job Insecurity*—Inherent stress with the superintendency is understanding the job is tenuous, but can be rewarding. An in-depth focus on promoting positive school board relations will help greatly with this concern.
- *Less Freedom of Expression*—The superintendency requires a leader to be very vigilant in all their actions, words used, and public demeanor.

- *Infrequent Relief and Strains on Family*—The superintendency requires focus on a 24/7 basis. There are few breaks (vacation periods), and as a result of this demanding work and schedule, family time is usually compromised.
- *Less Supporting Feedback*—The higher one rises in any organization, supportive, honest, and constructive feedback is difficult to receive.

As difficult as self-reflection may be, school leaders must occasionally assess their comfort with the list of costs and benefits and positively realign their beliefs and behaviors with their purpose (Branson, 2007; Runhaar, Sanders, & Yang, 2010). A leader who understands their overall purpose in life, and behaves consistent with that purpose, is more authentic and better understood by her or his followers in most situations that occasionally require "top-down" difficult actions and decisions (Runhaar et al., 2010). Moreover, grounding and a comprehensive understanding of leadership theory will assist educational professionals with the challenges they face on a daily basis.

Data collected in our Colorado superintendent study indicates there are numerous areas that need attention and further study related to the challenges of superintendent leadership. One area that is essential for a superintendent to completely understand is the importance of board–superintendent relationships, especially since one main jobs of a board of education is to hire the district's chief executive officer. Suggestions and techniques for helping superintendents to promote positive board–superintendent relationships (Kowalski, 2006) are outlined in Table 2.3. Positive superintendent–board relationships are essential for any school district to progress and positively impact the educational growth of all employees and students.

Leadership Theory

Leadership theory, in numerous iterations, has been studied extensively throughout the mid-nineteenth through the twentieth century as the concept of finding the right model to evoke behavioral responses throughout the organization has been driven by the need for achievement of organizational goals (Bernard, 1926; Blake, Shepard, & Mouton, 1964; Drath & Palus, 1994; Fiedler, 1967; House & Mitchell, 1974; Saal & Knight, 1988; Stogdill, 1974). History of the theory can be traced through numerous schools of thought beginning with the great man theory that emerged in the mid-19th century (Ololube, 2013) and evolved into today's numerous concepts of leadership growing out of transformational leadership theory (Alfian, 2016).

The main premise of great man theory was that leadership traits are inherent in the individual regardless of experience or education; however, this theory ignored both "situational and environmental factors that play

TABLE 2.3 Techniques for Promoting Positive School Board–Superintendent Relationships

Action	Description
Develop Norms	Agree how to treat each other, conduct business, deal with the public, conflict, and so forth.
Honesty	Be honest in all communications as lack of honesty destroys credibility.
Continuous, Two-way Communication	The board and superintendent must be constantly communicating—no favorites...everyone in the loop.
Fairness	Board members and superintendent must be fair, just, and caring in their associations.
Cooperation	Board/Superintendent relationships must be cooperative, not competitive. Relationship should not be a power struggle...it should be focused on helping each other.
Assistance	Superintendents must help assist board members to become effective.
Mutual Respect	Board and superintendent should honor each other's role, avoid usurping authority and never behave autocratically.
Commitment to Continuous Improvement	Yearly, the board and superintendent must focus on evaluations contributing to personnel performance, board performance, and improving relationships.
Trust	Studies continually cite "trust" as the most important element in relationships.
Effectiveness	Relationships are important due to the impact they have on the district. Say what you mean, and mean what you say, but don't say it mean!

a role in a leader's level of effectiveness" (Horner, 1997). The next wave of theory emerged in the 1930's and is known as trait theory, which incorporated the idea that leadership is dependent on innate personality traits such as technical skill, friendliness, and task motivation (Stodgill, 1974). The major criticism of trait theory was that although the identified traits may allow for leadership, they were difficult to measure (Bolden, Gosling, Marturano, & Dennison, 2003). In the 1960's contingency leadership theory emerged that asserted there is not one standard leadership style that will be effective across organizations. The limits of contingency leadership theories were that they were too general and subjective thus impossible to quantify (Naylor, 1999). In the following decade, transactional leadership emerged, which was characterized as a beneficial exchange between leaders and constituents through transactional exchanges (Alfian, 2016; Horner 1997). The benefits of transactional leadership theory were that transactional leadership theories are not encumbered by diversity or complexity of tasks and that the reward/consequence of the method are easy for people to understand; however, the theory tends to neglect human emotion and rewards motivated from a base-level (Bass & Bass, 2008). At the same time that transactional leadership theories were becoming popular, transformational leadership theories were coming into play. Transformational leadership theories incorporate the idea that a leadership approach can create change in both individuals and an organization through vision, which creates the capacity for both authentic interactions and professional opportunities (Burns, 1978). Several criticisms of transformational leadership included: too much reliance on one charismatic or popular leader, ambiguity in the leadership process, and issues related to measuring organizational outcomes (Evers & Lakomski, 1996; Stewart, 2006; Yukl, 1999).

With leadership theory evolving and changing based on our changing understanding of the world, is it possible to identify a consistent definition or formula of what motivates people to perform? In short, the answer to that question is no. Grounded in the review of leadership literature, there is not one universal definition of either a successful leadership model, which explains why leadership is a prevalent area of study across disciplines. Despite difficulties that arise in attempting to construct the appropriate model, two primary leadership paths are common within recent theory, one is a task-related focus and one is a people-related focus, and neither distinct path has been the determining factor in successful leadership (Amanchukwu, Stanley, & Ololube, 2015; Horner, 1997). The future of the theory appears to be headed toward new collaborative models that incorporate team-building, self-governance, and collaboration (Horner, 1997). Interestingly enough, Colorado superintendents are already well versed in these cooperative techniques.

Leadership Approaches, Theory in Action

The superintendent population we studied had an average age of 54, which means they were building critical leadership skills from the mid-1980s to the present. Concepts related to many forms of leadership theory, ranging from transactional leadership theory through team leadership behaviors, have shaped their perspectives to build diverse management methods dependent upon the individual situation in their districts. These leaders have learned to be familiar with the strengths and benefits of each numerous leadership models to assure flexibility and agility in a changing political environment. We found reoccurring themes of team building, self-governance, and collaboration emerge throughout the data collection cycle.

Superintendents are tasked with ensuring the implementation of federal and state mandates which are frequently unfunded or requires funding from a source that come from an already limited general budget (CDE, 2016b; Belansky et al., 2009; Johnson & Howley, 2015; Leachman & Mai, 2014; Ryley, 2012). Despite the resources accessible, the superintendency requires leadership that develops district and school conditions that allow for successful implementation of policy initiatives among an ever changing landscape of educational reform (U.S. Department of Education, 2015). This will necessitate a skillset of leadership practices that will promote change. Superintendents will need to envision new ways of meeting policy demands that call for equity and quality education for all students. Furthermore, these leaders will need to convey a clear sense of urgency and priority for implementation while being accountable to varied stakeholders.

Leithwood (1993) suggested that transformation leadership approaches may prove particularly useful when leaders are tasked with the challenges associated with the implementation of school reform initiatives. Leithwood, described transformational leadership as "those practices that foster significant growth not only in the overt practices of those experiencing leadership [. . .] but their capacities and motivations as well" (p. 4). While Leithwood (1993) focused on school-level processes, Leithwood (2016) later noted, that leadership practices identified at the school level could also be useful at the organizational level acknowledging that the representation of these practices would obviously be quantifiably different.

Leithwood and Jantzi (1999), identified 10 dimensions of leadership that incorporated not only transformational practices, but transactional or managerial practices as well. Leithwood and Jantzi contended that the transactional practices of leadership allowed for organizational stability. The full range of leadership practices they offered included: (a) building vision and goals, (b) providing intellectual stimulation, (c) offering individualized support, (d) symbolizing professional practices and values, (e) demonstrating high performance expectations, and (f) developing structures to foster participating in school decisions. Transactional or managerial strategies included: (a) staffing, (b) instructional support, (c) monitoring school activities, and (d) community focus. Therefore, as a transformational leader, the superintendent not only has to clearly communicate the purpose and goals of the initiative(s), but having the ability to garner motivation, capacity, and commitment at the organizational level are just as essential (Leithwood, 1993). Clear communication not only contributed to increased school effectiveness but motivation and commitment from stakeholders resulted in the engagement from others to become a part of the continual improvement effort (Leithwood, 1993).

The transformational and transactional leadership skills identified are closely aligned with the Professional Standards for Educational Leaders (2015). The standards for educational leaders serve to communicate expectations in regard to the complex work of educational leaders. Furthermore, the professional standards provide models of the values that reflect effective educational leadership. In the changing landscape of school reform, leadership becomes a salient feature in both the effective implementation of policy reform and in advocating for alternative ways to meet the needs of students. Leaders of the future will need to innovate, fast and boldly while maintaining a high level of tolerance for ambiguity and uncertainty, creating something that is both imaginative and useful (Hill, Travaglini, Brandeau, & Stecker, 2010).

While superintendents across the nation face tremendous odds in serving students and their communities, in Colorado, superintendents specifically in smaller rural districts are rising to the challenge (Belansky et al., 2009; Chin, Hammond, & Hickenlooper, 2012; Kaminsky, 2011; Mader, 2015). Colorado leaders in rural areas are attempting to think outside the box to meet the needs of students (Freeman & Randolf, 2013). For example, Mader (2015), reported that the Colorado Department of Higher Education is expanding five programs to help rural schools recruit and retain teachers and boost science, technology, engineering, and math programs. One of the state's programs is aimed at increasing grant funds to provide more professional development for teachers in rural areas and boost science, technology, engineering, and math (STEM) programs.

As rural schools grapple with hiring and retaining highly qualified teachers, providing quality education and instructional content to students is often compromised (Kaminski, 2011). School leaders have to become creative in how they will distribute human teaching capital so that equity and opportunity for learning is accessible to all students. Creative, innovation was a product of collaborative efforts between Colorado State University and the Board of Cooperative Educational Services (BOCES) in creating a distance learning program designed to meet the needs of high school students in rural districts. The distance learning program using an interactive video system allows students access to college preparatory, advanced placement, and vocational courses reaching over 1,000 students.

Another example of how rural superintendent are meeting the challenge of school reform is through the Colorado Innovation Schools Act (Chin et al., 2012). The Colorado Innovation Schools Act of 2008, was designed to allow flexibility for school districts through the implementation of structural changes that would address student and teacher needs. Applying to become an innovation school meant seeking change in school operations to better meet the needs of students. Twelve school districts within Colorado are currently participating in the program. Flexibility in hiring practices and instructional program structures are often needed in rural areas to do what is deemed best for district, school, and students. Some schools incorporated different instructional models such as Early Colleges or International Baccalaureate programs. Some schools opted for school improvement efforts by managing their workforces specifically with hiring practices which may have included alternate licensing requirements in an effort to obtain a teaching force that would be available for classrooms.

Other participating schools choose to manage school schedules and calendars differently increasing the instructional day or providing additional time to teacher collaboration and planning. One rural district focused its efforts on recruitment and retention strategies.

The use of networks particularly for smaller districts were great avenues for responding to change (Fox & Van Sant, 2011). Collaborative work can influence the direction and scope of the work creating professional capacity of school personnel and efficient operations and management of school resources. The Board of Cooperative Educational Services in Colorado is a model of sharing services and resources to rural schools. Given the challenges of rural school districts and to further collaborative efforts among rural districts, Colorado leaders have established a rural council to oversee the needs of rural education within the state (Fox & Van Sant, 2011). This council includes superintendents, BOCES representatives, professional associations, rural educators, and CDE in efforts aimed at problem solving issues pertinent to rural education. Colorado rural leaders now have an avenue to present their concerns and keep them front and center about the needs of their students in rural schools.

As the new teacher evaluation policy in Colorado, SB10-191 placed particular strain on leaders in rural communities, CDE developed a best practices research-based, self-assessment tool. The tool, the *Self-Assessment for a Healthy Human Capital System in Schools and Districts* (Ryley, 2012), was designed to provide a roadmap for districts to help build their knowledge in recognizing their capacity, strengths, and gaps in addition to identifying assistance and resources that might be provided by CDE to meet district and regional needs.

Superintendents are leading the way advocating for equity and professional capacity to meet the varied needs of students across the state. Through collaborative networking, they are able to communicate district needs and work within limited resources to implement reforms mainlining a clear and focused vision on students at the core.

SUMMARY AND CONCLUSIONS

Our analysis of the Colorado Superintendent Study revealed numerous themes. Within these themes we saw many juxtaposed perspectives and conflicting values that school leaders grappled with on a daily basis. The themes included contrasting areas and paradoxes such as: practice versus policy, theory versus application, and practitioner versus non practitioner views of schooling. However, the overarching theme that emerged from the study is the clash of cultures between Colorado superintendents and policy makers.

TABLE 2.4 Conflict of Cultures	
Colorado Superintendents	**Federal and State Policy Makers**
Focus on substance	Focus on perception
Building toward collaborative action	Top down mandates
Use resources wisely to advance system goals	Money does not matter for achieving results
Nurture a vision of schooling	Emphasis on performance measures
Accountable for things over which they have no control	Unaccountable for results of policies they create
Concerned with quality of end goal results (e.g., an improved society)	Concerned with narrow measure of performance indicators
Transformational Leadership	Transactional Leadership

Cultural leadership (House, Hanges, Javidan, Dorfman, & Gupta, 2004) offered an appropriate theoretical framework to describe the phenomena we observed in the data. Colorado superintendents live in a culture that is altruistic, while policy makers function in a political environment. One manifestation of this has been the cult of accountability imposed on public schools. The accountability movement and its dependence on performance measures is an ongoing hindrance negotiated by superintendents. Radin (2006), in her work on the subject exposed the flaws of the heavy-handed accountability policy perspective based on performance measures, which is a situation Colorado superintendents know all too well. Similarly, the late W. Edwards Deming was prescient when he predicted the adverse effects of education policies based on ratings, rankings, and mandating numerical goals without a method to reach them (Deming, 2000). Through our study, Colorado superintendents are telling us how they must steer their school districts around these hazards. Table 2.4 illustrates the conflict of cultures by way of contrast Colorado superintendents ascribe to professional codes of leadership that are imbedded in their training and seen in their professional standards (Kowalski, 2006; Northouse, 2012; National Policy Board for Educational Administration, 2015).

We end this chapter with a quote picked from over 300 comments gathered in the Colorado Superintendent Study; we believe it summarizes the voices and aspirations of Colorado superintendents well. Regarding Colorado public schools, "It is equal access and a promise for the future. Our schools are safe, productive learning environments where children thrive."

NOTE

1. All survey data referenced in this chapter can be accessed here: http://eric.ed.gov/?id=ED562366

REFERENCES

Alfian. (2016). How leadership style impacts the management information system: Quality—A theoretical study. *International Journal of Scientific Technology Research, 5*(6), 11–15.

Amanchukwu, R. N., Stanley, G. J., & Ololube, N. P. (2015) A review of leadership theories, principles, and styles and their relevance to educational management. *Management, 5*(1), 6–14.

Arnold, M. L. (2000). *Rural schools: Diverse needs call for flexible policies* (Policy Brief). Aurora: CO: Mid-Continent Research for Education and Learning.

Bass, B. M., & Bass, R. (2008). *The bass handbook of leadership: Theory, research, & managerial applications.* New York, NY: Free Press.

Belansky, E., Cutforth, N., DeLong, E., Ross, C., Scarbo, S., Gilbert, L., . . . Marshall, J. (2009). Early impact of the federally mandated local wellness policy on physical activity in rural, low-income elementary schools in Colorado. *Journal of Public Health Policy, 30,* 141–160.

Bernard, L. L. (1926). *An introduction to social psychology.* New York, NY: Holt.

Blake, R. R., Shepard, H. A., & Mouton, J. S. (1964). *Managing intergroup conflict in industry.* Houston, TX: Gulf.

Bolden, R., Gosling, J., Marturano, A., & Dennison, P. (2003). A review of leadership theory and competency frameworks: Edited version of a report for Chase Consulting and Management Standards Centre. University of Exeter Centre for Leadership Studies. Retrieved from http://www2.fcsh.unl.pt/docentes/luisrodrigues/textos/Lideran%C3%A7a.pdf

Branson, C. (2007). Effects of structured self-reflection on the development of authentic leadership practices among Queensland primary school principals. *Educational Management Administration & Leadership, 35*(2), 225–246.

Burns, J. M. (1978). *Leadership.* New York, NY: Harper & Row.

Chin, C., Hammond, R., & Hickenlooper, G. J. (2012). *Colorado Innovation Schools Act Annual Report.* Denver: CO: Colorado Department of Education.

Colorado Department of Education. (2016a, January 14). *Statewide preschool through 12th-grade student enrollment continues to grow.* Retrieved from http://www.cde.state.co.us/communications/20160114pupilmembership

Colorado Department of Education. (2016b). Understanding Colorado school finance and categorical program funding. Retrieved from http://www2.cde.state.co.us/artemis/edserials/ed55067internet/ed550672016internet.pdf

Colorado Department of Higher Education. (2016). *2016 Legislative Report Educator Preparation Report AY 2014–2015.* Retrieved from https://highered.colorado.gov/Publications/Reports/Legislative/TED/201602_TED_toGGA.pdf

Colorado School Finance Project. (2015). *Profile data: 2015 highlights.* Retrieved from https://cosfp.org/wp-content/uploads/StateProfileData/2015/ProfileDataHighlights_2015.pdf

Deming, W. E. (2000). *The new economics: For industry, government, education* (2nd ed.). Cambridge, MA: MIT Press.

Drath, W. H., & Palus, C. J. (1994). *Making common sense: Leadership as meaning-making in a community of practice.* Greensboro, NC: Center for Creative Leadership.

Ellis, K. P. (2008). Quality induction for teachers in rural schools. *School Administrator, 6*(9), 44–45.

Evers, C. W., & Lakomski, G. (1996). *Exploring educational administration: Coherentist applications and critical debates.* New York, NY: Elsevier Science.

Fiedler, F. E. (1967). *A theory of leadership effectiveness.* New York, NY: McGraw-Hill.

Freeman, G. G., & Randolph, I. (2013). Leadership strategies for maintaining success in a rural school district. *International Journal for Leadership in Learning, 1*(1), 1–18.

Fox, P., & Van Sant, D. (2011, January). *A rural needs study: Improving CDE services to rural school districts* (Research Report prepared for the Colorado Department of Education) Retrieved from the Colorado State Publication Library, Digital Repository: http://hermes.cde.state.co.us/drupal/islandora/object/co%3A10696

Great Education Colorado. (2016a). *Amendment 23 FAQs.* Retrieved from http://www.greateducation.org/statistics-faqs/funding-faqs/amendment-23/

Great Education Colorado. (2016b). *K–12 per pupil funding: Colorado versus national average.* Retrieved from: http://www.greateducation.org/resources/#14

Hill, L., Travaglini, M., Brandeau, G., & Stecker, E. (2010). Unlocking the slices of genius in your organization: Leading for innovation. In N. Nohria & R. Khurana (Eds.), *Handbook of leadership theory and practice* (pp. 611–654). Boston, MA: Harvard Business.

Horner, M. (1997). Leadership theory: Past, present, and future. *Team Performance Management: An International Journal, 3*(4), 270–287.

House, R. J., Hanges, P. J., Javidan, M., Dorfman, P. W., & Gupta, V. (Eds.). (2004). *Culture, leadership, and organizations: The GLOBE study of 62 societies.* SAGE.

House, R. J., & Mitchell, R. R. (1974, Fall). Path-goal theory of leadership. *Journal of Contemporary Business, 3*(4), 81–98.

Johnson, J., & Howley, C. B. (2015). Contemporary federal education policy and rural schools: A critical policy analysis. *Peabody Journal of Education, 90*(2), 224–241.

Kaminski, K. (2011, August). *Meeting high school highly qualified teacher requirements through distance learning.* Paper presented at the 27th Annual Conference on Distance Teaching & Learning, Madison, Wisconsin.

Kowalski, T. (2006). *The school superintendent, theory, practice, and cases.* Thousand Oaks, CA: SAGE.

Leachman, M., & Mai, C. (2014). *Most states still funding schools less than before the recession.* Washington, DC: Center on Budget and Policy Priorities.

Lee, R. J., & King, S. N. (2001) *Discovering the Leader in You.* San Francisco, CA: Jossey Bass.

Leithwood, K. (1993, October 29–31). *Contributions of transformational leadership to school restricting.* Convention of the University Council for Educational Administration, Houston, TX: The Ontario Institute for Studies in Education.

Leithwood, K. (2016). Department head leadership for school improvement. *Leadership and Policy in Schools, 15*(2), 117—140.

Leithwood, K, & Jantzi, D. (1999). Transformational school leadership effects: A replication. *School Effectiveness and School Improvement, 10*(4), 451–479.

Mader, J. (2015). Colorado offers more support to rural, understaffed schools. *Education Week*. Retrieved from http://blogs.edweek.org/edweek/rural_education/2015/01/colorado_offers_more_support_to_rural_understaffed_schools.html

Moller, M. R., Moller, L. L., & Schmidt, D. (2015). Examining the teacher pipeline: Will they stay or will they go? *Rural Educator, 37*(1), 25–38.

National Education Access Network. (2015). *School Funding Cases in Colorado*. Retrieved from https://cosfp.org/wp-content/uploads/HomeFiles/RegisFiscal Leadership/School_Funding_Cases_in_Colorado.pdf

National Policy Board for Education Administration. (2015). *Professional standards for educational leaders 2015: Previously the ISLLC standards.* Retrieved from https://ccsso.org/sites/default/files/2017-10/ProfessionalStandardsfor EducationalLeaders2015forNPBEAFINAL.pdf

Naylor, J. (1999). *Management.* Harlow, England: Prentice Hall.

No Child Left Behind Act [NCLB], 2001. Public Law PL 107-110.

Northhouse, P. (2012). *Introduction to leadership: Concepts and practice* (2nd ed.). Thousand Oaks, CA: SAGE.

Ololube, N. P. (2013). *Educational management, planning and supervision: Model for effective implementation.* Owerri, Nigeria: Springfield.

Radin, B. (2006). *Accountability culture: Challenging the performance movement.* Washington, DC: George Washington University Press.

Ramirez, A., Strawn, D., Clouse, W., & Radigan, P. (2015). Colorado School Superintendent Study, Academic Year 2014/15, Final Report. Retrieved from http://eric.ed.gov/?id=ED562366

Runhaar, P., Sanders, K., & Yang, H. (2010). Stimulating teachers' reflection and feedback asking: An interplay of self-efficacy, learning goal orientation, and transformational leadership. *Teaching and Teacher Education, 26,* 1154–1161.

Ryley, H. (2012, May). *Summary report: Exploring the potential impact of the Colorado healthy human capital self-assessment in rural districts.* Colorado Department of Education Educator Effectiveness Unit. Denver, CO. Retrieved from https://www.cde.state.co.us/educatoreffectiveness/humancapitalreport

Saal, F. E., & Knight, P. A. (1988). *Industrial/organizational psychology: Science and practice.* Pacific Grove, CA: Brooks/Cole.

Senate Bill SB10-191, Concerning Ensuring Quality Instruction Through Educator Effectiveness (EQUITEE), Colorado State legislature, Enacted 2010.

Stewart, J. (2006). Transformational leadership: An evolving concept examined through the works of Burns, Bass, Avolio, and Leithwood. *Canadian Journal of Educational Administration and Policy, 54,* 1–29.

Stogdill, R. M. (1974). *Handbook of leadership: A survey of theory and research.* New York, NY: Free Press.

Tekniepe, R. J. (2015). Identifying the factors that contribute to involuntary departures of school superintendents in rural America. *Journal of Research in Rural Education, 30*(1), 1–13.

U.S. Department of Education. (2015). *Every Student Succeeds Act (ESSA).* Retrieved from http://www.ed.gov/essa?src=rn.

Yukl, G. (1999). An evaluation of conceptual weaknesses in transformational and charismatic leadership theories. *Leadership Quarterly, 10,* 285–305.

CHAPTER 3

EFFECTIVE SYSTEMS' LEADERSHIP IN A RAPIDLY CHANGING ENGLISH EDUCATION SYSTEM

Ways Forward for U.S. Superintendents

Robin Precey
Christ Church Canterbury University

Terry Bennett
Executive Headteacher—London

This chapter traces the recent development of English compulsory state education and enables the reader to draw some comparisons between the English and U.S. education systems at present. It examines the current position with regard to system leaders in an increasingly dynamic, unpredictable English education system. The chapter traces the potential benefits and drawbacks of the new systems' leaders in England in terms of raising standards and closing the achievement gap between disadvantaged

The Contemporary Superintendent, pages 37–52
Copyright © 2019 by Information Age Publishing
All rights of reproduction in any form reserved.

students and their peers. There are lessons here, we hope, for the more established role of school superintendent in the United States in terms of what we know about future system leaders working in settings where accountability and autonomy are growing and where superintendents need to be even more effective in preparing their schools, staff and students for an increasingly globalised and exciting world. This is a goal shared by educators in the United States and England alike.

In writing as English educators we are well aware that, as George Bernard Shaw reportedly wrote, "England and America are two countries separated by the same language!" Despite this assertion, we believe there is sufficient common ground for shared lessons by system leaders working in both nations.

A BRIEF HISTORY OF RECENT SCHOOL EDUCATION IN ENGLAND: HOW HAVE THE NEW ENGLISH SYSTEMS EMERGED?

England is very different from the United States. It is smaller, with 53 million people, compared to 324 million and has a national rather than federal education system. Schools are largely funded nationally rather than locally. Until recently, this nationally determined education system was administered through a middle tier of 150 local authorities (LAs) compared to over 13,500 school districts in the U.S. In England there are:

- primary schools (students aged 4–11—similar to Elementary in the United States);
- secondary schools (students aged 11–18— similar to combined Junior and Senior High Schools. In England some areas secondary schools go from aged 11–16 with a separate college for the next two years).

However, in some LAs there are middle schools (similar to Junior High Schools) and Colleges (for 16–18 year olds). There are schools in some areas that select by academic ability at 11 years old, called grammar schools. There are faith schools representing the Church of England, Catholic, Muslim, Jewish, Sikh, Hindu and Quaker beliefs. There are specialist subject schools focusing, for example, on the arts, technology or sport. There are also single gender schools. All of these exist within the publicly funded system. It is a truly eclectic mix that has grown out of centuries of policies and practices. If you think of most criteria for school admissions, there is likely to be one to match them in England.

Recently central government in England has increased this heterogeneity as local authorities' powers have been reduced further and some LAs have all but disappeared. The government has strongly encouraged schools to convert to become academies over which the LAs have no authority. Their number grew dramatically from 203 in May 2010 to 4,515 in May 2016. Academies now constitute 61% of secondary schools and 14.5% of primary schools. The number is growing rapidly in parts of the country. There are also over 400 'free schools'; these are independent, state-funded schools that can be set up by parents or other interest groups, such as universities. Academies and free schools are directly funded by the Department for Education (DfE) and are directly accountable to the Secretary of State for Education, the chief minister for education in England and a member of the government's cabinet (executive body). Thus, academies and free schools circumvent the middle-tier. Added to this complexity are private (confusingly called 'public') fee-paying schools with 7% of school students.

In a further move to denude the influence of the middle-tier, and arguably to exert pressure on the quasi-independent national inspection service, Office for Standards in Education (Ofsted), a network of Regional School Commissioners (RSC) was established in 2014, each covering a geographical area of England. Rather than a replacement middle-tier, RSCs act as a proxy for the Secretary of State for Education. This role has attracted controversy. Firstly, the demarcation of responsibilities between the RSCs and Ofsted is blurred, leading to disagreements (Bloom, 2016). Secondly, RSCs are advised by Headteacher Boards (HTB), which are unelected and unaccountable and hold their meetings in secret. Members are appointed by the RSCs; headteachers of maintained (LA) schools are not eligible for membership. Thirdly RSCs are empowered to intervene in the affairs of maintained schools having precedence over the jurisdiction of LAs.

Alongside the demise of LAs, schools have formed their own arrangements to work together in several ways:

- Multi-Academy Trust (MAT)—Academy chains under a shared governance structure and sponsored by faith organizations, universities, businesses or even single entrepreneurs, e.g., ARK, Harris, Oasis.
- Federations where two or more maintained (i.e., local authority maintained) schools operate under the governance of a single governing body.
- Umbrella Trusts—partnerships of schools with a school improvement focus, such as THEP (Tower Hamlets Education Partnership in London), a 'school company' with charitable status owned by its member schools (THEP, 2017).

These partnerships between schools have emerged organically as opportunities have arisen. Some cover the whole country, others are localised; some are phase specific–primary or secondary, some are cross-phase; some have a faith ethos, while others are sponsored by wealthy benefactors.

All can be seen as new school systems, where a system is a group of schools that share some common governance, leadership and management. This may extend to use of resources as well as shared values and vision, e.g., the Oasis MAT is a Christian foundation. These system leaders have titles such as *Executive Principals, Executive Headteachers* or *CEOs* (Chief Executive Officer). In contrast to the headteacher role, which is clearly defined in legislation (Sections 35 and 36, Great Britain Education Act, 2002), there is no legal definition of a school executive headteacher or CEO.

The system leader's role is to make the system work through a leadership hierarchy with individual school site leaders. There are parallels with school superintendents in the USA in that they are responsible for the effective running and continual improvement of a group of schools.

THE CURRENT SITUATION WITH REGARD TO SYSTEM LEADERS IN ENGLAND

School system leaders are not a new phenomenon. Local Authorities, which were first established in 1902, are led by an individual, under various titles such as Director of Education or Chief Education Officer. However, these are a dying breed as the new academy and federation systems for schools have evolved, encouraged by central government, and this has seen the emergence of executive leadership roles. These new leaders generally are responsible for fewer schools than the LA Director of Education; their schools may be geographically dispersed and, in free schools and academies, their work may be monitored by government appointed National Schools Commissioners and the eight RSCs. The new system leaders have more direct control over what happens in the system in terms of its values and vision, as well as the strategic direction, and day-to-day management of individual schools within the group. There has been opposition to the notion of academies. For example, Smithers (2010) said that the plan to increase autonomy for schools will be divisive and disadvantaged children would lose out. However, it is now firmly embedded in government policy and unlikely to change in the near future. The system leaders described are here to stay in the English education structure. The rationale for the change in the system is that the new approach will lead to a more consistent and indeed systemic impact to improve children's education (Great Britain Academies Act, 2010). Lack of consistency of standards of teaching has been identified as one of the main obstacle to school improvement (Driessen & Sleegers, 2011)

Hargreaves (2010) argues that a school system can be self-improving and says that much of the responsibility then moves from both central and local government to the agencies in the schools. System leaders can more effectively lead school improvement because the sense of moral purpose can be communicated and shared better in smaller system than in the former LAs. However, although this may be more possible within these new systems, there are emerging concerns about the inconsistencies between these and the role of central government, through Ofsted, to monitor and promote consistency across the country. Following an inspection visit, Ofsted will rate a school as "outstanding," "good," "requires improvement" or "inadequate." This grading system has a predictable impact on the school's leadership direction and its marketability.

THE MAIN FEATURES OF ENGLISH SCHOOL SYSTEMS

There are at least four important features of this system and the leadership role in England, each with their own potential advantages and drawbacks. They are:

- the underpinning principles of autonomy, moral purpose and accountability;
- the growth of distributed leadership within the systems;
- the continued, resolute, focus on attainment (with some signs of a broadening curriculum);
- the development of national standards for system leaders.

These features (see Figure 3.1) are each complex and relate to each other in a variety of ways, some of which present new challenges as well

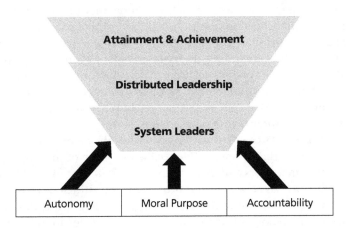

Figure 3.1 The key features of systems leadership in English schools.

as new opportunities, e.g., the relationships between moral purpose and accountability, between autonomy and distributed leadership, between accountability and achievement.

Systems Driven by Autonomy and Accountability

In England, there is a clear top tier. The national education system is led by the DfE in terms of curriculum, assessment and funding and by Ofsted in relation to a national inspection. It is all very well having a national curriculum and ways of judging schools, but there need to be levers that enable this to happen. What are these levers?

On October 18, 1976 the then-Prime Minister of England, James Callaghan, gave a speech in Ruskin College, Oxford University, that is widely regarded as having begun 'The Great Debate' within the country about the nature and purpose of public education. From this time a consistent twin-pronged policy for education has been pursued relentlessly by politicians, albeit with differing interpretations depending on the nature of the ruling government. These are the levers:

School Autonomy. Since the Great Britain Education Act (1988) schools have had control over their finances, with devolved budgets under local management of schools (LMS) along with the power to hire and fire staff. Head teachers have gradually had their powers increased, supported and challenged by Governing Bodies (analogous with the School Board in the United States).

School accountability. This autonomy is balanced, some would say subjugated, to the second policy lever: accountability. This occurs through an interconnected set of national strategies: delegated funding linked to student numbers; parental choice of schools; judgement by regular external published Ofsted inspection reports; the publication of examination league tables naming individual schools and freely available to all; performance management of staff including the system leaders. A major difference in England is that the processes leading to test outcomes form part of the (Ofsted) accountability judgement, not just the school's test performance itself (Supovitz, 2015). Leaders have power but, like football coaches, can lack job security if their team's performance slips.

Moral purpose. These extrinsic levers underpin the drive for school improvement, but perhaps more influential is the sense of moral purpose of individual system leaders and their desire to do their best for their students. Fullan (2002, p.1) argues that moral purpose is insufficient as our morality connects with something deeper – our spirituality. He writes about "a somewhat cumbersome term "moral purpose writ large" to indicate we are talking about principled behaviour connected to something greater than ourselves that relates to human and social development". How this moral purpose writ large manifests itself is the domain of the system leader, as long as their individual schools are succeeding in terms of their Ofsted rating and their performance data.

Central government and many systems leaders themselves would stress the inherent advantages of the evolution towards academy chains and federations in England, particularly in relation to autonomy. Hargreaves, seeing the self-improving school system as a family, calls these Family Virtues (Hargreaves, 2010). It allows systems the freedom to construct their own philosophies and implement methodologies to educate young people within the accountability checks.

- It frees up leaders to lead strategically ensuring that their system's values, vision and strategy match the operational management and ultimately lead to the desired student outcomes.
- It permits leaders to respond swiftly and appropriately to the latest national policy in a constantly changing landscape.

In this environment, much depends on the ability of the leaders and their relationship with their Governing body. Interestingly it has been difficult to recruit both systems leaders and governing body members. Despite the fact that system leaders are relatively well paid, recruitment is a problem (Wigdortz and Toop, 2016). Governing bodies are unpaid and vacancies can be very difficult to fill (James, Goodall, Howarth & Knights, 2014). The intense accountability and high workload required for both are contributing factors.

Schools are funded individually and it is not legally possible to vire funding between schools within a system. Increasingly, however, staff have contracts across a system, so they can be deployed in any of its schools. Repayments through one school charging another for services can help solve the funding issue. However, there are signs that some schools seek to charge parents for additional services (at present voluntary contributions), particularly as budgets are reduced. This is controversial in England; schools in deprived areas, where pupils have the greatest need, may find it difficult to secure funds from their families.

National Standards and Training for Systems Leaders That Are Fit for Purpose

The school district system within the U.S. has led to the well-established school superintendent role with a career path to reach that point and be effective. English schools have had to respond to some seismic shifts in education. After over sixty years of a settled middle-tier local authority model we now have a rapidly expanding model where the middle tier has been deliberately eroded. Further professional development for aspiring and existing system leaders has been needed. The National College for Teaching and Leadership (NCTL), previously the National College for School Leadership (NCSL) established in 2000, is an executive agency of the DfE. It has developed a new course for Executive Leaders (NPQEL). This blended learning program entails five coaching sessions, three online modules (in Teaching and Curriculum Excellence, Strategy and Improvement and Managing Resources and Risks), two 360 degree diagnostics, and a multi school improvement project. Those who successfully complete the NPQEL can be awarded two-thirds of a Master's degree.

It is useful to have standards for systems leaders in order prepare, select, guide practice and evaluate the performance of individuals, but there are dangers in these being overly prescriptive and so stifling creativity; some outstanding leaders are "responsibly maverick." In England the new *National Standards of Excellence for Headteachers* (DfE 2015) are forward thinking with an emphasis on values and procedures. There are four Domains (Qualities and Knowledge, Pupils (students) and Staff, Systems and Processes, the Self Improving School System) each have six standards which are aspirational and very useful to anyone seeking to create a world class school system. They are guidance, rather than compulsory but they provide appropriate challenge for leaders of school systems anywhere in the world.

A criticism is that they omitted the chance to stress the importance that leaders look after themselves. System leaders need to be values-driven focused on learning, smart and fit for purpose. However, if these Standards of Excellence are taken seriously in England they could make a real difference to ensure that the new order is better than that which preceded it.

It would seem that a revolution in the preparation and continuous professional development of system leadership in England is needed but, as is usual in education, evolution is the norm.

Systems Founded on Distributed Leadership

The English education system has developed since the 1970s to be highly hierarchical certainly when compared to most European systems. This may be due to a wide variety of factors such as the influx of management theory from (mainly from the United States), and additional resourcing under successive Labour governments from 1997 to 2010 along with increased legislation developing a perceived need for more specialist roles in schools. The autonomy–accountability agenda has exacerbated this hierarchical nature. For example, funding and responsibilities for children with special educational needs have grown following legislation such as the Great Britain Special Education Needs and Disability Act (2001). Hence most schools have specialist SEN provision led by a SEN coordinator who is likely to be part of the leadership structure and a team of non-teacher (support) staff. Typically, English schools have leadership teams and middle managers in a hierarchical formation, which can be complex and present a challenge in terms of communication. In order for this to be effective, it is vital that each part of the system is aware of others' roles and responsibilities.

The emerging school systems leaders have a larger pool of people to fill the roles at each level in the hierarchy. Transformational leadership can secure succession planning by identifying future leaders, providing bespoke professional development and anticipating future needs. In addition, system leaders can achieve economies of scale and avoid role duplication across the schools in their group by appointing cross-system curriculum leaders, specialist and administrative staff. English education currently has a recruitment crisis for both teachers ("English secondary schools", 2017; Pells and Khan, 2017) and leaders (Hazell, 2017). System leaders can offer potential applicants for role a number of benefits such as the opportunity to work across schools with consistent values and practices and thus gain a wider experience with greater opportunities for career progression. Most importantly through succession planning and growing their own leaders, system leaders can focus on retention to mitigate the expensive process of recruitment.

There are dangers in school systems becoming introspective. Effective system leaders are outward-looking, providing training and study visits to schools and businesses, sometimes including overseas study visits, although this is likely to be effected by the current funding pressures in England. The NCTL commissions organizations to run professional qualifications for aspiring and serving leaders as part of its brief. Currently it offers three programs below Executive leader. These are the National Professional Qualifications for middle leaders (NPQML), senior leaders (NPQSL) and headteachers (NPQH). At best these qualifications, along with relevant university-based Masters' programs and in-house professional development, enable system leaders to ensure that their teams have a greater understanding of their role to be more effective.

Systems Focused on Improving Student Achievement and Attainment and the Wider Curriculum

Sahlberg (2011) has written critically about the Global Education Reform Movement (GERM) which he claims has led to conformity and a slavish focus on valuing what can be measured. The PISA (Program for International

Students Assessment) international league tables for the attainment of 15 years old in reading, mathematics and science are an essential aspect of GERM and are taken very seriously by politicians particularly in Europe and Asia. Ball (2010) has argued that England has been at the forefront of this performativity culture. All who have an interest in education wish for education standards to rise, as Robinson (2010) says "who would want them to fall?" The PISA tables throw into sharp focus the use of public money in enabling young people to attain basic skills. In England they have driven policy leading to Acts of Parliament in 2006, 2010, 2011 and 2016 with a knock-on effect on spending priorities and practices in schools.

The English system is very much a market-oriented one with delegated funding based on student numbers, which are themselves determined by 'parental choice'. A school needs to attract students in order to stay open and in business. Each school's levels of attainment, and Ofsted rating, become significant in this context. In England, successive governments have professed high aspirations for young people. This may be encapsulated in the words of David Cameron, an ex- Prime Minister, as *"Raising the bar and closing the gap"* (Cameron, 2007). All those with an interest in education are aware of the wide variations between levels of attainment for different categories of students based on ethnicity, socio-economic deprivation, special educational needs, gender etc. The London Challenge was a highly successful school improvement program, launched by the Labour government in 2003 (Brighouse, 2015), that can justifiably claim to have both raised the bar and closed the attainment gap. The Department for Education and Science policy document "Transforming London Secondary Schools" (DfES, 2003) set out the aims of the program; to raise standards in the poorest performing schools; to narrow the attainment gap between pupils in London; to create more good and outstanding schools. It was designed to create a "step change" in the performance of London secondary schools.

The London Challenge initiative has been credited with securing a significant improvement in London's state education system. Ofsted reported in 2010 that "London Challenge has continued to improve outcomes for students in London's primary and secondary schools at a faster rate than nationally. London's secondary schools continue to perform better than those in the rest of England" (Ofsted, 2010, p.1). Programs of support for schools are planned with experienced and credible London Challenge advisers using a shared and accurate audit of need. Excellent system leadership and pan-London networks of schools allow effective partnerships to be established between schools, enabling needs to be tackled quickly and progress to be accelerated".

A more recent study identified the London Challenge as one factor in several that contributed to significant enhancements in student outcomes (Baars et al., 2015). The London Challenge program was initially aimed at secondary schools and was intended to run until 2008. It was subsequently extended until 2011 and expanded to include primary schools. Two additional City Challenge areas were established in the metropolitan areas of Greater Manchester and the Black Country in the west midlands in England.

These initiatives have demonstrated that improvement can be secured when they:

- are based on open, honest collaboration between schools so that they learn from each other's good practice,
- instil a forensic examination and understanding of performance data to guide actions for improvement focused in individual students, and investment in high quality leadership and
- encourage continuous professional development at all levels of the school hierarchy.

Lessons can be learned from the significant improvement in London schools and the emerging systems leadership landscape in England should make this more possible as collaboration within and between groups of schools in each system becomes the norm. A caveat is whether such collaboration between systems is achievable in a competitive market situation.

Changes in Measuring Attainment and the Wider Curriculum (Achievement) in English Schools: Implications for System Leaders

In England GERM, fuelled by PISA, has led to a reliance on measureable levels of attainment as the primary judgement of a school's success. The relationship between these student performance metrics and other important aspects of educational achievement that includes the wider curriculum (such as sport, music, drama, art), personal development skills (confidence, self-esteem, tolerance, emotional intelligence) and future skills (learning and innovation, digital literacy and career and life skills) (Trilling and Fadel 2009), has been imbalanced in recent years. Things are changing and the new systems are again able to make the changes happen more quickly. Once a school is graded by Ofsted as "Good" or "Outstanding" the +school leaders tend to focus on autonomy rather than accountability and take steps to broaden the curriculum.

Attainment and Progress—Some Changes for the Better

Until recently, the focus on attainment in England was simplistic and crude. In secondary education the measure was the test results for each

16-year-old student. To count as success a student had to attain in the top three (A–C) of the six pass grades (A–F) in each of five subjects (including English and Mathematics). These norm-referenced national examinations failed to recognise the achievements of many students who made great progress from low starting points yet did not meet the A to C level. In 2013, the government announced a new secondary school accountability system which was to be implemented from 2016 and show a more enlightened view on assessing and valuing what students learn: Attainment 8 and Progress 8.

Attainment 8 measures the achievement of a student across eight qualifications including mathematics (double weighted) and English (double weighted) and six further qualifications from the DfE (2017) approved list. This is similar to the previous system but in eight subjects instead of five.

Progress 8 aims to capture the progress a pupil makes from the end of primary school (age 11) to the end of secondary school (age 16). It is a value added measure, which means that students' results are compared to the actual achievements of other student with the same prior attainment. These new performance measures are designed to encourage schools to offer a broad and balanced curriculum with a focus on an academic core for 14-16 year olds. It rewards schools for the teaching of all their students, measuring performance across 8 subjects. Every increase in every grade a student achieves attracts additional points in the performance tables. Progress 8 does not identify individual students but rather provides a school-by-school comparison. The headline measures which now appear in the school published performance tables are:

- progress across 8 qualifications;
- attainment across the same 8 qualifications;
- percentage of students achieving the threshold grade in English and Mathematics General Certificate of Education examinations;
- percentage of students entering the English Baccalaureate;
- percentage of students achieving the English Baccalaureate;
- destinations (percentage of students staying in education or employment after the age of 16).

This focus on attainment in English schools over the last forty years means that learning-centred leadership, with its focus on classroom practice and pedagogy, has become more relevant. This is seen as the core purpose of schools and the core responsibility of all leaders especially those who lead the systems. System leaders are usually ex-headteachers, so have a grounding in learning and teaching. They are able to take a strategic view on improving levels and progress of attainment. They are increasingly doing this by ensuring good practice is identified and shared, deploying resources, including staff, in ways that foster equity. Strategic planning and resource management across a system is more likely to be successful with closer leadership and on a smaller scale than in the local authority model.

The Wider Curriculum: Achievement and Broadening What Is Valued to Include Other Aspects of Education

There is a real danger in this focus on attainment, albeit broadening to progress, in that we only value what can be measured. We do not allow children to live their lives. We measure their existence. Systems leaders can raise these other important aspects of a child's education up the priority list as long as the academic standards are high. This is not an either or situation as research shows that the other things (music, art, sport, drama, volunteering, community work etc.) build long term sustainable attitudes and skills such as confidence, purpose, resilience, enjoyment, mental health and wellbeing and a sense of belonging that can reinforce the desire and skills to achieve academically. Fielding (2006) argues that by centering schools on relationships recognising and celebrating all aspects of what it is to be human, the academic performance is also improved. Research studies (Kirwan and MacBeath, 2008) have also shown this to be true.

The Ofsted inspection process (Ofsted, 2016) does throw a spotlight on personal development and welfare. The inspection teams are expected to report, for example, on whether students are confident, self-assured learners. They form a judgement on students' attitudes to learning and pride in their achievements and their school. They comment on whether students' spiritual, moral, social and cultural development equips them to be thoughtful, caring and active citizens in school and in wider society.

English schools have a long tradition in extra-curricular learning as well but the standards agenda had diverted attention away from this as they have been pushed towards teaching to the test. There is a growing realisation that attainment and the wider curriculum go hand in hand and can support each other. In an accountability regime it can be a challenge to gather convincing evidence that "soft" outcomes can be evaluated. However, some interesting work is going on in this area; one example is International Quality Education Resource for Educational Leaders (iQerel). This is a website for school self-evaluation developed across five European countries that was launched in 2014 (Christ Church Canterbury University, 2014). It provides information and tools on how to evaluate a whole range of aspects of schooling including attainment, innovation and creativity, continuing professional development, belonging, relationships and trust, care, engagement, participation and community. It also offers advice on evaluating the underpinning of a school's education—slippery concepts such as equality, equity, social justice and globalisation.

In the former LA system in England it was often difficult to get and maintain momentum around such initiatives. Systems leaders steeped in learning are in a more powerful position to ensure consistency across schools so that both attainment and achievement are valued, resourced, celebrated and improving.

CONCLUSIONS: WHAT CAN WE LEARN?

System leaders can secure consistency of values, policies and practices. They can be outward looking enabling them to anticipate and prepare for threats and to seize opportunities. They can cross-pollinate good practice across the components of the system. They can monitor and evaluate teaching and learning to ensure that the best becomes the norm. They can deploy resources creatively to improve efficiency and narrow the attainment gap. They can create developmental opportunities for talented staff at all levels and so grow the systems' future leaders and so aid retention. All of these outcomes will have a beneficial impact on students' learning.

These are all possibilities, but none of this can happen without effective system leadership. The pressure is increasing on system leaders across the world and this is particularly true for England and the USA. PISA results and international standings fuel politicians' thinking. Policy-makers in both nations will be unhappy with their respective PISA rankings. Education is a cornerstone of peoples' lives. It is our investment in the future. Leadership matters (Day et al,. 2009) and, particularly, the leadership of school systems matters, as this sets the culture. An important feature of this is that people matter; therefore leadership that values people matters. As the twentieth century rolls on with its uncertainty, ambiguity and complexity, the development of transformational educational system leaders who value people must be a high priority. In England the new executive headteacher role forged in the furnace of autonomy and accountability and provides an opportunity for more radical, even revolutionary change.

The United States and England have very different education systems in terms of size and organisation, but both share a common goal: to provide the highest quality education for all students. We may be two countries separated by a common language, but we share this common purpose. System leaders have the responsibility and privilege to breathe life into that purpose. Although the English developments may seem somewhat laissez-faire with the drawbacks that brings, the new schools systems in England offer a potential to raise standard of education for all students. A culture driven by autonomy and accountability, emerging aspirational national standards and training for system leaders, a history of distributed leadership in schools and the redefinition of student attainment as well as a renewed interest in a broader definition of student achievement make it more possible to raise the bar AND narrow the gap.

REFERENCES

Ball, S. (2010). The teacher's soul and the terrors of performativity. *Journal of Education Policy, 18*(2), 215–228.

Bloom, A. (2016, March 2). Sir Michael Wilshaw hits back at 'faceless' schools commissioners. *Times Education Supplement.*

Brighouse, T. (2015). Local Authorities and the London Challenge. *London Councils.* Retrieved from https://www.londoncouncils.gov.uk/download/file/fid/14885

Barrs, S., Bernardes, E., Elwick, A., Malorite, A., McAleavy, T., McInerney, L., & Riggall, A. (2014). *Lessons from London schools: Investigating the success.* London, England: CfBT Education Trust.

Cameron, D. (2007). *Raising the bar, closing the gap.* Speech by David Cameron, November 20, 2007. Retrieved from http://conservative-speeches.sayit.mysociety.org/speech/599738

Christ Church Canterbury University. (2014). *Erasmus+ funding awarded to develop school leadership across Europe.* Retrieved from https://www.canterbury.ac.uk/news-centre/press-releases/2014/press-release.aspx?instance=2363

Day, C., Sammons, P., Hopkins, D., Harris, A., Leithwood, K., Gu, Q., . . . Kington, A. (2009). *The impact of school leadership on pupil outcomes: Final report.* London, England: Department for Children, Schools and Families.

Department for Education. (2015). *National standards for excellence for headteachers.* London, England: Author.

Department for Education. (2017). *Progress 8 and Attainment 8.* London, England: Author.

Department for Education and Science. (2003). *London challenge: Transforming London secondary schools.* London, England: Author.

Driessen, G. and Sleegers, P. (2011). Consistency of teaching approach and student achievement: An empirical test. *School Effectiveness and School Improvement, 11*(1), 57–79.

English secondary schools "facing perfect storm of pressures." (2017, April 29). *The Guardian.*

Fielding, M. (2006). Leadership, personalization and high performance schooling: Naming the new totalitarianism. *School Leadership & Management, 26*(4), 347–369.

Fullan, M. (2002). Moral purpose writ large: The pressing goal is to infuse spiritual force into all educators. *The School Administrator Web Edition,* September 2002. Retrieved from: http://michaelfullan.ca/wp-content/uploads/2016/06/13396048660.pdf

Great Britain Academies Act 2010, ch. 32.

Great Britain Education Reform Act 1988, ch. 40.

Great Britain Special Educational Needs and Disabilities Act 2010, ch. 10.

Hargreaves, D. (2010). *Creating a self-improving school system.* Nottingham, England: NCSL

Hazell, W. (2017, May 9). Recruitment crisis: "I switched to teaching so I could make a difference." *Times Educational Supplement.*

James, C., Goodall, J., Howarth, E., & Knights, E. (2014). *The state of school governing in England*. Bath: National Governors' Association.

Kirwan, T., and MacBeath, J., (2008). *ECM Premium Project: School leadership, Every Child Matters and school standards*. Retrieved from National College for School Leaders http://dera.ioe.ac.uk/9160/1/download%3Fid%3D18633%26filename%3Decm-premium-project-case-studies.pdf

Office for Standards in Education. (2010). *London Challenge*. Manchester, England: Author.

Office for Standards in Education. (2016). *School inspection handbook*. Manchester, England: Author.

Pells, R., & Khan, S. (2017, February 21). Teacher shortages at "crisis" point as pupil numbers set to soar, MPs warn. *The Independent*.

Robinson, K. (2010). *Changing education paradigms*. TED.com. Retrieved from https://www.ted.com/talks/ken_robinson_changing_education_paradigms

Sahlberg, P. (2011). *Finnish lessons: What can the world learn from educational change in Finland?* New York, NY: Teachers College Press.

Smithers, A. (2010, June 27). Letting schools do their own thing is a recipe for chaos. *The Independent*. Retrieved from http://www.independent.co.uk/news/education/schools/alan-smithers-letting-schools-do-their-own-thing-is-a-recipe-for-chaos-2007722.html

Supovitz, J. (2015). Building a lattice for school leadership: Lessons from England. *CPRE Policy Briefs*. Retrieved from http://repository.upenn.edu/cpre_policybriefs/7

THEP, (2017). *Tower Hamlets Education Partnership*. Retrieved from https://the-partnership.org.uk/about-us

Trilling, B., & Fadel, C. (2009). *21st century life skills: Learning for life in our times*. San Francisco, CA: Wiley.

Wigdortz, B., & Toop, J. (2016). *The School Leadership Challenge: 2022*. London, England: Future Leaders Trust, Teaching Leaders and TeachFirst.

CHAPTER 4

SUPERINTENDENTS WHO LEAD FOR OPTIMAL LEARNING

Nine Insights

Jim Brandon
University of Calgary

Paulette Hanna
Red Deer College

Kent Donlevy
University of Calgary

Dennis Parsons
University of Calgary

Though it is widely acknowledged that the professional practice of the contemporary Canadian school superintendent is increasingly complex and incredibly demanding (Alberta Teachers' Association, 2016; Hetherington, 2014; Parsons, 2015; Parsons & Brandon, 2017), many superintendents do manage to devote a high proportion of their time to building, supporting,

The Contemporary Superintendent, pages 53–72
Copyright © 2019 by Information Age Publishing
All rights of reproduction in any form reserved.

and assuring quality leadership and quality teaching across their districts. In fact, the learning focused leadership of Alberta school superintendents contributes significantly to the success of the provincial school system—a school system that is consistently rated as one of the best in the world (Barber, Whalen, & Clarke, 2010; Coughlan, 2017; Hargreaves & Fullan, 2012; Hargreaves & Shirley, 2012a, 2012b).

This chapter illuminates nine insights about the leadership practices employed by six Alberta superintendents whose steadfast focus on educator and student learning have yielded positive results within their school systems. These insights stem from our recent collective case study that examined a number of ways that superintendency teams lead learning in highly successful and learning oriented Alberta school districts (Brandon, Hanna, & Negropontes, 2015, 2016; Brandon, Hanna, Donlevy, & Parsons, 2018). The purpose of the study was to better understand the *overall* instructional leadership practices of these six superintendency teams who had been identified as leaders of educator and student learning. To this end, we collected and analyzed qualitative data from 23 focus groups and 16 individual interviews that accessed the perspectives of 53 principals, 33 middle-level district leaders, and 28 superintendency team leaders. In addition, we gathered evidence from field notes, observations, and documentary sources. An online survey was also administered to 48 participants in the larger study to augment the qualitative data as reported in Brandon et al. 2015 and 2016, as well as Brandon et al. 2018. This chapter is based solely on the qualitative portion of the study.

With the February 7, 2018 approval of three professional practice standards by the Minister of Education, the timing could not be better for superintendents to learn from these insights in view of these new provincial expectations that place even greater priority on optimal learning for all Alberta students. The three standard documents all focus on optimal learning for all students and each conceptualizes professional practice in similar ways.

> Quality *teaching* occurs when the teacher's ongoing analysis of the context, and the teacher's decisions about what pedagogical knowledge and abilities to apply result in optimum learning for all students. (Alberta Education, 2018a)
>
> Quality *leadership* occurs when the leader's ongoing analysis of the context, and the leader's decisions about what leadership knowledge and abilities to apply, result in quality teaching and optimum learning for all students in the school. (Alberta Education, 2018b)
>
> Quality *superintendent leadership* occurs when the superintendent's ongoing analysis of the context, and the superintendent's decisions about what leadership knowledge and abilities to apply, result in quality school leadership, quality teaching, and optimum learning for all students in the school authority. (Alberta Education, 2018c)

In each standard statement, professional practice is based on the professional's reading of the context and the application of the professional's judgement about the professional knowledge and skills that will most likely lead to optimum learning for *all* students. All three standard documents are structured in the same manner: one standard, six to nine required competencies, and several optional indicators. For the first time in history, there is a strong throughline in the professional practice expectations for teachers, principals, and superintendents. It is an opportune time for superintendents to apply lessons learned from insights into the ways that highly successful and learning oriented superintendents enact their district leadership practices. Concentrating district leadership efforts on the nine overlapping areas of practice that emerged as themes from our collective case study, provides a manageably coherent and research-informed approach to the superintendency in complex times.

This chapter unfolds in six parts, beginning with an overview of the Alberta context, followed by a short description of the six individual school districts. The conceptual framework that situated the study in the existing research literature is presented before the collective case study research design is explained. We then focus on the nine cross-case themes that were developed through more detailed analysis of individual case findings and emerging themes. Discussion in the concluding section sheds light on ways in which insights from the larger themes may be used to guide superintendency team practice in other settings.

THE ALBERTA CONTEXT

Alberta's school system serves the province's 606,627 students in 1,868 schools organized into 62 school districts. The system employs 41,000 full- and part-time teachers, each of whom is professionally prepared and provincially certificated in accordance with the provincial *Teaching Quality Standard* (Alberta Education, 2018a). In addition to their university level teacher education, beginning teachers are only granted permanent certification on the recommendation of their school superintendents following two full years of successful teaching. Individuals wanting to become teachers need to have a bachelor's in education or possess a recognized university degree supplemented by completion of a teacher preparation program leading to a provincially approved *interim certificate.*

Within Alberta's public school system, 135,720 (22.3%) of the students attend one of the 372 Catholic schools, 5,565 (1%) attend 34 Francophone schools, and another 7,547 (1.2%) are enrolled in one of the 18 public charter schools operated by the 13 public charter school authorities. Public schools in the province are operated by 41 public, 16 Catholic, and five

Francophone publicly elected school boards. Of the choices available to parents in the province, only 4% opt for private education.

SIX HIGHLY SUCCESSFUL ALBERTA SCHOOL DISTRICTS

The six school districts we selected for the study can be described as *highly successful* and *focused on learning*. Although many Alberta school districts could be described in these ways, we made our final determinations from a longer list to gain insights from the perspectives of district and school leaders in a range of rural and urban settings, public and separate school boards, and a variety of geographic locations across the province. We further decided to focus on districts that had not previously been studied through research conducted through the support of the College of Alberta School Superintendents (Brandon, Hanna, Morrow, Rhyason, & Schmold, 2013; Friesen & Locke, 2010).

Table 4.1 presents a summary of key demographic information for each district in the order in which we gathered the data over the spring, summer, and fall of 2014: Chinook's Edge School Division, St. Albert Public Schools, Westwind School Division, Holy Family Catholic Regional Division, Fort McMurray Catholic Schools, and the Calgary Board of Education.

CONCEPTUAL FRAMEWORK

Evidence to support the claim that district leadership does play a significant role in improving student *success*—student engagement, learning, and

TABLE 4.1   District Demographic Information

District	Students	Teachers FTE	Schools	District Notes
Chinook's Edge School Division	10,768	580	43	Large Rural Central Alberta
St. Albert Public Schools	7,202	387	14	Small Urban Edmonton Region
Westwind School Division	4,326	248	13[a]	Small Rural Southern Alberta
Holy Family Catholic Regional Division	2,165	158	9	Small Urban/Rural NW Alberta
Fort McMurray Catholic Schools	5,482	315	10	Small Urban NE Alberta
Calgary Board of Education	110,165	6,035	225	Large Urban Calgary Region

[a] plus 19 Hutterite Brethren schools

well-being—has been documented in an increasing number of recent studies. Of the research reports featured in our review of the literature, three are viewed as seminal studies that together provide a general overview of the most compelling evidence of school district leadership contributions to student success. Leithwood's (2010a) meta-analysis of 31 published reports identified 12 common characteristics of high performing districts. Louis, Leithwood, Anderson, and Wahlstrom's (2010) massive study investigated school and district links to student learning over a 6-year period. They underlined the importance the district leadership in four areas: setting direction, developing people, redesigning the organization, and managing the instructional program. The meta-analysis of school system leadership by Marzano and Waters (2009) provided substantive evidence that district leadership matters and "that when district leaders are carrying out their leadership responsibilities effectively, student achievement across the district is positively affected" (p. 5).

The *Alberta Framework for School System Success* (Brandon, Hanna, Morrow, Rhyason, & Schmold, 2013) was founded on these three seminal studies of district leadership impact as well as additional current research in this same vein. It features 12 research verified leadership dimensions organized within four areas of collective practice as outlined in Table 4.2. Whereas each of the dimensions is a system leadership quality positively correlated to student learning, the four practice areas—*vision and direction setting, capacity building, relationships* and *system design* have been established to formulate a conceptually coherent structure for thinking and acting from the perspective of a district leadership team member.

Leading Learning at the District Level

We were guided by research from a variety of sources, but organized within five Alberta framework dimensions that we believed to be more

TABLE 4.2 The Alberta Framework for School System Success	
Vision and Direction Setting	**Relationships**
Dimension 1: Focus on Student Learning	Dimension 7: System Connections
Dimension 2: Curriculum and Instruction	Dimension 8: Parent–Community Engagement
Dimension 3: Uses of Evidence	Dimension 9: School Board Leadership
Capacity Building	**System Design**
Dimension 4: System Efficacy	Dimension 10: System Alignment
Dimension 5: Leadership for Learning	Dimension 11: System Improvement
Dimension 6: Professional Learning	Dimension 12: Leveraging Technology

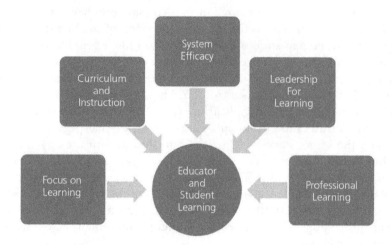

Figure 4.1 Conceptual framework.

specifically applicable to informing district instructional leadership practices: (a) a district wide focus on student learning (Framework Dimension 1); (b) the alignment of curriculum, instruction, and assessment (Framework Dimension 2); (c) system efficacy (Framework Dimension 3); (d) expecting and supporting instructional leadership at the both the district and school levels (Framework Dimension 5); and (e) research informed approaches to professional learning (Framework Dimension 6).

In maintaining a clear *chain of evidence* our interview protocols and survey items were derived from the study's five-dimension conceptual framework (Yin, 2009). As a conceptual consolidation of specific district leadership practices that impact student outcomes, the framework was then used as an organizational guide for the coding, descriptive, and report writing processes we employed.

RESEARCH DESIGN

Our collective case study design addressed the following research question: "In what ways do successful superintendency teams lead educator and student learning?" The qualitative interviews, focus groups, field notes, observations, documents, and artifacts allowed for a rich and in-depth exploration of perspectives in each of the six cases. Evidence was collected through 23 focus groups and 16 individual interviews. In total, 114 educational leaders participated: 53 principals, 33 central office leaders, and 28 superintendency team leaders.

The focus was on six Alberta school districts as *instrumental cases* (Creswell, 2012) to illustrate and illuminate ways through which Alberta school superintendency teams lead educator and student learning. Evidence from multiple-case studies is "often considered more compelling, and the study is therefore regarded as being more robust" (Yin, 2009, p. 53) and is a "common strategy for enhancing the external validity or generalizability of your findings" (Merriam, 1998, p. 40). The determination of the six specific cases was purposeful. We selected six school districts that could be described as *highly successful* and *focused on learning*. With the help of the Ministry of Education, we considered districts whose Annual Educational Results Reports showed strengths on three measures: (a) student achievement, (b) provincial survey results (on such factors as safe and caring environment, school satisfaction, and program quality), and (c) school completion rates.

Data collection and analysis in the six district cases were informed by collective case study or multicase methods (Creswell, 2012; Merriam, 1998; Stake, 1995, 2006; Yin, 2009). A case study is an in-depth exploration of a bounded system (e.g., activity, event, process, or individuals) based on extensive data collection (Creswell, 2007). "*Bounded* means that the case is separated for research in terms of time, place or some physical boundaries" (Creswell, 2012, p. 465). In collective case study, multiple cases are described and cross-referenced to better understand the phenomenon under investigation. The phenomenon investigated within the bounded system of the Alberta school system in 2014 was "school and district leader perceptions of the ways superintendency teams in successful and learning focused school districts lead educator and student learning" (Brandon, Hanna, & Negropontes, 2015, p. 19). Such inquiry called for a range of research methods to do justice to the complexity of the case and to facilitate cross-case analysis and explanation.

Research team members traveled to each of the six districts to collect data through 23 focus groups and nine individual interviews (Brinkman & Kvale, 2015). In total, 114 educational leaders participated in our inquiry: 53 principals, 33 middle level leaders, and 28 superintendency team leaders—including seven chief superintendents. In keeping with the requirements of case study research (Merriam, 1998; Stake, 1995, 2006; Yin, 2009), multiple sources of evidence were gathered and analyzed during our inquiry.

As a former school superintendent and two former deputy superintendents with more than 60 years of experience on senior leadership teams in five Alberta school districts, we have tried to transparently locate ourselves as researchers through all phases of this study. Our histories as district leaders *positioned* us as *insiders* in this research (Andres, 2012, p. 18). From this position, we were able to gain access to school district personnel, documents, and artifacts quite readily. Through our vantage points as experienced members of the superintendency and as career long advocates of *overall instructional leadership* we were able to continuously collect, analyze, and interpret data through the lens of our professional experiences. As researchers who have transitioned away from the daily life worlds of practicing educational leaders and into the academic and consulting domains, we were also positioned as *outsiders* in this research. From this vantage point, we were consciously committed to adhering to the principles of mixed methods and collective case study research.

NINE CROSS-CASE THEMES

Though the insights provided in each of the six cases detailed in Brandon, Hanna, and Negropontes (2015) are important and will be of interest to both practitioners and policy makers, the primary purpose of collective case study was to enhance understanding of the phenomenon of *overall* instructional leadership as practiced by superintendency teams in highly successful and learning focused school districts. Individual cases were studied to gain understanding of the complex meanings of this phenomenon in some of its situations (Stake, 2006, p. 41). Each case summary illuminated one contextualized set of approaches used by a superintendency team in its specific geographic, social, economic, and educational setting. Building on the findings and emerging themes from these individual illustrations, our cross-case analysis identified the nine larger themes that are the subject of this section.

The nine major themes discussed below are based primarily on our further analysis of the qualitative data. The cross-case theme development process was ongoing and continuous over the entire course of the study, early in our investigation we began to identify and discuss commonalities among the cases and to generate a list of possible themes. In a second stage, one team member took the lead in formalizing and describing the cross-case themes following data collection from all six settings. In stage three, a second researcher reviewed the surveys and began blending the two data sources. In stage four, selected research literature was consulted to deepen our understanding of the mixed data and to aid our interpretations and assertions. All of us were engaged in critically reviewing the analysis as it evolved into findings, themes, and assertions.

Further evidence of the utility of the five dimensions of the Alberta framework that served as our conceptual framework (Table 4.1) is provided in the first five of the cross-case themes. Our research benefited from the use of this conceptual lens from the design of interview and survey questions, through the collection of both sets of data, and into the analysis and interpretation phases. The ways we utilized our conceptual framework acknowledged Merriam's (1998) observation: "In multicase or cross-case analysis, the use of predetermined questions and specific procedures for coding and analysis enhances the generalizability of findings in the traditional sense" (p. 208).

During the individual and focus group interviews we took note of how well versed principals, middle level leaders, and superintendency team members were in current research literature. Almost every educational leader we encountered was able to speak passionately and eloquently about a wide range of credible evidence informed leadership practices. What was even more impressive was their orientation to action. It is one thing to know what should be done; it is quite another challenge to move evidence informed ideas into sustained action. Most of the school and district leaders we encountered were striving to practice in ways that were framed by what they judged to be contextually appropriate *best available evidence.*

As we engaged with the participants and analyzed the data, it became apparent that the role of the Alberta framework was significant, if not always consciously so. Many aspects of this document were reflected in the language and actions of district leaders. This alignment may be related to the engagement of some members of the superintendency teams in the development of the framework and related professional learning opportunities over the previous 7 years, the availability of the College of Alberta School Superintendents (CASS) publication of the framework to all superintendency team members or other related research based professional learning opportunities.

Cross-case themes six through nine are based on findings that do not fit neatly within the Alberta framework. These final four themes illuminate district leadership practices that are not specifically delineated in our conceptual framework. Themes six through nine speak to the overwhelmingly positive impact of learning-oriented relationships and collaborative leadership at the district level.

Theme One: Focusing on Student Success

Participants in all six settings articulated that their districts were highly focused on student success: learning, engagement, and well-being. Educators at every level indicated that their work was guided and in many cases, inspired, by a clear learning vision that was understandable, attainable, and forward looking. The learning direction encouraged educators to help improve life chances for all students.

Our first cross-case theme underlines the benefits of intentionally focusing district energy and efforts on teaching and learning. The senior leaders in this study were committed to developing and acting on a widely shared vision and focus on student learning and well-being in the 21st Century. In this respect, the work of the six superintendency teams aligned with and added to research claims that leadership practices aimed at creating such a widely shared sense of purpose can have a significantly positive impact (Elmore & Burney, 1998; Friesen & Lock, 2010; Leithwood, 2010a, 2011, 2012;

McLaughlin & Talbert, 2003; Togneri & Anderson's, 2003; Wahlstrom, Louis, Leithwood, & Anderson, 2010). The theme also supports the need for attention to be placed on engaging students intellectually, academically, and socially to more fully support student learning and welfare for the immediate and longer terms (Willms, Friesen, & Milton, 2009).

Theme Two: Enabling Engaging Instruction

Many of the senior teams called upon principals, learning coaches, learning leaders, and central office leaders to invest heavily in teaching strategies designed to more deeply engage all students. Holy Family emphasized the consolidation of professional learning about teaching and learning, rather than continually engaging in new initiatives. The intent was to sustain support to schools in their efforts to increasingly provide highly engaging forms of instruction to all students. The five principles of Friesen's (2009) *Teaching Effectiveness Framework* were being extensively utilized across the Calgary Board of Education to support collaborative teacher efforts to design learning tasks that more consistently engage students in worthwhile and engaging work.

Theme Three: Fostering Collective Efficacy

Consistent with the direction charted by existing research, each of the senior leadership teams provided quite extensive opportunities for staff to develop expertise relevant to achieving the district's goals. Steering committees for initiatives; professional learning community groups; one on one meetings of principals with the superintendent; administrator retreats with the school trustees every 2 years; district organizational health committees; long service awards; professional development, including book studies and in-basket activities; and administrators council are all examples of the variety of structures in place at St. Albert Public to engage and to build individual and collective capacity.

The data that generated cross-case theme three were extensive and varied. The structures and norms deliberately established in the districts produced a continuum of interconnected school and system leader networks wherein educators worked together toward achievement of system goals. Bandura (1977, 1986, 1989, 1997) provided the research foundations that explain the persistence in solving problems and effortful responses to challenges that we heard about in the focus groups and are characteristic of high levels of efficacy. Leithwood (2010a) and his colleagues (Louis, Leithwood, Anderson, & Wahlstrom, 2010; Leithwood, Anderson, Louis, 2012) found that a sense of collective efficacy on the part of a district's principals was a significant factor in accounting for district effects on student achievement. The ways that the districts in our study built collective efficacy ran parallel to what Leithwood, Anderson, and Louis (2012) found. Districts contribute most to school leaders' sense of efficacy through five strategies: (a) unambiguously assigning priority to the improvement of student achievement and instruction; (b) investing in the development of instructional leadership; (c) ensuring that personnel policies support the selection and maintenance of the best people for each school; (d) emphasizing teamwork and professional community; and (e) providing worthwhile programs of professional development, aimed at strengthening their capacities to achieve shared purposes (p. 119).

Theme Four: Scaffolding Overall Instructional Leadership

A large volume of data related to theme four came forward. Participants from all levels were eager to describe school and district approaches to instructional leadership and most participants viewed this as the core work of the district leadership team.

The expectation that principals should be knowledgeable about the quality of their teachers' instruction was universally understood and applied in all six districts. These expectations played out in nuanced ways in each system. Holy Family and Fort McMurray Catholic, for instance, expect principals to spend a specified percentage of their time in classrooms. Westwind, St. Albert, and Chinook's Edge have similar expectations, but take a more general approach. In all these cases, the intention is to create relationships of expectation and support within schools. Interactions with teachers are often structured around questions such as "How is this making a difference for student learning? What can we do to help?" In CBE, interviewed principals indicated that they were expected to be knowledgeable of the quality of their teachers' instruction. In addition, each principal viewed "leading teacher learning" as an important part of the role.

Cross-case theme four—*scaffolding overall instructional leadership*—illustrates how persistent senior leader commitment to the development of instructional leadership is progressing in the six district settings. To a considerable degree, the efforts of district leaders in our study aligned with the growing research base of how school districts can do this important work well (Anderson & Louis, 2012; Barber et al., 2010; Louis & Wahlstrom, 2012; Robinson, 2011; Robinson, Lloyd, & Rowe, 2008; Togneri & Anderson, 2003; Wahlstrom, 2012). Increasingly, these leaders were working to improve instructional leadership practices in what Wahlstrom (2012) found to be two complementary categories: *Instructional Ethos* and *Instructional Actions.* These participants were working broadly to build professional community to generate benefit through the establishment of school and district cultures that support continual professional learning. At the same time, they were working to enhance school leader capacity to supportively engage with individual teachers to promote professional growth in classroom settings.

Theme Five: Strengthening Professional Learning

The qualitative evidence collected in the six districts underlined the high value placed on professional learning. At both the district and school levels, most of the time spent on professional learning was clearly aimed at enhancing and supporting teaching and learning. Senior leaders were acting on Firestone and Riehl's (2005) conclusion that "districts play a key role in supporting instructional reform by being the primary designers and deliverers of learning opportunities for teachers, and if they do so in a focused, coherent fashion they can influence teaching practice" (p. 316).

Cross-case theme five—*professional learning*—underlined the benefits of intentionally focusing district resources on building teaching and learning capacity through effective professional learning. District leaders were committed to ongoing and sustained educator learning. In several instances, their efforts reflected current research on how to effectively improve leading and teaching practice through focused and responsive professional learning. In other cases, intentions were good, but approaches were less tightly connected to the research. Evidence supporting the importance of professional learning was claimed in 21 of the 33 studies reported in Leithwood's (2010a) review. This was the largest number of studies reporting evidence about any of the 12 dimensions of high-performing districts. We expect to a continuing evolution toward the more evidence driven professional learning, as identified in an increasing number of studies (Bredeson & Johansson, 2000; Firestone & Riehl, 2005; Leithwood, 2010a; Opfer, Pedder, & Lavicza, 2011; Pritchard & Marshall, 2002; Timperley, 2011; Timperley, Wilson, Barrar, & Fung, 2007).

Theme Six: Leading Learning Through Superintendency Teams

This is one of the fundamental ideas that has run through our study from conception to execution. From our past experiences working as members of senior leadership teams in five Alberta districts, we had a strong, shared faith in the importance of team leadership and team learning grounded in the literature by Senge (1990). The benefits of the district leadership group working as a team in their collective efforts to lead educator and student learning became increasingly prominent during each successive data collection visit.

Superintendency teamwork was seen by participants to contribute to student success in a number of ways. Under the overall leadership of the superintendent, central leadership teams in these districts were working together to establish and support clear expectations for school leadership practice. They coordinated organized opportunities for teachers and principals to engage in relevant and targeted professional learning that connected to the strategic focus of the district. Participants repeatedly noted that the most significant focus of the superintendency teams was on student learning and achievement. All participants viewed this as the core work of the district leadership team.

Under the overall leadership of the superintendent, central leadership teams in these districts were working together to establish and support clear expectations for school leadership practice. They coordinated organized opportunities for teachers and principals to engage in relevant and targeted professional learning that connected to the strategic focus of the district. Participants repeatedly noted that the most significant focus of the superintendency teams was on student learning and achievement. Almost all participants viewed this as the core work of the district leadership team.

The unique role of the chief executive and chief educational officer in each district was quite well understood and very much appreciated as a distinct and challenging position by all participants. What was even more greatly appreciated was the way in which the superintendents in this study were working with their senior leadership colleagues to provide coherent, coordinated, and focused leadership of the learning agenda in the districts. Their work in this regard is linked with evidence in a number of recent studies (Louis & Wahlstrom, 2012; Wahlstrom, 2012; Wahlstrom, Louis, Leithwood, & Anderson, 2010a, 2010b). Leithwood's (2010b) second CASS sponsored research study of district improvement processes concluded that the district leadership team is the single most important influence on district turnaround processes and that the superintendency team should be held directly accountable for tasks it is uniquely positioned to accomplish (p. 28).

Theme Seven: Building Purposeful Professional Relationships

In addition to what participants said about the nature of educator relationships within the district using such terms as—open, supportive, trusting, and reciprocal—we also formed our own thoughts in this direction through reflection on and dialogue about each of our data collection visits. With very few exceptions, participants were cordial, relaxed, and proud to be engaged with each other in conversation about the ways in which they were working together with their colleagues at various levels to support teacher and student learning. It was clearly and consistently evident to us that professional working relationships and relational trust (Bryk & Schneider, 2002) were strong across the cases. Professional relationships characterized by high levels of relational trust, reciprocity, and collaboration. Moreover, these professional relationships were built with a shared focus on enabling student success. Establishing purposeful relationships was an ongoing intentional high priority for the superintendency teams in this study. Efforts in this direction are supported by evidence from several recent studies (Bryk & Schneider, 2002; Louis & Wahlstrom, 2012; Robinson, 2011; Timperley, 2011; Wahlstrom et al., 2010a, 2010b).

Two claims from this existing research were particularly well linked to the evidence we gathered. First, Louis and Wahlstrom (2012) found that "leadership practices targeted directly at improving instruction have significant effects on teachers' working relationships and indirectly on student achievement" and that "when principals and teachers share leadership, teachers' working relationships are stronger and student achievement is higher" (p. 25). The effect occurs "largely because effective leadership strengthens professional community, a special environment within which teachers work together to improve their practice and improve student learning" (p. 25). Similarly, Timperly (2011) underlined the importance professional learning community, which she described as a group of professionals committed to working together to learn about their practice for the purpose of improving student learning. Significantly, it is important for educators in this arrangement to focus on student learning through respectful, trusting relationships and collaborative inquiry for deep learning based on evidence.

Theme Eight: Accessing External and Internal Expertise

All six of the districts in this study utilized external expertise to grow capacity and to develop local expertise, particularly the areas of research based instruction, assessment, and instructional leadership. Access to experts was a critical component of ongoing professional learning. External experts were often asked to support district efforts in areas of specific needs. For the most part this expertise was very targeted and purposeful while still allowing for some individuality at the school level. Particularly, in rural districts where access to a cadre of internally trained facilitators or researchers is limited, external experts provided support to the superintendency team.

Though many professional learning opportunities were facilitated internally in the CBE, Alberta's largest district has also benefited from a continuing partnership with the Galileo Educational Network (GENA) at the University of Calgary. Sharon Friesen, Candace Saar, and others on the GENA team have worked extensively to foster pedagogical leadership and they are now helping to strengthen shared instructional leadership across the system through their monthly work with 700 learning leaders from across the system.

When experts were integrated into professional learning, the districts worked to ensure there was continuity and alignment with the priorities of the district, especially with the focus on student learning and building instructional leadership capacity. In keeping with a philosophy of professional learning grounded in work, follow-up with the experts or members of the superintendency team or school leaders was part of the planning and implementation process. Cross-case theme eight—*accessing external and internal expe*rtise—illustrates several ways that highly successful and learning focused school districts were working with trusted experts to help build leadership, pedagogy, and assessment. These efforts are supported by recent research by a number of scholars (for instance, Friesen, 2009; Friesen & Lock, 2010; Hargreaves & Fullan, 2012; Hatano & Oura, 2003; Robinson, 2011; Timperley, 2011; Timperley et al., 2007). In our view, the larger intent of these district efforts to build internal capacity is to develop what Timperley (2011) describes as *adaptive expertise,* which is characterized by deep pedagogic or leadership knowledgeable that can be retrieved, organized, and applied to address shifting challenges and needs.

Theme Nine: Collaborative Leadership Learning

In addition to what participants said about their work to build collaborative leadership learning structures and communities within their settings, we also mined data from other interview segments. In particular, responses related to the focus on learning, system-wide efficacy, leadership for learning, and professional learning portions of the interview protocol yielded rich insights to inform theme nine.

The variety of approaches to leadership learning observed in our study support the view that there is no one best way to become a more competent school or district leader. No standardized template dictates a one size fits all mandate for leadership development. Rather, our study suggests that districts enable and benefit from multiple forms of leadership learning.

These highly successful and learning focused districts were committed to development of instructional leaders in every school and at the central office. Each district was on its own journey of collaborative leadership learning. It could be said they were on a continuum of development. Some were fully engaged in instructional leadership while others were not as far along the path, but all were committed to focusing on student learning. Some were very tightly coupled with a model guiding their actions, while others were more loosely coupled—bound together by a shared vision but more flexible in how individual schools approached implementing a strong focus on student learning and providing instructional leadership.

Although there were multiple pathways, there were common strategies employed to move in the direction of collaborative leadership community building. Each district had organizational structures that enabled collaboration, leadership and alignment, such as: classroom support teachers, learning coaches, instructional leadership teams, professional learning communities, administrative meetings, beginning administrator or teacher programs. Collaboration, mentorship, and adequate resources, including time, were evident in each opportunity. Processes were in place that also built capacity like engagement in research or implementation of specific programs or models. Each district recognized prior learning and created a scaffold to new learning. Districts recognized that having only a few priorities all focused on student learning was a leverage point that energizes people to work together.

Our final cross-case theme—*collaborative leadership learning*—draws attention to the multiplicity of ways that the superintendents in this study capitalized on the benefits of collective, shared, and distributed leadership to foster enhanced leadership capacity and to support aspiring and novice leaders in their systems. Their collaborative orientation leverages collective efforts to support overall instructional leadership that scaffolds teaching directed toward student success. This work is supported by a number of studies (for instance, Anderson & Louis, 2012; Barber, Whelan, & Clark, 2010; Elmore & Burney, 1998; Leithwood, 2010a, 2011, 2012; Louis, Leithwood et al., 2010a, 2010b; Louis & Wahlstrom, 2012; McLaughlin & Talbert, 2003; Robinson, 2011; Timperley, 2011; Togneri & Anderson's, 2003; Wahlstrom et al., 2010a, 2010b). The theme also supports the Togneri and Anderson (2003) finding that most high performing districts provide intensive long-term opportunities for principals to further develop their capacities as instructional leaders.

CONCLUDING REMARKS: FROM INSIGHT TO ACTION

We offer these nine *insights for superintendency teams* from the perspective that "most fields informed by the social sciences have imperfect evidence available to inform their practices" and, as such, "judgments are rightly based on the best available evidence, along with the practical wisdom of those actually working in the field (Leithwood, Louis, Anderson, &

Wahlstrom, 2004, p. 9). The nine insights about the ways in which successful superintendency teams lead educator and student learning are based on the research team's reasoned judgment and assertational logic about the extent to which the findings and themes of this study are transferable and can be used to guide practice in other settings.

Our larger study (Brandon et al., 2015) illustrated how superintendency teams lead learning in three ways. First, it provided six detailed descriptions of the work of superintendency teams in six school districts. Each case summary stands as one contextualized set of approaches used by a superintendency team in its specific geographic, social, economic, and educational setting. Second, the first five of the nine cross-case themes provide evidence of the power of the five dimensions of our conceptual framework—these dimensions do, in fact, enable district leaders to *frame leadership research in action*. Cross-case themes six through nine speak to the overwhelmingly positive impact of evidence informed practice, judicious use of expertise, and collaborative leadership learning at the district level.

REFERENCES

Alberta Education. (2018a, February). *Teaching quality standard*. Edmonton, Canada: Author.

Alberta Education. (2018b, February). *Leadership quality standard*. Edmonton, Canada: Author.

Alberta Education. (2018c, February). *Superintendent leadership quality standard*. Edmonton, Canada: Author.

Alberta Teachers' Association. (2016). The role of the superintendent and the teaching profession. Edmonton, Canada: Author.

Andres, L. (2012). *Designing and doing survey research*. Thousand Oaks, CA: SAGE.

Anderson, S., & Louis, K. S. (2012). The district difference: A new perspective on the local challenges for improvement. In K. Leithwood & K. Seashore Louis (Eds.), *Linking Leadership to student learning* (pp. 181–202). San Francisco, CA: Jossey-Bass.

Barber, M., Whelan, F., & Clark. M. (2010). *Capturing the leadership premium: How the world's top school systems are building capacity for the future*. Retrieved from http://www.mckinsey.com/clientservice/social_sector/our_practices/education/knowledge_highlights/~/media/Reports/SSO/schoolleadership_final.ashx

Bandura, A. (1977). Self-efficacy: Toward a unifying theory of behavioral change. *Psychological Review, 84,* 191–215.

Bandura, A. (1986). *Social foundations of thought and action. A social cognitive theory.* Upper Saddle River, NJ: Prentice Hall.

Bandura, A. (1989). Human agency in social cognitive theory. *American Psychologist, 44*(9), 1175–1184.

Bandura, A. (1997). *Self-efficacy: The exercise of control.* New York, NY: W. H. Freeman.

Bredeson, P., & Johansson, O. (2000). The school principals' role in teacher professional development. *Journal of In-Service Education, 26*(2), 385–401.

Brandon, J., Hanna, P., Donlevy, J. K., & Parsons, D. (2018). Leading learning: Lessons from successful superintendency teams. *Asian Educational Studies, 2*(4), 57–73.

Brandon, J., Hanna, P., Morrow, R., Rhyason, K., & Schmold, S. (2013). *The Alberta framework for school system success.* Edmonton, Canada: Henday.

Brandon, J., Hanna, P., & Negropontes, D. (2015, November). *Superintendents who lead learning: Lessons from six highly successful school systems.* Report prepared for the College of Alberta School Superintendents, Edmonton, Canada.

Brandon, J., Hanna, P., & Negropontes, D. (2016, April). *Superintendents who lead learning: Final report.* Paper presented at the American Educational Research Association Annual Meeting, Washington, DC.

Brinkman, S., & Kvale, S. (2015). *Interviews: Learning the craft of qualitative research interviewing.* Los Angeles, CA: SAGE.

Bryk, A., & Schneider, B. (2002). *Trust in schools: A core resource for improvement.* New York, NY: Russell Sage.

Coughlan, S. (2017, August 2). How Canada became and education superpower. *BBC News.* Retrieved from http://www.bbc.com/news/business-40708421

Creswell, J. (2007). *Qualitative inquiry and research design: Choosing among five approaches* (2nd ed.). Thousand Oaks, CA: SAGE.

Creswell, J. (2012). *Educational research: Planning, conducting, and evaluating quantitative and qualitative research.* Boston, MA: Pearson Education.

Elmore, R., & Burney, D. (1998). *Continuous improvement in Community District #2, New York City.* Retrieved from http://citeseerx.ist.psu.edu/viewdoc/download?doi=10.1.1.1011.464&rep=rep1&type=pdf

Firestone, W., & Riehl, C. (2005). *A new agenda for research in educational leadership.* New York, NY: Teachers College Press.

Friesen, S. (2009). *What did you do in school today? Teaching effectiveness: a framework and rubric.* Toronto: Canadian Education Association. Retrieved from https://www-deslibris-ca.ezproxy.lib.ucalgary.ca/ID/239075

Friesen, S., & Lock, J. (2010). *High performing school systems in the application of 21st century learning technologies: Review of the research.* Calgary, Canada: University of Calgary.

Hargreaves, A., & Fullan, M. (2012). *Professional capital: Transforming teaching in every school.* New York, NY: Teachers College Press.

Hargreaves, A., & Shirley, D. (2012a). *The global fourth way: The quest for educational excellence.* Thousand Oaks, CA: Corwin.

Hargreaves, A., & Shirley, D. (2012b). The international quest for educational excellence: Understanding Canada's high performance. *Education Canada, 52,* 10–13.

Hatano, G., & Oura, Y. (2003). Commentary: Reconceptualizing school learning, using insight from expertise research. *Educational Researcher, 32,* 26–29.

Hetherington, R. (2014). *Decision-Making and the superintendency* (Unpublished doctoral dissertation). University of Alberta, Edmonton, Alberta.

Hightower, A. M. (2002). *San Diego's big boom: District bureaucracy supports culture of learning.* Retrieved from https://eric.ed.gov/?id=ED499096

Leithwood, K. (2010a). Characteristics of school districts that are exceptionally effective in Closing the Achievement Gap. *Leadership and Policy in Schools, 9*(3), 245–291.

Leithwood, K. (2010b, June). *Turning around underperforming school systems: Guidelines for district leaders.* Paper prepared for the College of Alberta School Superintendents, Edmonton, Canada.

Leithwood, K. (2011, April). *District effectiveness framework.* Paper presented at the Annual Pre-Conference of the College of Alberta School Superintendents. Edmonton, Canada: College of Alberta School Superintendents.

Leithwood, K. (2012). Core practices: The four essential components of the leader's repertoire. In K. Leithwood & K. Seashore Louis (Eds.), *Linking Leadership to student learning* (pp. 57–67). San Francisco, CA: Jossey-Bass.

Leithwood, K., Aitken, & Jantzi, D. (2006, April). *A review of transformational school leadership research.* Paper presented at American Educational Research Association, Montreal, QC.

Leithwood, K., Anderson, S., & Louis, K. S. (2012). Principal efficacy: District-led professional development. In K. Leithwood & K. Seashore Louis (Eds.), *Linking Leadership to student learning* (pp. 119–141). San Francisco, CA: Jossey-Bass.

Leithwood, K., Louis, K. S., Anderson, S., & Wahlstrom, K. (2004). *Review of research: How leadership influences student learning.* New York, NY: The Wallace Foundation.

Louis, K. S., Leithwood, K., Anderson, S., & Wahlstrom, K. (2010). *Learning from leadership: Investigating the links to improved student learning: Final report of research findings.* New York, NY: The Wallace Foundation. Retrieved from https://www.wallacefoundation.org/knowledge-center/Documents/Investigating-the-Links-to-Improved-Student-Learning.pdf

Louis, K. S., & Wahlstrom, K. (2012). Shared and instructional leadership: When principals and teachers successful lead together. In K. Leithwood & K. Seashore Louis (Eds.), *Linking leadership to student learning* (pp. 25–41). San Francisco, CA: Jossey-Bass.

Marzano, R., & Waters, T. (2009). *District leadership that works: Striking the right balance.* Bloomington, IN: Solution Tree Press.

McLaughlin, M., & Talbert, J. (2003). *Reforming districts: How districts support school reform.* Retrieved from https://www.education.uw.edu/ctp/content/reforming-districts-how-districts-support-school-reform

Merriam, S. (1998). *Qualitative research and case study applications in education.* San Francisco, CA: Jossey-Bass.

Opfer, D., Pedder, D., & Lavicza, Z. (2011). The influence of school orientation to learning on teachers' professional learning change. *School Effectiveness and School Improvement: An International Journal of Research, Policy and Practice, 22*(2), 193–214.

Parsons, D. (2015). *The impact of the office of superintendent of schools on the personal lives of superintendents* (Unpublished doctoral dissertation). University of Calgary. Calgary, Canada.

Parsons, D., & Brandon, J. (2017, April). *The impact of the office of superintendent of schools on the personal lives of superintendents.* Paper presented at the American Educational Research Association Annual Meeting. San Antonio, TX.

Pritchard, R., & Marshall, J. (2002). Professional development in "healthy" vs. "'un-healthy" districts: Top 10 characteristics based on research. *School Leadership and Management, 22*(2), 113–41.

Robinson, V. (2011). *Student-centered leadership.* San Francisco, CA: Jossey-Bass.

Robinson, V., Lloyd, C., & Rowe, K. (2008). The impact of leadership on student outcomes: An analysis of the differential effects of leadership types. *Educational Administration Quarterly, 44*(5), 635–674.

Senge, P. (1990). *The fifth discipline: The art and science of the learning organization.* New York, NY: Doubleday.

Stake, R. (1995). *The art of case study research.* Thousand Oaks, CA: SAGE.

Stake, R. (2006). *Multiple case study analysis.* New York, NY: The Guilford Press.

Timperley, H. (2011). *Realizing the power of professional learning.* London, England: Open University Press.

Timperley, H., Wilson, A., Barrar, H., & Fung, I. (2007). *Teacher professional learning and development: Best evidence synthesis iteration (BES).* Wellington, New Zealand: Ministry of Education.

Togneri, W., & Anderson, S. E. (2003). *Beyond islands of excellence: What districts can do to improve instruction and achievement in all schools.* Retrieved from http://www.learningfirst.org/publications/districts

Wahlstrom, K. (2012). An up-close view of instructional leadership: A grounded analysis. In K. Leithwood & K. Seashore Louis (Eds.), *Linking Leadership to student learning* (pp. 68–86). San Francisco, CA: Jossey-Bass.

Wahlstrom, K., Louis, K. S., Leithwood, K., & Anderson, S. (2010). *Learning from leadership: Investigating the links to improved student learning: Executive summary of the research findings.* New York, NY: The Wallace Foundation. Retrieved from https://www.wallacefoundation.org/knowledge-center/Documents/Investigating-the-Links-to-Improved-Student-Learning-Executive-Summary.pdf

Willms, D., Friesen, S., & Milton, P. (2009). *What did you do in school today? Transforming classrooms through social, academic and intellectual engagement.* Toronto, Canada: Canadian Education Association.

Yin, R. (2009). *Case study research. Design and methods.* Thousand Oaks, CA: SAGE.

CHAPTER 5

SUCCESSION PLANNING FOR ADMINISTRATIVE POSITIONS

Supporting Order During Tumultuous Transitions

Mark E. Deschaine
Central Michigan University

Raymond W. Francis
Central Michigan University

Superintendents of today have to respond quickly to issues and initiatives on a number of local, state, and national fronts. Quite often, the most important areas they have to deal with involve personnel issues within their own district. Superintendents that want to improve the quality and caliber of their educational programs need to attend to the quality and caliber of the administrators responsible for those programs. The hiring, mentoring, and retaining of quality lead administrators is a difficult process at best, and one that is often overlooked by superintendents who are responding and reacting, as opposed to building formative and proactive supports in their

The Contemporary Superintendent, pages 73–92
Copyright © 2019 by Information Age Publishing

personnel approaches and hiring practices. This chapter presents a framework that allows superintendents to proactively begin the search for quality front line administrators before the need arises.

LITERATURE REVIEW

School superintendents work in an educational system that is complex and extensive, where individual units often compete for the limited attention and resources of the school district leadership. Multiple actors and stakeholders often operate autonomously within an intricate adaptive system (Collins, 2013), with ultimate accountability resting within the superintendent's office. School superintendents are required to deal with an inordinate amount of daily demands that seldom provide an opportunity for them to be proactive in their orientation related to personnel issues. Many of the areas that compete for a superintendent's time are related to finance, policy, compliance, accountability, and educational integrity. This often creates an environment where it is difficult for superintendents to proactively think about future needs when they are currently embroiled in a large and wide variety of immediate needs. Symbiotically, it also creates a situation where the attention and focus of researchers interested in educational administration issues often have to focus their research attention and efforts on more pressing issues. Both researchers and practitioners often have to focus on things of pressing need as opposed to issues related to longitudinal impact. "While increasing proportions of school districts are responding to [these] demographic, policy, and reform pressures, very little empirical work has examined their practices associated with intentional leadership succession planning" (Russell & Sabina, 2014, p. 602). Superintendents and researchers interested in gaining useful information related to succession planning activities for front line administrators have to look carefully to find solid content about the topic. This chapter will provide a quick overview of the topic, and provide a suggested process improvement framework that will allow superintendents to deal with the issue of succession planning for front line building administrators and principals proactively, from a firm position based upon assembling a strong institutional knowledge base and memory from which to draw content and resources.

What exactly do we mean by succession planning? What are the key features, and why should they be of interest to school superintendents? Most of all, what are the key features of succession planning that school superintendents should attend to according to researchers in the field?

Succession Planning in the Academic Literature

Although we have an extensive literature base on succession planning in other areas such as business, health care, and public administration (Garman & Glawe, 2004; Pynes, 2004; Russell & Sabina, 2014; Schall, 1997), little research has been conducted related to the way that school districts and educational institutions intentionally engage in succession planning (Zepeda, Bengtson, & Parylo, 2011; Russell & Sabina, 2014). To exacerbate the situation further, public organizations (such as school districts) do not engage in the process of succession planning as well as their counterparts in private organizations (Hargreaves & Fink, 2006; Zepeda et al., 2011), thus leaving a vacuum for researchers interested in conducting empirical investigation into the topic. This is becoming more of an issue as the number of open front line administrative school principal positions appear to be increasing at a rapid pace.

According to the United States Bureau of Labor Statistics (2008), qualified individuals looking for positions as a school principal are entering a field considered "excellent," since approximately 40% of school administrators will need to be replaced (Russell & Sabina, 2014; United States Department of Labor, 2000) due to retirement issues (Gates, Ringel, & Santibanez, 2003). Even with extensive openings for school principal positions, many school districts have a difficult time securing high-quality principal candidates to fill their position openings (Russell & Sabina, 2014). "The job is simply too complex, too poorly constructed, too isolating. School leaders lack the ongoing support and development required to maintain and foster sustained commitment" (RAND, 2014, p. 1). Beteille, Kalogrides, and Loeb (2012) suggest that "more than one out of every five principals leaves their school each year" (p. 904). Schmidt-Davis and Bottoms (2011) describe a situation where "Each year, about 20 percent of the nation's 90,000 public school principals leave their jobs, leaving more than 18,000 schools with a new principal each fall" (p. 1). The RAND Corporation (2014) states that one quarter of the nation's school principals leave their positions within their schools on an annual basis. That situation becomes exacerbated because, again, according to RAND (2014), 50% of the new principals that fill those vacancies quit after only serving 3 years in their roles.

> Turnover among principals currently is at an unsustainable level, and the quality of the pool of leaders available to step up in the next few years is suspect. Better succession planning for school leaders offers a viable solution to these problems. (Schmidt-Davis & Bottoms, 2011, p. 1)

All of this leaves school superintendents asking "How do I best meet the need for filling administrative vacancies?" We contend that a proactive process, based upon resources currently available, can help meet the reactive need for administrative succession planning.

For our purposes, we believe that the definition posited by Wallin, Cameron, and Sharples (2005) is a good starting place for understanding where succession planning fits into the conceptualization of the process orientation shared by the authors. "Succession planning is a process by which an organization assures necessary and appropriate leadership for the future through a talent pipeline with the capabilities of sustaining an institution's long-term goals" (p. 26). It is complimented by the work of Russell and Sabina (2014) who state that succession planning involves "the explicit design and implementation of programs to identify and develop high-quality principal candidates" (p. 600). Even though both of these definitions focus more on the behavioral attributes of the candidates under consideration to fulfill the open positions, we agree with the direction the definitions are taking. Our emphasis is not so much on the leadership capabilities or predispositions that candidates bring to the position, we focus more on a certain set of processes that we feel are necessary so that proper decisions are rendered and supported. We believe that a solid process will result in a solid product. Organizations that attend to and adhere to these processes will have a better likelihood of identifying, growing, supporting, and maintaining frontline administrative personnel.

The Need to Address Succession Planning

Even though school superintendents' attention is stretched and divided, the information that we have on the potential turnover for frontline school administrators should cause us pause, and provide an impetus for the field is to focus on the need to identify, train, grow, and maintain the educational leaders of school buildings for the future. Future educational leaders find themselves having to deal with an inordinate amount of issues and responsibilities. The process improvement guidelines that we suggest for succession planning takes into account the changing landscape often experienced by instructional leaders, were accountability to student achievement measures and fiscal responsibility often are primary concerns of billing principles. "Leadership succession planning is a means to identify the need for systematic and purposeful change in education" (Ryan & Gallo, 2011, p. 132).

THEORETICAL UNDERPINNINGS OF THE PROCESS IMPROVEMENT GUIDELINES

In order to better understand the process that we advocate, we feel it important to take a very cursory look at some of the theoretical underpinnings that drive our suggested interventions. Many of these theorists are well known to the educational community, while a couple may not be as utilized. However, taken as an aggregate, they form a supportive theoretical background to our process improvement guidelines. The process improvement framework posited by the authors is based on accepted theory espoused by Schön (1983) in his work on reflective practice, Hord (1997) with her work on change processes, Kolb (1984) who focused on experiential learning, Knowles (1984) emphasis on adult learning theory, and Deming (1950) and his work on statistical and process improvement. It would be beyond the scope of this chapter to provide an extensive narrative on each: We will explicate their significance later in the chapter when specific examples are provided. Coverage of appropriate knowledge management structures will also be covered, and the ways that information is collected, shared, and utilized impact not only the process, but the stakeholders impacted by the hiring decision making.

PROCESS IMPROVEMENT GUIDELINES APPLIED TO SUCCESSION PLANNING

The process improvement guidelines utilize a five stage process that can be utilized to support superintendents wishing to engage in proactive succession planning for frontline administrators. These guidelines are an effective structure to address both current and future personnel need through the utilization of communication and feedback channels throughout the organization. The utilization of these guidelines helps establish an effective and positive organizational culture that allows programs to identify the salient needs necessary to appropriately fill open administrative positions. At first glance, these stages might appear somewhat rudimentary and painfully obvious. However, we believe that a focused consideration of each element will provide significant insights and opportunities for superintendents to find the resources currently available within their program to help make better personnel planning and implementation decisions.

Each stage of the process improvement guidelines (Figure 5.1) aligns to provide specific results related to succession planning, and ultimately leads to the next. Between each stage, there is a reflective and recursive pause that allows organizations to thoughtfully consider the resources at their disposal, the information and capabilities that are needed, and a way to effectively come to some resolution or ultimate direction. This ongoing reflective process allows participants to utilize support, feedback, and guidance mechanisms needed to move the organization forward. The five stages of the process improvement guidelines include:

- Prepare
- Prioritize

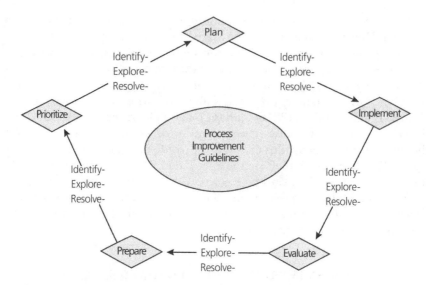

Figure 5.1 Stages of the process improvement guidelines.

- Plan
- Implement
- Evaluate

Stage 1: Prepare for the Succession Planning Process

When personnel prepare for succession planning, they are engaged in activities that get the entire process ready for further action. It is more than just getting ready for the process: The preparation stage is an overt activity that provides all stakeholders an opportunity to identify the goals and objectives for the process. The emphasis is on anticipating, formulating, acquiring, arranging, assembling, strengthening, fortifying, bracing, and adjusting materials, methods, expectations, and resources necessary to proactively support the succession process. This allows the development of an evaluation mechanism whereby each individual's contribution can be identified and utilized (Goldhaber, Liddle, & Theobald, 2013), and provides for a clarification of the role each individual will play in the succession planning process (Laurillard, 2013).

In addition, existing information related to the requirements for the position can be assembled and considered by all stakeholders. An intentional effort is made to identify what we currently know about the requirements for the position, what do we need to know about the requirements, taking time to identify the resources that are currently available within the district, articulate the resources that need to be acquired to move forward with the process, and the identification of any potential direction that the organization needs to have in place before any major worker decisions are completed. The authors believe that the preparation phase is often overlooked in previous models that focus on continuous improvement. Without a solid understanding of what is currently available, what is needed, and where the organization needs to go to obtain the appropriate resources to move forward with the process, poor decisions often result. Because of the potential for significant harm to the decision, we do not believe that most organizations focus enough on the preparation stage.

A big part of the preparation phase is to have the organization draw upon its currently existing resources. This often requires a superintendent to utilize existing management structures so they may be able to identify what is currently known, and to take the necessary steps to obtain any information or support that is either nonexistent, completely lacking, or is not overtly evident.

The emphasis here is to take a holistic view of the entire succession planning process, to view it from a systems perspective. Individual parts and pieces all are identified, and the interrelationship between these are examined and considered. This overview process looks at the forest, as a whole, while trying to understand and identify the various types of trees that exist not only in number but in location, the impact that each tree has on the whole, and the resources necessary to implement the entire scope of the project. Neely (2005) stated that in order "to help teams reach their potential, have them look at the macro view of processes" (p. 19). Effective preparation involves looking at only the individual pieces of the curricular process, but also tends to the final outcome of the interactions between various people and pieces.

Although it is important to consider the individual parts of the entire system, we need to be incredibly careful that we do not lose sight of the greater whole. "Focusing in on the details of the process will overlook the larger view and possibly even major process weaknesses" (Neely, 2005, p. 20). Therefore, it is necessary for individuals preparing for succession planning to take a tempered view of the entire process, and fully understand all the individual pieces that impact the outcome of the whole.

Stage 2: Prioritize for the Succession Planning Process

Superintendents that are responsible for guarding the succession planning process are encouraged to identify and set priorities in order to be effective (Rimm-Kaufman, Storm, Sawyer, Pianta, & LaParo, 2006). These priorities are natural outcome and flow directly from the Preparation Stage, and are used to identify the attributes and situations requiring the greatest attention in order to ensure that a common understanding is developed amongst all stakeholders. Prioritization provides a vehicle that allows trans-formative cultural shifts (Weber & Mitchell, 1996) to occur within the origin organization.

During the prioritization stage, individuals engaged in the succession planning process make value judgments as to what are the most salient or important aspects and features that need to be attended to during the process. Individuals need to make intellectual decisions based upon existing data, and reflect upon the needs of the organization that impact the identification, acquisition, training, induction, and maintenance of a newly hired principal. Although very difficult to achieve, it is important that the organization attempt to leave any emotional or political influences at the door when priorities are identified. Effective prioritization requires organizations to take a careful, measured, holistic, and reflective look at what their current situation is, the steps that need to occur to make things happen, and to provide an idea of direction as to where the organization goes to effectively plan for the succession of front-line administrators.

Stage 3: Plan the Activities Specific to the Succession Planning

As alluded to earlier, planning is often the first step that many authors consider when they discuss quality improvement initiatives (Benneyan & Chute, 1993; Bocean, 2011; Bushell, 1992; Dahlgaard, Kristensen, & Kanji, 1995). It is quite common and natural for organizations to want to immediately start planning for the arrival of a new administrator. It is a significant occurrence in the life of any educational organization. However, we believe that teams that immediately move to this stage in the process without taking the time to adequately and fully prepare for, and prioritize the important elements related to the succession plan often overlook not only important but potentially long-lasting elements that have direct impact on the success or failure of the planning process. In order for a plan to be the most effective in meeting the multitude of demands placed upon the organization by the varied stakeholders with a vested interest in the outcome, we believe that solid preparation and prioritization is essential in order to develop appropriate and holistic succession plans. Taking the time to go through these first two stages helps establish a "planning culture" (Hess, Johnson, & Reynolds, 2014, p. 3) that creates an "organizational commitment to ongoing planning and continuous improvement" (p. 3).

Bocean (2011) provides a framework to help guide the organization through the planning process. This allows the superintendent to define the parameters required for the succession planning process, and to determine the boundaries that will guide the delineation of responsibilities for the team. It is important to also include accountability checks that are intentionally embedded into the process at regular and recurring intervals in order to assure that all elements of the succession plan are being attended to on an orderly and regular basis. There is also an intentional identification and allocation of organizational resources to ensure that all processes, projects, and operations that occur during the succession planning process are in alignment to ultimately support the decisions made. The authors feel that planning needs to be inclusive enough to not only recognize, but consider the many different moving parts that impact the succession planning process. There is a strong emphasis on the identification and articulation of individual needs during the planning process so that all stakeholders that need to be represented have a say in the outcome. Successful organizations need to have an effective plan to help guide them through the implementation of the succession planning process in order to help ensure that all salient aspects are covered and attended to during the remaining stages of the process.

Stage 4: Implement the Activities Specific to the Succession Planning

Contrary to popular belief, the implementation stage of the succession planning process is not characterized by organizational inaction. Instead, it becomes vitally important that all salient aspects of the succession process are attended to through recursive and reflective activities to ensure that the plan is approached greatly and effectively implemented. The utilization of the organization's knowledge management structures is key during the implementation phase. These structures provide the information and support necessary to ensure that all stakeholders responsible for the implementation of the succession plan are acting in accordance with the direction that they have been prescribed.

We believe that during the implementation stage of the succession plan, all of the actors are not only involved in the process and need to perform their assigned tasks, but they need to be not only deliberate in their actions and implement their charge with fidelity but to also take the time to identify the features that are occurring in the moment and to document these for assessment and evaluation purposes. These formative assessment activities are intentionally built into the process to help ensure that all participants are not only meeting their specified roles and responsibilities, but also are providing the information and knowledge necessary to help document any glitches that occurred in the previous three stages.

Stage 5: Evaluate the Succession Planning Process

During the evaluation stage, the focus is not just on identifying the success or failure of the succession planning process, but rather to take a much broader and systematic view that is more inclusive in scope. It is during this stage where the actions and activities of those involved in the succession planning process are holistically looked at to make sure that the elements identified were appropriately tended to. This provides an organizational accountability on a broad scale in order to ascertain how the alignment of the many working parts of the system ultimately interacted to meet the goals of the organization.

All summative evaluation artifacts, assessments, and information are stored and maintained within the organization's knowledge management structure. Although evaluation is often considered to be a terminal activity, the authors firmly believe that the wealth, breath, and depth of information obtained through a reactive succession planning process can be utilized proactively in the future when other opportunities arise. Often the evaluation stage that occurs for the hiring of one administrator often becomes, and forms the basis of the preparation stage for subsequent succession planning processes.

Knowledge Management Structures and Processes

Up to this point we have alluded to the idea of a knowledge management structure contained within the organization. Quite often organizations have a variety of data and information at their disposal, but they seldom take the time to put it into one consistent and cohesive format or site so that the richness of the information can be drawn upon on a moment's notice to meet the district's needs. We strongly encourage superintendents that are proactive in their orientation to take a careful and considered look at how they not only obtain data and information, but how they store and manage these resources for distribution to stakeholders throughout the organization. We believe that through the utilization of knowledge management structures, reflective and recursive thought is not only enabled, but enhanced as organizational stakeholders have the opportunity to draw upon a consistent and rich resource base upon which the district is organized and maintained.

Between each stage there is an opportunity for the stakeholders involved in the succession planning process to engage in formative and reflective assessment and evaluation in order to identify the areas where things are going right as well as going wrong. Through a process of identification, exploration, and resolution (Francis, 1992), organizations are able to collect information and data in the moment that is potentially germane to appropriate functioning during each stage, and movement to the next. Reflection occurs when an individual identifies issues, events, or topics are identified and refined by the individual or the group participating in the process. When individuals explore they examine events from multiple perspectives and engage in a reflective exploration of available research and information in order to explore the many aspects of the topic or the event. When an issue gets to the resolve stage, common understanding and direction is established for future action and this often results in a statement of belief or practice that informs a rationale for support, a demonstration of understanding, or a statement of action to be taken to move to the next level.

The authors believe that superintendents who create formative and summative knowledge management structures that utilize the identify, explore, resolve (IER) principles have an opportunity to enhance the process, not only in the present, but also for future utilizations. Knowledge management structures that utilize the IER component take considerable organizational commitment, time, and attention so that they are consistently maintained and utilized effectively to help implement initiatives with fidelity. Although these knowledge management structures require superintendents to allocate considerable resources, the authors believe that these investments will pay off during the current as well as future succession planning events. In fact, the return on investment for knowledge management structures go beyond succession planning process, the information contained within the structures can be utilized for other parts of the organization that deal with finance, staffing, personnel, organizational need, or school culture and climate.

APPLICATION OF THE BENEFITS
OF AN ESTABLISHED PROCESS

The remainder of this chapter focuses on applying the elements of the process improvement guidelines for succession planning (a) for frontline administrators that have to lead without an ideal governance structure, (b) to incorporate the process to enhance student growth, and (3) to engage stakeholders in the school and in the local community in helping them make decisions as to who is selected to lead the school.

Leading Without Ideal Governance Structures

Even under the best situations, the job of the superintendent is demanding and challenging. Quite often the only group that the superintendent has to rely on for support and direction is the school board. However, it is fanciful to think that all school board members approach their responsibilities to this district in the same fashion. There are times when board members have ulterior motives for serving, and these often do not provide the superintendent with appropriate or effective governance structures. In the absence of any consistent support or direction from a school board, a superintendent often has to rely on their own ability to create order out of chaos. This requires the administrator to function on the basis of past experience (Kolb, 1984), engage in reflective thought (Schön, 1983), and understand that their school board members might have significant areas for professional development (Knowles, 1984).

Quite often, lack of ideal governance structures are a result of lack of consistency in the vision of the individual stakeholders with the reality of the situation. Inconsistency between reality and vision often leads to inconsistent or ineffectual interventions. This can have significant deleterious impact on superintendents wishing to lead affective succession planning processes. Without solid leadership from the board, in the areas of policy and procedures, it becomes difficult for superintendents to effectuate change and manage school culture through the process of succession planning.

Quite often the leadership styles of the board are not in alignment with the organizational needs, and the superintendent often finds themselves having to not only lead those above them but simultaneously support those below them within the organizational structure. It is during these times that a solid and consistent external locus of control can be implemented upon the organization. We believe that the process improvement guidelines provide such a support for superintendents that are dealing with lack of leadership issues from those above them, while enhancing their leadership impact for those below them as they engage in succession planning.

Superintendents that find themselves in situations with less than appropriate support and governance structures often have to rely upon past practice, and the results of their previous decisions to guide current or future problem-solving. This can be very difficult during times when the superintendent has to not only identify quality school administrators to guide the program, but also must unilaterally put into place parameters and structures that might not exist due to the inactivity or inability of the school board. We believe that the structured and developmental approach that the process improvement guidelines offers organizations that are engaging in succession planning in the best of situations, provide a significant level of support to superintendents that may find themselves having to engage in this important activity often independent of their school board structure, interest, support, or ability.

The focus that we place on the preparation stage will provide superintendents that are not in ideal situations and opportunity to very honestly reflect upon the resources that they currently have available to support them and their organization as they go through the succession planning process. The preparation phase identifies both the positive and negative elements that currently exist within their organization. Taking the time to proactively assess and establish what currently exists within the organization, both positive and negative, and to reflectively consider the impact that this has on the succession planning process, offers a superintendent proactive insight into potential problems and pitfalls that they may find themselves in.

Prioritization is a key element for all succession planning projects. However, when the superintendent is left to their own devices due to the fact that they do not have the support or governance structure necessary, taking the time to strategically prioritize issues and elements may be key to the success or failure of their succession planning initiative. Taking the time to make conscious note of the rate, sequence, intensity, and duration of a change initiative as significant as the hiring of a new building administrator needs to take into account the idea that change is a process not an event (Hord, 1997). Intentionally and deftly sequencing the various moving elements required for the succession planning process often requires that the superintendent engage in making tough decisions, intentionally elevating certain situations or stakeholders above the needs and desires of others. This reflective process (Schön, 1983) allows the superintendent to potentially identify outcomes in a way that unanticipated ones are potentially reduced or negated.

Planning becomes very significant for superintendents who do not have the support or ideal governance structures necessary for adequate succession planning. The elements that are not in existence in the organization need to be identified, so alternative routes of progression can be identified. Understanding that planning is the third stage in the process for succession planning allows the superintendent to build in emotional and intellectual buffers for the organization. Not rushing into a planning phase, provides a superintendent time to collect the information identified in the two previous stages so that holes that are in existence can potentially be filled. Delaying the planning phase also allows the superintendent the ability to reach out to key stakeholders that might be responsible for the less than ideal governance supports in an attempt to muster a change in position.

Knowledge management structures and the IER process provide school superintendents of potential wealth of resources that are often overlooked during times of stress and conflict. Superintendents that find themselves in unsupportive situations often have to rely upon themselves, their abilities, past organizational initiatives, and existing resources to help identify and meet current and future demands. Superintendents that proactively take the time to document, assess, and evaluate past incidences and occurrences through formative and summative assessment have a potential gold mine of support available to help guide and direct them in their decision-making in

the future. Knowing how past occurrences of the hiring of school administrators was accomplished and the impact that it had on the school community provides the superintendent with valuable insight as to ways that they
might want to proceed during this current initiative. Having a knowledge
base to understand the success or failure of past hiring decisions often is
the only support a superintendent might have when they have to lead without an ideal governance situation.

Assessment to Perpetuate Student Growth

With the advent of high-stakes testing within the public schools, many
school administrators responsible for leading the instructional quality of the
programs in their buildings often find themselves overwhelmed and stressed
to a point where they cannot handle the external pressures. As we have seen
in the introduction of this chapter, there has been significant turnover in administrative staff, and quite often this has to do with lack of student achievement on a year-to-year basis, and the stress that the situation places on them
personally and professionally. Due to this stress, may leave the profession
through retirement, or self-select themselves out, thus leaving a need for
school superintendents to find adequate administrative replacements.

The process improvement guidelines have the potential to be a great
support for superintendents finding themselves in a situation where they
need to identify new school administrators who are able to impact student
achievement. The 5 stages of the framework, along with the knowledge
management IER structure, provide the support necessary for superintendents to launch a succession plan. Taken as a whole, the process improvement guidelines provide a developmentally sequences process, that attends
to the details necessary to identify appropriate school administrators.

As we have seen, the process improvement guidelines place a great deal
of emphasis on the value of assessment; both formative and summative.
Although the steps above focused primarily on the succession planning for
school administrators, we believe that the framework also has utility when
looking at assessment as a whole. As an aside, superintendents reading this
chapter might consider taking the time to try and apply stages listed here as
they attempt to impact instructional quality and student outcomes in their
district. However, that is beyond the scope of this chapter, yet, it is also well
within the purview of this chapter.

Superintendents needing to fill school administrative positions because
they find themselves without an effective instructional leader that is up to
the challenge of guiding academic improvement efforts have a powerful
tool through the process improvement guidelines. These guidelines can
be utilized to help the superintendent identify, hire, and support school

leaders that can help meet the instructional needs of their school district. The time consuming process of hiring a new principal, in this scenario, is exacerbated by the fact that there has not been an effective program to adequately increase student academic achievement. This situation often occurs in organizations that have not had an alignment of initiatives, that are reflective and recursive, that have at its core implementation with fidelity. In addition, effective programs that are able to positively impact student achievement often depend on data and information contained within consistent knowledge management structures. As we have seen, and as we will see, the process improvement guidelines assist with all of these issues.

Utilizing the stages of preparing and prioritizing are key to the identification of school administrators who are intentionally hired to meet academic achievement issues. Any superintendent needing to fill an administrative need due to poor student performance would do well to carefully attend to these first two stages. Preparation stage would require the superintendent to have a good understanding of exactly what is occurring academically within the building, and to gather information related to the way instruction has been conducted within the program. Having a solid understanding of the materials and methodologies being used by the teachers, as well as the technological innovations and integrations, along with their ability to differentiate instruction and meet individual student needs are all vitally important information for the school superintendent to have as an attempt to hire a new educational leader. Having access to all of this information through existing knowledge management structures, as well as the IER process provides the superintendent a tremendous amount of support as they work through the preparation and prioritization phases. Without taking the time to engage in these two important stages, a school superintendent might be planning for the succession of a school administrator for the wrong reasons, knowing exactly why you need some specific individual with specific capabilities is vitally important for superintendents as they try to hire someone to meet instructional quality needs.

During the implementation phase of the succession planning process, it becomes vitally important for the superintendent to continue to engage in the IER and knowledge management acquisition process. This level of reflection (Schön, 1983) helps ensure that instructional quality and the capabilities of the future administrator are forefront in everyone's mind as they attempt to identify an individual that is hired specifically to help increase student achievement. Having a solid understanding of the skill sets, attributes, and experiences of any future school administrator needs to be a constant consideration during the implementation phase.

During the evaluation stage, the superintendent has an opportunity to identify the impact that their hire has had on meeting student achievement needs. Succession planning often leads to succession management, and it is during the evaluation stage where the school superintendent has the ability to assess the newly hired principal's capabilities in meeting student needs. If additional supports are needed through professional development or training, coursework, or retooling, the school superintendent can utilize many of the features contained in the process improvement guidelines to help identify and direct the school administrator to give them the experiences and abilities that they are lacking in order to meet the academic and achievement needs of the students within the program.

The utilization of the process improvement guidelines for succession planning offers a school superintendent the ability to identify the needed attributes and qualities that need to be a part of the person hired for school programs to meet student achievement needs.

Engage School and Community Members in Succession Planning

Out of the three scenarios presented in this chapter that we used to provide examples of the process improvement guidelines, this one has probably the most direct applicability. The entire five step process that we articulate has a strong emphasis on the inclusion of input from all salient stakeholders within the organization. With this input, there is a strong emphasis on openness and transparency. We firmly believe that all decisions need to have the consideration from, and to the greatest extent input from all stakeholders impacted by that decision. Engaging school and community members in the succession planning process is vitally important, and often when appropriate engagement does not occur, the results are disastrous. Individuals ultimately hired as principals to meet building needs, often find themselves embroiled in a culture that they are not prepared for due to political or emotional hard feelings about the way the process had been handled. Disastrous results often ensue when the plans developed for the administrative succession do not include the needs of the broader school, and when the ultimate decision is made, it becomes apparent that the community was not taken into account.

During the preparation stage of the succession planning, superintendents have the opportunity to gain the feedback and consensus from the impacted community members about the areas or attributes that they would like to have attention paid to during the succession planning process. These preparation activities provide the community an opportunity to collectively problem solve and go through a visioning process that leads to community and consensus building about the processes to be utilized, as well as the attributes being looked for in the new educational leader.

Having this process implemented with fidelity, with a reflective and recursive process being built onto the system provides support for the outcome.

Allowing for a communal prioritization process that identifies salient aspects of the succession plan allows for transparency and input from all interested. The additional aspect of taking copious notes, and continual assessment from community input through the IER process allow for the collection of vital artifacts and information that will be included in the knowledge management structure. This information will assist the organization as they move forward, not just in the hiring of the new administrator, but also when preparation for future community interactions occur.

Allowing community members to sit in on the planning and implementation phase, allow opportunities for participation of selected community members. Care must be given at this juncture in the way that these individuals are selected and announced. There is a huge potential for organizational backfire if it is assumed that specific community members were intentionally selected for inclusion over others, based on some political consideration. Identification of a transparent process for the consideration and selection of the members from the community minimizes the likelihood that people will be unhappy with the decision.

Often school superintendents have difficult times identifying effective strategies or best practices necessary for effective stakeholder engagement. We believe that the process improvement guidelines can be utilized to support stakeholder analysis of need for succession planning. By going through and attending to each of the five steps in the process improvement guidelines, a school superintendent can do a cursory review of stakeholder need, and this activity can become an introductory preparation for succession planning. We believe that one five-step process ultimately leads to others, and often initial opportunities to utilize process improvement guidelines lead to successive more important processes. Such is the case here. By utilizing the process improvement guidelines for stakeholder analysis, the superintendent has the ability to effectuate change through the identification of organizational culture and stakeholder need.

CONCLUSION

In this chapter, we have provided school superintendents concerned with succession planning a process that they can follow to help guide their organization as they bring on key employees to meet the important needs of their school programs. The process improvement guidelines provide the appropriate support and direction necessary to assist superintendents as they direct individuals within the organization through the succession planning process. "Ultimately, it is the collective efforts of workers who either perform or fail to perform their jobs that counts" (Elmuti, Kathawala, & Wayland, 1992, p. 42). The hiring of a school administrator impacts many organizational stakeholders, and often this impact is felt in personal and differing ways. We believe that it is important for all stakeholders to have an open and significant share in the responsibility and the hiring of a new building later. This means that the superintendent has to take a great deal of time to assemble the resources and individuals necessary to go through the succession planning process. However, we believe that this process is much more elaborate than most think, there is often more involved than just looking at how individual actors perform an act in their collective roles and responsibilities. We believe that the utilization of the process improvement guidelines provides the supports necessary that increase the likelihood of establishing an effective succession planning experience for all stakeholders. We believe the process improvement guidelines provide superintendents a developmentally sequenced series of stages that our intentionally designed to allow stakeholders to be reflective and recursive in their roles, as they methodically work through the process of hiring an effective school administrator.

REFERENCES

Benneyan, J., & Chute, A. (1993). SPC, process improvement, and the Deming PDCA circle in freight administration. *Production and Inventory Management Journal, 34*(1), 35–40.

Beteille, T., Kalogrides, D., & Loeb, S. (2012). Stepping stones: Principal career paths and school outcomes. *Social Science Research, 41*(4), 904–919. doi:10.1016/j.ssresearch.2012.03.003

Bocean, C. G. (2011). Project based organization—An integrated approach. *Management & Marketing, 9*(2), 265–273.

Bushell, S. (1992). Implementing plan, do, check and act. *The Journal for Quality and Participation, 15*(5), 58–62.

Collins, M. (2013). Local solutions for national challenges? Exploring local solutions through the case of a national succession planning strategy. *Educational Management Administration & Leadership, 41*(5), 658–673.

Dahlgaard, J., Kristensen, K., & Kanji, G. (1995). Total quality management and education. *Total Quality Management, 6*(5), 445–456. doi:10.1080/09544129550035116

Deming, W. E. (1950). *Elementary principles of the statistical control of quality.* Tokyo, Japan: JUSE.

Elmuti, D., Kathawala, Y., & Wayland, R. (1992). Traditional performance appraisal systems: The Deming challenge. *Management Decision, 30*(8), 42–48. doi:10.1108/00251749210022203

Francis, R. W. (1992). *Issues in establishing rural professional development schools*. A paper presented at the Annual National Rural and Small Schools Conference. Manhattan, KS.

Garman, A. N., & Glawe, J. (2004). Succession planning. *Consulting Psychology Journal: Practice and Research, 56*(2), 119–128.

Gates, S. M., Ringel, J. S., & Santibanez, L. (with Ross, K. E., & Chung, C. H.). (2003). *Who is leading our schools? An overview of school administrators and their careers*. Santa Monica, CA: RAND.

Goldhaber, D., Liddle, S., & Theobald, R. (2013). The gateway to the profession: Assessing teacher preparation programs based on student achievement. *Economics of Education Review, 34*, 29–44.

Hargreaves, A., & Fink, D. (2006). Redistributed leadership for sustainable professional learning communities. *Journal of School Leadership, 16*(5), 550–565.

Hess, M., Johnson, J., & Reynolds, S. (2014). A developmental model for educational planning: Democratic rationalities and dispositions. *International Journal of Educational Leadership Preparation, 9*(1), 1–10.

Hord, S. M. (1997). *Professional learning communities*. Austin, TX: Southwest Education Development Laboratory.

Knowles, M. S. (1984). The adult learner: A neglected species (3rd ed.). Houston, TX: Gulf.

Kolb, D. (1984). *Experiential learning as the science of learning and development*. Englewood Cliffs, NJ: Prentice Hall.

Laurillard, D. (2013). *Rethinking University Teaching: A Conversational Framework for the Effective Use of Learning Technologies*. New York, NY: Routledge.

Neely, M. (2005). Prepare for the perfect day. *Industrial Management, 47*(6), 19–24.

Pynes, J. (2004). The implementation of workforce and succession planning in the public sector. *Public Personnel Management, 33*(4), 389–404.

Rimm-Kaufman, S. E., Storm, M. D., Sawyer, B. E., Pianta, R. C., & LaParo, K. M. (2006). The Teacher Belief Q-Sort: A measure of teachers' priorities in relation to disciplinary practices, teaching practices, and beliefs about children. *Journal of School Psychology, 44*(2), 141–165.

Russell, J. L., & Sabina, L. L. (2014). Planning for principal succession: A conceptual framework for research and practice. *Journal of School Leadership, 24*, 599–639.

Ryan, T. G., & Gallo, M. (2011). A descriptive examination and synthesis of leadership succession. *International Journal of Educational Reform, 20*(2), 132–152.

Schall, E. (1997). Public-sector succession: A strategic approach to sustaining innovation. *Public Administration Review, 57*(1), 4–10.

Schmidt-Davis, J., & Bottoms, G. (2011). *Who's next? Let's stop gambling on school performance and plan for principal succession*. Atlanta, GA: Southern Regional Education Board.

Schön, D. A. (1983). *The Reflective Practitioner: How Professionals Think in Action* (Vol. 5126). New York, NY: Basic Books.

RAND. (2004). *The careers of public school administrators: Policy implications from an analysis of state-level data*. Santa Monica, CA: Author. Retrieved from http://www.rand.org/content/dam/rand/pubs/research_briefs/RB9054/RB9054.pdf

U.S. Bureau of Labor Statistics. (2008). *Occupational outlook handbook*. Retrieved from http://www.bls.gov/oco/

U.S. Department of Labor. (2000). *Occupational outlook handbook*. Washington, DC: U.S. Government Printing Office.

Wallin, D., Cameron, D. W., & Sharples, K. (2005). Succession planning and targeted leadership development. *Community College Journal, 76*(1), 24–28.

Weber, S., & Mitchell, C. (1996). Betwixt and between: The culture of student teaching. In Z. Moore (Ed.), *Foreign language teacher education: Multiple perspectives* (pp. 301–316). Lanham, MD: University Press of America.

Zepeda, S. J., Bengtson, E., & Parylo, O. (2011). Examining the planning and management of principal succession. *Journal of Educational Administration & Society, 50*(2), 136–158.

CHAPTER 6

ETHICS AND THE SUPERINTENDENCY

Denver J. Fowler
Franklin University

Perhaps now more than ever, ethics is at the forefront of school leadership, especially as it applies to the superintendency at both the state and district levels in the United States. "The role of school-district superintendents in the United States of America has evolved since the introduction of the position during the middle of the 19th Century (Björk, Kowalski, & Browne-Ferrino, 2014, p. 1). In fact, others have even argued superintendents' role as applied scientist and social activist (Fusarelli & Fusarelli, 2005). Moreover, school board-superintendent relationships continue to be arduous (Alsbury, 2003; Mountford, 2004). Despite such impediments, stakeholders, including students, staff, parents, community members, and business owners, expect their superintendent to lead, and to do so in an ethical manner. However, it would be a disservice to the reader to merely suggest that the need for superintendents to lead ethically is either revolutionary or evolutionary. In contrast, one might contend that this ideal may in fact be both. That is, we might contend that what is considered to be ethical leadership within the educational setting has gradually and continually been developed over the years through

The Contemporary Superintendent, pages 93–107
Copyright © 2019 by Information Age Publishing
All rights of reproduction in any form reserved.

an array of standards (Fowler, 2018) that exist supporting the need for ethical leadership by school leaders (evolutionary). Nevertheless, in more recent years, we have seen numerous ethical scandals by both district and state superintendents (Associated Press, 2017; Blasius, 2018; CNN, 2013; McVicker & Devine, 2014; Schneider, 2018), causing a dramatic shift and focus on ethics as it applies to the superintendency (revolutionary). Thus, this chapter aims to highlight the recent research as it applies to ethics, more specifically, ethical leadership perspectives and the superintendency, while supporting the need for additional research, discussion, and debate on this particular topic. After all, superintendents should "fulfill(s) all professional duties with honesty and integrity and always act(s) in a trustworthy and responsible manner" (American Association of School Administrators, 2016). To do otherwise, is negligence, and has serious implications and consequences for the very stakeholders in which superintendents serve, namely, school aged children. Nonetheless, as previously mentioned, we continue to see ethical scandals by superintendents across our nation and we continue to see the solemn consequences of such unethical behavior and decision-making (Associated Press, 2017; Blasius, 2018; CNN, 2013; McVicker & Devine, 2014; Schneider, 2018). As the focus continues to shift on ethics and the superintendency (revolutionary) and the array of standards supporting the need for ethical school leaders continues to be reexamined, modified and re-released (evolutionary), one might contend that above all, ethics is truly the heart of leadership, and perhaps especially, as it applies to the superintendency, where the very nature of the work itself is multifaceted and extremely demanding on a daily basis (Björk, 2005).

The study of ethics and leadership can be traced back to Socrates, Aristotle, Plato and the Ancient Greeks, dating back as far as 300 B.C. Still, such philosophical writings on ethics tends to be discounted and often ignored by researchers (Ciulla, 2014). Ethics research can be somewhat of a moving target. That is, most, if not all of us, generally speaking, know right from wrong, rather we serve in a leadership capacity or not. However, we continue to see virtuous people make unethical decisions (Carucci, 2016), and we continue to see great district leaders do the same (Associated Press, 2017; Blasius, 2018; CNN, 2013; McVicker & Devine, 2014; Schneider, 2018). Studying ethics can be a difficult task for scholars and researchers alike (Clowney, 1992; Koepsell, 2015; Peters, 1966). As Peters (1966) so aptly wrote, what makes ethics so distinctive "is that it is concerned with the analysis and justification of answers to practical questions where 'practical' is contrasted with 'theoretical'" (p. 17). Oftentimes, researchers and scholars are trying to determine how we can ensure ethics is at the forefront of all leadership, including educational leadership (Beckner, 2004; Oliver, 2015; Rebore, 2014; Strike, 2007; & Strike, Haller, & Soltis, 2005). Unfortunately, too often, researchers and scholars are analyzing the aftermath of unethical decision-making. For example, this inclination alone tends to make it difficult to understand (and research) how a given individual who has led an organization ethically for several decades, makes one unethical decision that brings down the entire organization, as well as destroying said leaders' credibility, and possibly, employment and future (Carucci, 2016). To be clear, "researchers study leadership to understand how and why it works and does not work" (Ciulla, 2005, p. 325). Nonetheless, we must continue to be innovative in our research, not only as it relates to ethics in general, but how ethics applies to educational leadership, namely, the superintendency. Superintendents at both the state and district levels are widely considered to be the chief executive officer (CEO) in both our state education systems and school districts (Björk, 2005; Browne-Ferrigno & Glass, 2005). Thus, there is little doubt the decisions made by state and district level superintendents have a lasting impact on the stakeholders they serve and lead, as well as a collective influence on national education outcomes in comparison to other nations around the globe. Although diminutive extant research is focused on ethics as it relates specifically to the superintendent at both the state and district levels, there is research being conducted in this arena (Fowler, Edwards, & Hsu, 2018; Fowler & Johnson, 2014). This research will be invaluable to both state and district level superintendents, as well as the very stakeholders in which they serve. Moreover, the results of this research will be valuable to individuals (e.g., professors of educational leadership) and educational leadership programs that prepare aspiring school leaders for the superintendency. In addition, one could argue that this research will be beneficial to the individuals who represent national organizations and associations who have influence on, and often play a significant role in the creation of the very standards that are used for accreditation in educational leadership programs across the nation.

Again, the purpose of this chapter is to highlight recent research on the topic of ethics as it applies to the superintendency. More specifically, the chapter will focus on research of the ethical leadership perspectives of state and district level superintendents, and how those perspectives vary according to state education/school district characteristics and state/district leader demographics. Additionally, opportunities and suggestions are offered in an effort to share resources for state/district level superintendents, specifically as it relates to possible sources of ethical guidance, with an overlying purpose to support the need for ongoing ethics discussions amongst state/district level superintendents, as well as those individuals who prepare aspiring school leaders (i.e., professors of educational leadership), and the very stakeholders in which they serve. Finally, the content of this chapter is written in an effort and attempt to support the need for additional research on ethics and the superintendency amongst scholars and researchers alike.

ETHICS AND THE SUPERINTENDENCY

Ethics with regards to the superintendency, is not a new concept, and ethics continues to be at the forefront of school leadership at the state, district, and building levels. Yet, little research exists focused specifically on the ethical dimensions of school leadership, particularly as it pertains to the superintendency. Nonetheless, one can easily access a bulk of literature on how school leaders should lead, from a philosophical or theoretical perspective. However, much of this content is not supported by research, rather, it is written in the form of self-help style books without any research to support the content, and as previously reported, is often ignored by researchers (Ciulla, 2014). Furthermore, much of the extant literature on leadership ethics applies to the business sector, and moreover, apply more to business ethics versus leadership (Ciulla, 2005; Hitt, 1990; Paine, 1996). Thus, how does one determine what literature to reference with regard to ethics, and more specifically, leadership ethics, as it applies to school leadership? Likewise, if researchers often ignore ethics literature (Ciulla, 2014), why would we suspect our practitioners, namely state/district superintendents, are utilizing it. The truth is, it is most likely they are not utilizing this literature, and the great quest continues to determine what extant literature is relevant, supported by research, and can be applicable to both state/district level superintendents on the job. "One of the greatest difficulties in researching leadership is sorting out articles that have leadership in the title, that are basically traditional management articles" (Ciulla, 2005, p. 324). One might argue that we do not simply want great managers leading our state education systems/local school districts. Rather, we might demand individuals to be well-versed instructional leaders who have the capacity to improve instruction and academic achievement, while also having the necessary management skills required to effectively (and ethically) lead their school district and/or respective state education system.

Ethics, in some way, shape, or form, appears throughout the standards driving the content (and accreditation) of our educational leadership preparation programs in the higher education setting throughout the United States. In fact, within the Professional Standards for Educational Leaders released in 2015, an entire section is dedicated to "Ethics and Professional Norms" (National Policy Board for Educational Administration, 2015, p. v). Additionally, other historically prominent standards guiding educational leadership programs around the nation such as the Interstate School Leaders Licensure Consortium (ISLLC) Standards (Council of Chief School Officers, 2008) and National Educational Leadership Preparation (NELP) standards (formerly known as the ELCC Leadership Standards) (National Policy Board for Educational Administration, 2016) respectively, include standards and language on ethics. Likewise, the largest and oldest association in the United States representing school superintendents has an entire code dedicated to ethics and release a monthly magazine with a section dedicated to ethics titled the Ethical Educator (American Association of School Administrators, 2016). Thus, there is little doubt that there has been a focus on the importance of school leaders leading with integrity. "School administrators encounter situations almost on a daily basis that require personal judgments to be made that involve ethical decisions" (Oliver, 2015, p. xix). Today, superintendents at both the state and district level(s) are held accountable for effectively responding to societal issues that are the result of current social trends in their districts and states (Bryant, 2011; Campbell, 2008; Wilcox & Ebbs, 1992; Fowler & Johnson, 2014). "Over the last decade, the role of leadership in developing ethical conduct has become an area of increased interest due to the large number of ethical scandals by leaders across the globe" (Fowler & Johnson, 2014, p. 12). However, ethical scandals continue to remain prevalent in the educational setting (Associated Press, 2017; Blasius, 2018; CNN, 2013; McVicker & Devine, 2014; Schneider, 2018). Perhaps most infamous, the cheating scandal by the superintendent of Atlanta Public Schools, who also happened to be the former National Superintendent of the Year in the United States, which led to prison time for many school leaders and educators in the district (CNN, 2013). Others exist in the education setting as well, in recent years, the state superintendency in the state of Ohio was rocked by ethical scandals. In fact, the state of Ohio named three state superintendents in as many years, the first two fired amidst ethical scandals (Fowler & Johnson, 2014). Worth noting, at least a dozen more district superintendents in the state of Ohio were under investigation for what investigators termed data scrubbing during this same period of time (Bush, 2017; Fowler & Johnson, 2014; Neese, 2017). In recent years, major ethical scandals in leadership have plagued major corporations and organizations such as Penn State University, Enron, Tyco, WorldCom, Arthur Anderson, the entire U.S. housing market and the many notorious banks involved, and many more. With so many ethical scandals in recent years, one has to wonder if we have a competency issue or if we have an ethical issue? Perhaps Sternberg (2009) answers this question best when he reported that "smart and knowledgeable people ran those agencies and institutions" so "the question is not whether or not the people had sufficient knowledge; it's whether they used that knowledge ethically" (p. 34).

As previously reported, one could argue that the state/district superintendents are the CEO of their respective state education systems and/or local school districts (Björk, 2005; Browne-Ferrigno & Glass, 2005). Thus, it is imperative that we ensure such leaders lead ethically and do so with the thought in mind that their decisions have major influence and consequences affecting all stakeholders; students, staff, parents, community members, and business owners. That is, their decisions have implications, and one might contend that researchers must be proactive (versus reactive) with regards to the study of ethical leadership in states/schools. If not, in the end, and sadly, the students do not have the opportunity to complete another grade or hit pause every time such leaders make unethical decisions. In contrast, they keep marching forward and matriculating from grade-to-grade until graduation, all while researchers, lawyers, investigators, and the like, are often trying to sift through the evidence, decide what happened, where did things go wrong, why, and how to fix the problem as quickly as possible, all while students attend school each day. This is the predicament, we know research on ethics and the superintendency is important, however, we continue to see a lack of research in this arena. If ethics is truly the heart of leadership (Ciulla, 2004), then why does so little research focus on ethics as it applies to the state/district superintendency?

RECENT RESEARCH ON ETHICS AND THE SUPERINTENDENCY

As previously reported, the topic of ethics as it relates to school leadership and the superintendency is not a new concept. In fact, dating back to 1996, School Administrator (a national superintendent practitioner focused magazine released monthly by The School Superintendents Association, more widely known as the American Association of School Administrators [AASA]), included one word on the front cover of their October 1996 issue, the word was ethics. This particular issue included four articles on the ethical dimensions of decision-making by superintendents. In addition, AASA includes a section in their monthly magazine titled Ethical Educator (see: http://www.aasa.org/SAethics.aspx) that draws on actual circumstances to raise an ethical decision-making dilemma in K-12 education, and furthermore shares how practicing and retired superintendents would respond. Nonetheless, articles on ethical school leadership are not lacking. A simple Google search on ethical school leadership will return over 23 million results, again, mostly written from a philosophical or theoretical view, while often lacking the research or references to support the content. The fact is, ethics as it applies to the state/district superintendency continues to be an area of focus, however, little to no research is being conducted in this arena specifically as it applies to ethics and the superintendency.

In more recent years, some researchers have begun to shine light on the importance of the ethical leadership perspectives of both district and state superintendents in the United States, more specifically, as it relates to their own leader demographics and state education/school district characteristics (Fowler, Edwards, & Hsu, 2018; Fowler & Johnson, 2014). The results of this research are beginning to shed light on not only the ethical leadership perspectives of the superintendents in the studies, but also how they relate to other constructs both as it applies directly to the superintendent as well as the state/district in which they serve. For example, in a study by Fowler and Johnson (2014), the researchers determined that the ethical leadership perspectives of superintendents in the state of Ohio were significantly statistically correlated with school leader demographics (e.g., age, gender, and highest educational degree obtained) and school district characteristics (e.g., student achievement). More specifically, the researchers found that the older a superintendent was, the more strongly positive their ethical leadership perspectives were. This outcome may suggest that with more experience, a superintendents ethical decision-making improves. The researchers also found that female superintendents had stronger ethical leadership perspectives than male superintendents. This finding was particularly significant in that the superintendency at both the state/district levels in the United States, continues to be dominated by males (Grogan & Brunner, 2005; Brunner & Kim, 2010). In fact, and perhaps worth mentioning with regards to this specific outcome, the only country in the world that is dominated by female superintendents is Israel. In a study by Glass (2000), it was determined that of the estimated 13,728 district superintendents in the United States, only 1,984 were women (AASA, 2017). In the same article, it was reported that 72 percent of all K-12 educators in the United States are women (AASA, 2017). In addition, Fowler and Johnson (2014) found that superintendents who held doctoral degrees, had slightly stronger ethical leadership perspectives than those superintendents who held a Master or Bachelor degrees. This outcome may imply that the ethical leadership perspectives of superintendents is sharpened through the completion of a degree program and accompanying coursework. Perhaps one of the most significant findings of this study, was the fact that superintendents who had more strongly positive ethical leadership perspectives, also led school districts with higher student achievement, further supporting the need for ethical leaders in our schools. This study, for conceivably the first time, was able to show a significant statistical correlation between the ethical leadership perspectives of superintendents and student achievement. As we know, student achievement almost always determines a school's success (or failure) in educating its students. A similar study focused on the ethical leadership perspectives of state superintendents in the United States, including the District of Columbia and the Department of Defense, was launched by Fowler, Edwards, and Hsu (2018). This study found that state superintendents had only a slightly positive mean score ($M = 3.8$) on the Ethical Leadership Scale (ELS) used in the study, and the ELS mean scores ranged from ($M = 2.10$–$M = 5.0$). Thus, showing quite a bit of variation in the ethical leadership perspectives of state superintendents in the United States, including the Department of Defense and the District of Columbia. This outcome is significant for two reasons: (a) it is rare to see a score below 3.0 on the ELS (Brown, Harrison, & Trevino, 2005); and (b) it shows that at least some of the state superintendents in the United States have negative ethical leadership perspectives. The focus of these studies was to determine if the ethical leadership perspectives of superintendents vary according to state education/school district characteristics and state/school leader demographics, and the researchers found that they did in fact vary. Nonetheless, more research will be required in order to support the findings of the aforementioned studies.

There is no doubt that direct and profound ethical implications as a result of the actions of such school leaders carries influence on both their organizations and corresponding stakeholders (Calabrese & Roberts, 2001; Fowler & Johnson, 2014). However, we continue to see a lack of research focused on ethics in education, especially as it relates to the superintendency at any level (state or district). Again, if ethics is truly the heart of leadership (Ciulla, 2004), we must make it a priority to support and encourage research on ethics, and specifically, as it applies to the superintendency.

A SOURCE OF ETHICAL GUIDANCE FOR STATE AND DISTRICT SUPERINTENDENTS

The extant research implies that superintendents do in fact take and complete coursework in their superintendent license programs that is focused on ethics (Fowler, Edwards, & Hsu, 2018; Fowler & Johnson, 2014). However, the research also indicates that most superintendents only complete one (or two) ethical leadership courses in their degree/licensure programs. For example, the majority of superintendents ($n = 65$) in the Fowler and Johnson (2014) study had only completed two ethical leadership courses and ($n = 66$) only completed one ethical leadership course - as part of their degree/licensure programs, many of which held Doctoral degrees. Furthermore, in the Fowler, Edwards, and Hsu (2018) study on state superintendents in the United States, Department of Defense, and District of Columbia, the majority of state superintendents only completed one ethical leadership course in their degree programs. In most cases, principal/superintendent license programs often include ethics within their school law course. If not for the content, within the title anyway (e.g., Law and Ethics in Education, School Law and Ethics, etc.). Additionally, the majority of state superintendents did not complete any type of mentoring program/experience in their superintendent license programs (Fowler, Edwards, & Hsu, 2018), whereas in the Fowler and Johnson (2014) study, the majority of superintendents did in fact complete a mentoring program/experience as part of their superintendent license program ($n = 123$). Perhaps also worth noting, and somewhat interesting, is that the majority of state superintendents in the Fowler, Edwards, and Hsu (2018) study did not have a valid superintendent license, further complicating the analysis as it applied to coursework completed as part of a superintendent licensure program. Nevertheless, based on the results of this research, we might ask ourselves where state and district superintendents look to for an excellent source of ethical guidance?

When this question was posed to both practicing state and district level superintendents (Fowler, Edwards, & Hsu, 2018; Fowler & Johnson, 2014) their answers were quite intriguing. For example, when superintendents were asked what state/school characteristics affected their ethical leadership perspectives, they implied items such as community norms, size of budget, state/school culture, and expectations of stakeholders were all items affecting their ethical leadership perspectives (Fowler, Edwards, & Hsu, 2018; Fowler & Johnson, 2014). However, when the same superintendents were asked if they believed their ethical leadership perspectives were affected by their own leader demographics, items such as individual morals, experience on the job, individual ethical code, personal values, and upbringing were all responses and emergent themes (Fowler, Edwards, & Hsu, 2018; Fowler & Johnson, 2014). Essentially, the results of these studies suggest that state/district superintendents do not look to items such as ethical coursework in their degree programs, ethical standards, codes of ethics, and the like, to guide their ethical leadership perspectives. In contrast, based on the results of these studies, they rely on and trust their personal values, upbringing, community norms, and even the size of budget (to name a few) to guide such perspectives. Now the question is, Is this good enough? That is, can we simply trust that state/district superintendents had a good upbringing, so we know they will be ethical in all that they do? I do not believe so, in fact, I believe it is a major disservice to all stakeholders, including students, staff, parents, community members, and business owners. In the 21st Century, we must do a better job preparing our state/district superintendents. We must dig deeper and get to the roots of ethical decision-making and how we can prepare leaders to make consistent ethical decisions based on what is best for their stakeholders, namely their students. We must ask ourselves what exactly qualifies as ethical in the educational context? What characteristics and traits are associated with ethical leadership? and, What is the application of leadership ethics within the school setting? (Lynch, 2015).

Let's take a moment to reflect on and analyze the outcomes from the extant research shared within this chapter. In both studies, it was apparent that state/district superintendents used their personal values, upbringing, community norms, and even budget size to guide their ethical compass. Now, I do believe community/state norms should be taken into consideration as a state/school superintendent, however, what if those norms in and of themselves are not ethical? Since, in many ways, the state/school superintendents refereed to their upbringing as the major source of guiding their ethical leadership perspectives, might we consider how this alone might falter? I once heard a sermon by a preacher who discussed how our upbringing tends to be circulative, that is, a cycle. We all tend to think we were raised properly because we often only truly understand and know how we were raised, that is, our upbringing. Then, we tend to raise our children the same way, and those children tend to raise their children the same way, and so on. We have this mindset that, I turned out fine, so I must have been brought up fine enough as well. Unfortunately, this is all to true and an extremely hard cycle to break. Perception is reality, and again, most of us think we were raised properly no matter how good (or bad) it might have been. Thus, when hiring state/school superintendents, we are putting a lot of faith into their upbringing, as, based on the extant research (Fowler, Edwards, & Hsu, 2018; Fowler & Johnson, 2014), they are not necessarily looking elsewhere for ethical guidance. Personally, I believe this is a big gamble, and furthermore, I believe we can do better. Local and state school boards must appoint and elect the best individuals to serve as their state/school superintendent. However, we must continually point such individuals in the right direction when it comes to a source of ethical guidance.

Fortunately, many national and state organizations, including State Departments of Education, have ethical codes and standards in place that address ethics, and in some cases, specifically, as it applies to state/district superintendents. Perhaps most notably, AASA has a code of ethics for educational leaders. As previously mentioned, AASA is The School Superintendents Association in the United States representing public school district superintendents across the nation. This code of ethics serves as an excellent resource for educational leaders, including state/district superintendents. In more recent years, and as previously reported, the Professional Standards for Educational Leaders, which were released in 2015, have dedicated an entire section to "Ethics and Professional Norms" (National Policy Board for Educational Administration, 2015, p. v). Additionally, other prominent standards guiding educational leadership programs around the nation such as the Interstate School Leaders Licensure Consortium (ISLLC) Standards (Council of Chief School Officers, 2008) and National Educational Leadership Preparation (NELP) standards (formerly known as the ELCC Leadership Standards) (National Policy Board for Educational Administration, 2016) include language and standards on ethics for district level leaders. Furthermore, many state Departments of Education have a code of ethics and standards of conduct for both educators and administrators, including superintendents. For example, in the state of Mississippi, there are 10 standards all focused on the ethical conduct of licensed educators and administrators (Mississippi Department of Education, 2016). Although professional development and training is available to both educators and administrators with regards to these standards and code of conduct, unfortunately, not every educator and administrator attend and/or register for such trainings and professional development. In addition, other national organizations such as the National Association of Secondary School Principals and National Association of Elementary School Principals, as well as state organizations in each state such as the Mississippi Association of School Superintendents and the Mississippi Association of School Administrators, often have standards and/or a code of ethics, often easily accessible by state/district superintendents and school leaders. Perhaps the strongest effort to provide ethical guidance to state/district superintendents, is postulated in a monthly column in AASA's School Administrator national magazine. In this column titled Ethical Educator, which is accessible in hard copy format (the monthly magazine) or via the Internet (see: http://www.aasa.org/SAethics.aspx), realistic scenarios are highlighted in order to raise an ethical decision-making dilemma in the PreK–12 educational setting. In addition, four panelists (who are currently superintendents or retired superintendents, and in the past, have included professors, as well as executive directors and presidents of national education organizations) provide their own resolutions to each dilemma. This scenario based learning (SBL) can provide an authentic experience for state/district superintendents, while also allowing such individuals to grapple with and think through the decision-making process of the panelists without real-life consequences. In recent years, SBL has garnered much support as an effective tool in teaching any content, especially as it applies to problem-based or case-based learning (Clark, 2009; Kindley, 2002; Savery, 2006). Within this chapter, I have included my personal recommendations with regards to a excellent sources of ethical guidance for state/district superintendents (see Table 6.1). In addition, it is my recommendation

TABLE 6.1 Sources of Ethical Guidance for State/District Superintendents

Source (and Year Released)	Location of Source	Notes
Professional Standards for Educational Leaders (2015)	http://www.ccsso.org	Latest Standards created for Educational Leaders.
The American Association of School Administrators (AASA) Code of Ethics (2016)	http://www.aasa.org	AASA is the oldest organization representing superintendents in the United States.
National Educational Leadership Preparation (NELP) Standards (2016)	http://www.ucea.org	Reference Standard 2, aligned with PSEL standards.
Interstate School Leaders Licensure Consortium (ISLLC) Standards (2008)	http://www.ccsso.org	Reference Standard 5.0

Note: Another source of ethical guidance for state/district superintendents is the code of ethics provided by the department of education in their respective state, as many state departments of education provide a standard of conduct and/or code of ethics for all educators, administrators, and superintendents.

that both state/district superintendents and professors charged with preparing them, consult these sources on a regular basis, and continue to have ongoing ethics discussions with and amongst colleagues, as well as the very stakeholders in which they serve, including students, staff, parents, community members, and business owners.

CONCLUSION

This chapter has focused on ethics and the superintendency. Furthermore, this chapter highlighted the recent research that is being conducted in this arena, as well as some of the findings of this research as it applies to the ethical leadership perspectives of state/district superintendents and how those perspectives vary according to other constructs including state/district leader demographics and state education/district characteristics. Additionally, sources for ethical guidance were shared as possible valuable references for both aspiring and practicing state and district superintendents. The chapter has most certainly supported the need for ongoing and additional research to be conducted on ethics and state/district superintendents. As such research is continually conducted, perhaps we can begin to determine the ethical leadership perspectives of state/district superintendents, as well as what affects these perspectives, all in an effort to better prepare and further support aspiring and practicing school leaders at both the state and district levels.

Finally, one might argue that the need for district/state superintendents to lead ethically is neither revolutionary or evolutionary. In fact, one might contend it is both. As previously reported, standards and codes of ethics are constantly reexamined, reimaged, rewritten, adopted, and rereleased (Fowler, 2018). Thus, in some ways, this idea of superintendent leading ethically is evolutionary. However, due to the numerous ethical scandals in recent years by both district and state superintendents, we have witnessed a histrionic shift and focus on ethics as it applies to the superintendency (both at the state and district levels). Thus, in some ways, this idea of superintendents leading ethically is revolutionary. Needless to say, ethics will remain at the forefront of education, especially as it applies to the superintendency. Furthermore, ethics should remain an important topic of discussion for researchers, scholars, and practitioners alike. In addition, ethics should be (or in some cases, become) prevalent within leadership preparation programs throughout our nation and around the globe, perhaps especially in programs leading to superintendent licensure. If ethics is truly the heart of leadership, might we start there? If not, I strongly believe we are doing a disservice not only to the aspiring district/state superintendents, but to the very stakeholders in which they serve, namely students, and these students will become our future society. By ensuring ethics is at the forefront of the superintendency, we model for future generations what is perhaps the most vital aspect of leadership; ethics.

REFERENCES

Alsbury, T. (2003). Superintendent and school board member turnover: Political versus apolitical turnover as a critical variable in the application of the dissatisfaction theory. *Educational Administration Quarterly, 39*(5), 667–698.

American Association of School Administrators. (2016). *Code of ethics for educational leaders.* Retrieved from http://www.aasa.org/content.aspx?id=1390

American Association of School Administrators. (2017). *Where are all the women Superintendents?* Retrieved from http://aasa.org/SchoolAdministratorArticle.aspx?id=14492

Associated Press. (2017). *Superintendent quits in wake of school district sex scandal.* Retrieved from https://www.usnews.com/news/best-states/pennsylvania/articles/2017-09-27/superintendent-quits-in-wake-of-school-district-sex-scandal

Beckner, W. (2003). *Ethics for educational leaders.* New York, NY: Pearson Education.

Björk, L., Kowalski, T., & Browne-Ferrigno (2014). The school district superintendent in the United States of America. *Educational Leadership Faculty Publications.* Retrieved from https://ecommons.udayton.edu/cgi/viewcontent.cgi?article=1011&context=eda_fac_pub

Björk, L. G. (2005). Superintendent-board relations: An historical overview of the dynamics of change and sources of conflict and collaboration. In G. J. Petersen & L. D. Fusarelli (Eds.), *The district superintendent and school board relations: Trends in policy development and implementation* (pp. 1–22). Charlotte, NC: Information Age.

Blasius, M. (2018). *Scottsdale superintendent and top administrator fired over financial scandal.* Retrived from https://www.abc15.com/news/region-northeast-valley/scottsdale/scottsdale-superintendent-and-top-administrator-fired-over-financial-scandal

Brown, M., Harrison, D., & Trevino, L. (2005). Ethical leadership: A social learning perspective for construct development and testing. *Organizational Behavior and Human Decision Processes, 97,* 117–134.

Browne-Ferrigno, T., & Glass, T. E. (2005). Superintendent as organizational manager. In L. G. Björk & T. J. Kowalski (Eds.), *The contemporary superintendent: Preparation, practice and development* (pp. 137–61). Thousand Oaks, CA: Corwin Press.

Brunner, C., & Kim, Y. L. (2010). Are women prepared to be school superintendents? An essay on the myths and misunderstandings. *Journal of Research on Leadership Education, 5*(8), 276–309.

Bryant, C. (2011). Exploring ethical leadership: A superintendents' professional learning project. *Education Canada, 51*(5).

Bush, B. (2017). Five years in, cases linger in Columbus schools data cheating scandal. *Columbus Dispatch*. Retrieved from http://www.dispatch.com/news/20170616/ five-years-in-cases-linger-in-columbus-schools-data-cheating-scandal

Calabrese, R., & Roberts, B. (2001). The promise forsaken: neglecting the ethical implications of leadership. *International Journal of Education Management, 15*(6), 267–275.

Campbell, D. (2008). Leadership qualities that promote positive racial teacher–student relationships. *Leadership for Educational and Organizational Advancement, 1*(4).

Carucci, R. (2016). Why ethical people make unethical choices. *Harvard Business Review*. Retrieved from https://hbr.org/2016/12/why-ethical-people -make-unethical-choices

Ciulla, J. (2014). *Ethics, the heart of leadership* (3rd ed.). Santa Barbara, CA: Praeger.

Ciulla, J. (2005). The state of leadership ethics and the work that lies before us. *Business Ethics: A European Review, 14*(4), 323–335.

Ciulla, J. (2004). *Ethics, the heart of leadership*. Westport, CT: Greenwood.

Clark, R. (2009). *Accelerating expertise with scenario based learning*. Learning Blueprint. Merrifield, VA: American Society for Teaching and Development.

Clowney, D. (1992). *Why (and how) to study ethics*. Retrieved from http://users.rowan .edu/~clowney//cmp/ETHINKS.HTM

CNN. (2013). *Former Atlanta schools superintendent reports to jail in cheating scandal.* Retrieved from https://www.cnn.com/2013/04/02/justice/georgia-cheating -scandal/index.html

Council of Chief State Officers. (2008). *Educational Leadership Policy Standards: ISLLC 2008*. Washington, DC: Author.

Fowler, D. (2018). *The 21st century school leader: Leading schools in today's world*. Ontario, Canada: Word & Deed.

Fowler, D., Edwards, R., & Hsu, H. (2018). An investigation of state superintendents in the United States: Ethical leadership perspectives, state leader demographics, and state education characteristics. *Athens Journal of Education, 5*(3), 209–246.

Fowler, D., & Johnson, J. (2014). An investigation of ethical leadership perspectives among Ohio school district superintendents. *Education Leadership Review of Doctoral Research, 1*(2), 96–112.

Fusarelli, B. C., & Fusarelli, L. D. (2005). Reconceptualizing the superintendency: Superintendents as social scientists and social activists. In L. G. Björk & T. J. Kowalski (Eds.), *The contemporary superintendent: Preparation, practice, and development* (pp. 187–206). Thousand Oaks, CA: Corwin Press.

Grogan, M., & Brunner, C.C. (2005). Women superintendents and role conception: (Un)troubling the norms. In L. G. Björk & T. J. Kowalski (Eds.), *The contemporary superintendent: Preparation, practice, and development* (pp. 227–250). Thousand Oaks, CA: Corwin Press.

Hitt, W. D. (1990). *Ethics and leadership: Putting theory into practice*. Columbus, OH: Battelle Press.

Kindley, R. W. (2002). *Scenario-based e-learning: A step beyond traditional e-learning*. Retrieved from http://www.learningcircuits.com/2002/may2002/kindley.html

Koepsell, D. (2015). *Is studying ethics (or anything) worth it?* Retrieved from https://www.centerforinquiry.net/blogs/entry/is_studying_ethics_or_anything_worth_it/

Lynch, M. (2015) *The eight principals of ethical leadership in education.* Retrieved from http://www.theedadvocate.org/the-eight-principles-of-ethical-leadership-in-education/

McVicker, L., & Devine, R. (2014). *Ex-sweetwater superintendent gets 2 months in jail in corruption case.* Retrieved from https://www.nbcsandiego.com/news/local/Ex-Superintendent-Gets-2-Months-in-Jail-Jesus-Gandara-264991981.html

Mississippi Department of Education. (2016). *Mississippi Educator: Code of Ethics, Standards of Conduct* [Brochure]. Jackson, MS: Author.

Mountford, M. (2004). Motives and power of school board members: implications for school board-superintendent relationships. *Educational Administration Quarterly, 40*(5), 704–741.

National Policy Board for Educational Administration. (2016). *National Educational Leadership Preparation Standards for District Leaders.* Retrieved from http://www.ucea.org/2016/05/01/comment-on-the-new-nelp-standards-for-leadership-preparation-today/

National Policy Board for Educational Administration. (2015). *Professional Standards for Educational Leaders 2015.* Reston, VA: Author.

Neese, A. W. (2017). More Columbus schools data scandal official finally facing state discipline. *Columbus Dispatch.* Retrieved from: http://www.dispatch.com/news/20170816/more-columbus-schools-data-scandal-officials-finally-facing-state-discipline

Oliver, C. G. (2015). *Leading with integrity: Reflections on legal, moral, and ethical issues in school administration.* Bloomington, IN: AuthorHouse.

Paine, L. S. (1996). *Cases in leadership, ethics, and organizational integrity.* New York, NY: McGraw-Hill/Irwin.

Peters, R. S. (1966). *Ethics and education.* New York, NY: Routledge.

Rebore, R. (2014). *The ethics of educational leadership.* New York, NY: Pearson Education.

Savery, J. R. (2006). Overview of problem-based learning: Definitions and distinctions. *Interdisciplinary Journal of Problem-Based Learning 1*(1).

Schneider, J. (2018). *N.J. mystery pooper scandal: Questions pile up as superintendent stays silent.* Retrieved from: http://www.nj.com/education

Sternberg, R. J. (2009). We need to teach for ethical conduct. *The Educational Forum, 73,* 190–198.

Strike, K. (2007) *Ethical leadership in schools: Creating community in an environment of accountability.* Thousand Oaks, CA: Corwin Press.

Strike, K., Haller, E., & Soltis, J. (2005). *The ethics of administration.* New York, NY: Teachers College Press.

Wilcox, J., & Ebbs, S. (1992). *The leadership compass: Values and ethics in higher education.* ERIC Clearinghouse on Higher Education. Washington DC. George Washington University. Washington DC. School of Education and Human Development.

CHAPTER 7

INCLUSIVE LEADERSHIP

**Breaking Down Isolated Practice
and Developing a Culture of Inquiry
to Increase Student and Adult Learning**

Deborah M. Telfer
University of Cincinnati

Aimee Howley
Ohio University

Martha L. Thurlow
University of Minnesota

This chapter examines the commitments and practices of superintendents in districts identified for their work to close achievement gaps between students with disabilities and other students as part of district efforts intended to improve learning for all students. We call these districts "inclusive" because they intentionally employ high-leverage educational strategies to address the needs of all students, primarily by giving them meaningful opportunities to progress through the general education curriculum. We use

The Contemporary Superintendent, pages 109–132
Copyright © 2019 by Information Age Publishing
All rights of reproduction in any form reserved.

the term *inclusive leadership* as a way to describe the coherent set of practices deployed intentionally by superintendents and other educational leaders in these districts to promote greater equity and thereby to promote the academic growth of all students.

Our understanding of what inclusive leadership entails is empirically based—derived from data that were collected through the National Center on Educational Outcomes' Moving Your Numbers (MYN) project. MYN researchers analyzed interviews, documents, and artifacts from 10 case study districts to support generalizations about the leadership and other organizational practices that were deployed widely across these inclusive districts. This chapter briefly describes superintendents' innovative work to foster meaningful change across the 10 districts; then it characterizes inclusive leadership practices in greater detail by examining three case studies.

WHAT ARE MOVING YOUR NUMBERS DISTRICTS?

The 10 districts, which varied considerably in terms of their locations within regions of the country, locales (e.g., rural, urban, suburban), and demographics, were all recognized as exemplary for their success in reducing achievement gaps between students with disabilities and their counterparts who did not have disabilities.[1] Interpretation of interview data showed that the districts' efforts on behalf of the equitable treatment of all students resulted from (and also helped to build and sustain) a set of practices that fit with the research teams' understanding of what it meant for a district to be "inclusive."[2]

How Were Districts Identified?

To identify districts in the United States that demonstrated success in closing achievement gaps, MYN researchers first asked for nominations from the MYN Advisory Board, state directors of special education, other educational leaders, and advocates. Once a district had been nominated, an MYN researcher reviewed district data and contacted district leaders to learn more about district-wide commitment to students with disabilities and students from other marginalized groups as well as the superintendent's willingness to allow the district to serve as a case-study site.

How Were Data Collected and Analyzed?

When a superintendent agreed to allow the district to participate, the lead researcher from the MYN team arranged to meet with district leaders and other district educators to learn more about the practices the district was using. Interviewees in each district included the superintendent and/or deputy superintendent, curriculum leaders and other central office staff, special education director, principals, and a few teachers. In most cases, the interviews were face-to-face; a few involved conversations by phone. The researcher used a set of semi-structured interview questions to guide the conversations, and she used field notes to maintain detailed records of what each participant said. In the field notes for each interview, the researcher recorded exact quotes to the greatest extent possible.

The researcher analyzed the data through iterative reading and coding of field notes to identify similarities and differences in the practices used across the districts. She also shared preliminary findings with members of the MYN Advisory Board, who posed questions requiring her to demonstrate how quotes from district educators supported generalizations about the practices the districts were using. This process as well as careful efforts to maintain an audit trail contributed to the trustworthiness (e.g., credibility, dependability) of the research findings.

THEMATIC FINDINGS: MYN DISTRICT PRACTICES

Analysis of coded data pointed to six key practices observed in MYN districts and supported strongly by superintendents in the districts. Four of the practices required the direct involvement of superintendents and other central administrators: focusing goals district-wide, using data well, monitoring improvement efforts, and fostering a culture of inquiry. The other two practices, while clearly requiring support and oversight from a district's superintendent, primarily involved the ongoing work of teachers, administrators, and related-service personnel within the district's schools: selecting and implementing shared instructional practices and engaging deeply in efforts to improve instruction. The discussion of findings below briefly describes the four key practices that depended most closely on the actions of superintendents.

Focusing Goals

Superintendents and other central administrators clearly identified and continually referred to inclusive education as a core value, and they mobilized support for it by paring back district goals to those that were most attentive to the high-level academic achievement of all learners. One district adopted Universal Design for Learning (UDL) as the organizing framework for helping all students "learn to use their minds well." According to the superintendent in another district: "Our [purpose] is to help all kids learn at high levels." A central administrator in one of the districts offered a similar perspective when he described the district's aim of having "good instruction going on for all kids." In the largest of the case-study sites, sustained focus on making schools responsible for ensuring the academic success of all students resulted from the long-term commitment of the superintendent who, unlike many counterparts in large urban districts across the United States, has served the district for more than three decades, two in the role of chief executive officer.

Using Data Well

Systematic work to base improvement efforts on data about academic performance was a significant feature of the leadership strategy used in all of the districts. The districts incorporated assessments of different types to meet different purposes, using curriculum assessments to support instructional planning and using aggregated and disaggregated state achievement-test data to keep track of continuous improvement district wide. As the superintendent of one district explained,

> Data allowed us to look in the mirror in an honest way. We have tons of data, and we're moving away from collecting all kinds of data to becoming much more intentional and collecting what we need to make better decisions about instruction.

The districts also relied on data to evaluate the use of inclusive practices and the outcomes of those practices. For example, some of the districts had procedures for direct observation of teaching to ensure that inclusive practices were being deployed effectively in classrooms. Most kept track of indicators of inclusiveness such as changes in the percentage of students on IEPs and changes in achievement comparisons across subgroups.

Monitoring Improvement Efforts

The superintendents in all of the districts ensured that monitoring arrangements were in place to promote consistency in the implementation of agreed-upon practices and to gauge progress toward the accomplishment of desired results. For example, they instituted cycles of monitoring district wide to make sure that all schools were routinely basing instructional decisions on relevant data. They also made use of organizational structures (e.g., teams of educators at each level of the system—grade level or department, school, and district) in ways that promoted the bidirectional flow of information about both the fidelity of implementation and the outcomes of improvement efforts.

Monitoring in the districts also contributed to capacity building because the systematic review of practices district wide allowed leaders to identify the educators who were using the most effective and inclusive strategies. Once these exemplar educators had been identified, leaders were able to codify the effective strategies the exemplar educators were using and share those strategies widely with other educators through professional development (PD), coaching, and other types of support. One central administrator described this approach:

> We've found that the talent is typically in the school district. It's about mobilizing the talent and using PD from inside out. [We] may have a consultant that comes in and works with the existing talent pool, and [we] use institutional resources with guidance from the consultant, but we begin that movement/improvement from within rather than have a template imposed. . . .

Fostering a Culture of Inquiry

Intentional application of the three leadership practices described above led to widespread understanding of and respect for data-based decision-making. Furthermore, the demystification of data that came with routine review of quantitative and qualitative information as part of the decision-making process encouraged educators in the 10 districts to reflect on their own practice and feedback from peers and administrators as a basis for modifying or refining the instructional strategies they deployed. As a central administrator in one of the districts noted,

> We don't really have professional learning communities in the traditional sense as we've focused intensely on a different kind of team process that is a bit more systemic and a bit less autonomous. . . . One of our next steps is to augment our teaming processes to include collaborative teacher teams using standards-based common formative assessments focused on how students are progressing toward the Common Core State Standards. We strive to continuously refine our approach as the research community establishes new best practices yet, as an organization, we try to only take on new practices that are vetted in rigorous research.

SUPERINTENDENTS WHO LEAD: THREE CASE-STUDY VIGNETTES

The case study vignettes described here illustrate the important role of the district, and district leadership, in initiating, implementing, and sustaining improvement efforts on behalf of all learners. In each district, the super-intendent set clear expectations and direction for change, intentionally distributed leadership, required and aligned resources to support collab-orative learning among teachers and other personnel to build the instruc-tional capacity of the school system, and communicated—frequently, regu-larly, and in multiple ways—a common mission based on a commitment to excellence and equity for every learner.

Bartholomew Consolidated School Corporation

Intentional and focused actions were clear indicators of the leader-ship strategy endorsed by the superintendent and used throughout the Bartholomew Consolidated School Corporation (BCSC).[3] In this district, which served approximately 12,000 students in suburban Columbus, Indi-ana (a community located about 40 miles south of Indianapolis), actions supporting the learning of all students reflected the commitments of key leaders, notably the superintendent, the director of elementary education, the director of secondary education, and the director of special education.

Described by the *Smithsonian Magazine* (December 2005)[4] as a "verita-ble museum of modern architecture" (p. 1), the community of Columbus, Indiana rallied around BCSC's use of UDL (Rose & Gravel, 2013; Rose & Meyer, 2002) as a strategy for promoting deeper learning on behalf of ev-ery student. According to Bill Jensen, director of secondary education, the use of UDL enabled district personnel "to become architects of our own learning, support all staff in being self-directed learners willing and able to learn from structured failure, and replicate effective instructional practice across the district."

A commitment to deeper learning, repeated by the superintendent in varied communications to the BCSC and larger community, is reflected in the district's mission statement: "Deeper Learning is our individualized ap-proach for preparing all learners to succeed in a competitive global economy and democratic society and to tackle the complex issues they will encounter."

The Character of the Change

Until the early 2000s, BCSC—like many school districts in the country—supported multiple, and often misaligned, priorities as illustrated by each of the district's 18 schools having what Assistant Superintendent for Human Resources Teresa Heiny called "its own unique perspective and unique cul-ture." In the 1990s, the district began to examine its practices for improving learning using the *Baldrige* criteria,[5] revealing the need to shift from relying on "random acts of improvement" to aligning core work for improving instruction and achievement on a district-wide basis.

District personnel learned early in the planning process that something was needed, not only to align and improve learning opportunities for all students, but also to bring all staff at all levels of the district together around shared priorities. As Heiny noted, developing a common language was essential in being able to work across schools and build the capacity of personnel to improve instruction and learning for all children.

In 2003, BCSC began the implementation of UDL in one elementary school that was selected as a pilot school by the Indiana statewide initiative, *Promoting Achievement through Technology and Instruction for all Students* (PA-TINS). This early effort, geared toward developing professional and organizational capacity to meet the needs of students with a wide range of learning characteristics, provided BCSC with the unifying framework needed to focus and align work and make significant improvements. Following the pilot year, the UDL process was implemented at Northside Middle School, and soon after extended to become the district's instructional framework—organizing improvement efforts in all schools.

Rather than viewing disability as a deficit, or characterizing UDL as a strategy that is limited to improving outcomes for students with disabilities or learning difficulties, BCSC conceptualized the district's use of UDL as an approach that would benefit all children as they entered and progressed through the school system. George Van Horn, director of special education and member of the district's core leadership team explained:

> UDL is about creating the learning environment, not creating curriculum or a piece of instruction for a child. We will never just arrive. That's why there has to be a continuous improvement mentality focusing on growth for everyone, not just a focus on closing subgroup gaps, which often obscure the starting point and can be closed because better scores are dropping, not because lower scores are rising. We're committed to making sure curriculum and instruction is for all students; we want growth for everyone. Our UDL work has always been about all kids; it has never been only about special education.

UDL, developed by the Center for Applied Special Technology (CAST),[6] supports the development of resourceful, knowledgeable, goal-directed, and motivated learners by providing all children and youth with *multiple means of representation* (to give them multiple ways of acquiring information and knowledge), *multiple means of action and expression* (to give them multiple ways of demonstrating what they know), and *multiple means of engagement* (to give them a variety of levels of challenge, support, and relevance to help them stay engaged in learning and to support meaningful connections to others).

The district's use of UDL has evolved since 2003 and is foundational to many other aspects of district operation, particularly those involving building the capacity of all personnel to continually improve their own and each other's practice. BCSC continues to invest in UDL through the assignment of educators to serve as UDL coordinators, PD to develop capacity in the application of UDL strategies, and teacher evaluation aligned with UDL principles. Former UDL Coordinator Loui Lord-Nelson captured the essence of the district's use of UDL as an improvement strategy: "It's the consistent and persistent conversations that teachers have around working with, understanding, and challenging the (UDL) framework, and the impact on student learning, that lead to growth."

Persistent and consistent conversations about instructional practice contributed to changes in attitude, expectations, and beliefs, as noted by sixth-grade teacher Gail Koors: "UDL has given us the common language and prompts, and has allowed us to look at what a child *can* do."

Superintendent Leadership

Changes in central office structure accompanied the initiation of UDL as the district's framework for improving learning. Under Superintendent John Quick's leadership, BCSC changed the central office structure to support more collaborative work across departments (e.g., special education, elementary education, secondary education). "The superintendent allowed us to take a leadership role in moving UDL forward in the district. We began to talk and work together on behalf of all students," recalled Van Horn.

Quick—who served as BCSC superintendent for 13 years and, prior to that, as assistant superintendent and principal in the district—believed that sharing leadership was essential to making and sustaining improvements. Not only did he support the district leadership team (DLT), he also worked with the school board to help them understand the benefits of UDL—a focus board members have sustained for more than 13 years. In addition, Quick drew on UDL principles as the foundations for a high school renovation project to construct more flexible learning environments. According to Van Horn, Superintendent Quick firmly rooted UDL in the district's improvement process to ensure that every school improvement plan, including facilities plans and resource allocation plans, were attentive to UDL principles. These actions helped establish UDL as a significant core value undergirding the district's culture.

From Quick's own perspective, district-wide change occurred for three reasons. First, increased focus led to meaningful collaboration among the director of special education, director of elementary education, and director of secondary education who together conveyed the importance of UDL as BCSC's instructional framework to others across the district. Second, the employment of a coordinator with expertise in the implementation of UDL throughout the district provided local capacity for helping educators learn and apply UDL strategies. Finally, efforts to give competent teachers within the district opportunities to share their classroom practice with other teachers throughout the district allowed informal leaders to exert a significant influence on instructional practice district wide.

Overall, the major contributions of Superintendent Quick, who retired at the end of the 2015–2016 school year, included the following: (a) the creation of a culture with shared expectations for collaborative learning to take place at all levels—across departments within central office, between central office and schools, across classrooms, and as a unifying force with school board members; (b) widespread reliance on inquiry as the basis for instructional discourse; and (c) deep and competent implementation of UDL district wide. These contributions, moreover, were durable.

In recruiting a new superintendent, the school board made it clear that UDL was and would remain the district's framework and the core of BCSC's efforts to support higher levels of learning for all children. Jim Roberts assumed the superintendency in July 2016. One of his first acts was to attend the district's annual weeklong UDL Institute along with about 150 teachers from across the district, sending the clear message that the district will stay the course. Van Horn commented, "Dr. Roberts listens, asks good questions, and learns. His presence at the Institute was very noticeable to teachers; we couldn't have hoped for more."

Val Verde Unified School District

"Passion and purpose," according to current Superintendent Michael McCormick, are at the heart of the Val Verde Unified School District's commitment to ensure that all students are "future ready" (i.e., ready for both college *and* career upon graduation). This commitment has, over the past 10 years, motivated significant improvements in the Val Verde Unified School District. A first step in realizing improvements involved setting a few very direct but ambitious goals. For example, one of the most important goals has been to ensure that all students are reading at grade level by the end of third grade.

Located directly east of Los Angeles, Val Verde encompasses a 67 square mile area in a mixed rural and suburban region of Riverside County and enrolls 19,841 students. Approximately 1,875 staff members in 22 schools serve the district's students, 82% of whom are economically disadvantaged and 22% of whom are English learners. Rather than using demographics associated with poverty or race (74% are Hispanic, 18% are African American, and there are more Val Verde children living in foster care or group homes than in any other part of Riverside County) as a justification for holding low expectations for student learning (i.e., a deficit perspective), the Val Verde administration and teaching staff have altered both their discourse about student learning and their instructional practices. Then Superintendent Michelle Richardson, who was filling the role at the time of the initial interviews, described the district's commitment:

> For every single child, regardless of race, creed, or disability, our job is to give them the skills to be able to work, to be a productive member of society, and to make a difference in the world, no matter where they start.

The Character of the Change

The district began its improvement process in 2007 when state assessment results pointed to significant gaps in learning for subgroups of students. When interviewed originally, Superintendent Michael McCormick (then assistant superintendent for educational services) recalled, "I'm sad to say it was standardized and national assessment that drove our attention to students with disabilities, but it did." According to former director of special education, Vicki Butler, "Suddenly students in special education: their scores counted. So it was easier to sell the idea of inclusion to principals and regular education teachers and the importance of giving these students a rich curriculum."

Val Verde staff began to use state assessment data to identify trends and critical needs, but they went further in their use of relevant data to make ongoing decisions about instructional design and delivery with the goal, according to Deborah Bryant, director of assessment and accountability, of "getting to 100% proficiency." The district therefore created a standards-based accountability system that allowed all staff—teachers, administrators, related services personnel such as school psychologists—to access and use relevant performance data. District leaders, with guidance from the superintendent and associate superintendent, provided targeted PD to support all staff in their use of data as a basis for instructional decision-making. They also engaged board members in efforts to examine the organizational health of the district. McCormick recalls that board members "saw their role as setting clear direction, maintaining fiscal solvency, and creating and maintaining policy that helped sustain a focus on the district's goals. Their leadership has increased coherence across the district; they own our goals."

The district initiated structural changes that fostered cross-departmental collaboration and shared learning. During the 2007–2008 school year, McCormick moved the special education department out of student services and into rducation services, to send the clear message that the district's work was intended to improve learning for all students, regardless of label, and reinforcing the district's commitment to an assets perspective toward the learning of all students in the district. Current director of special education, Troy Knudsvig, elaborated: "Unlike most other districts, the Department of Special Education is attached to education services because the first question we ask is, 'Do we have good instruction going on for all kids?'"

The district empowered collaborative teams, at the district, school, and teacher level, to support collective learning and instructional capacity building. District leaders provided all teachers and related services personnel with access to high-quality instructional materials and training in data analysis and in the use of effective instructional practices. Coupled with more effective use of data at all levels, these changes provided support mechanisms that enabled all educators to change their routine practices and ways of thinking about teaching and learning. As a result, educators across the system developed a common language for talking about their efforts to improve learning on behalf of all students, and staff began looking at and taking responsibility for school-wide and district-wide issues, not only issues in their own classrooms or other, more narrow spheres of influence. According to Richardson, the district was very prescriptive and directive in making sure core work was implemented by all personnel, and that all personnel were given the same information and received the same training.

Middle school Principal Jim Owens reflected that while his job as instructional leader hadn't changed much, the way that principals operated across the district changed significantly. "What's different here is that principals don't do their own thing. We're looking at district issues, helping each other through our own jobs-alike meetings, and there isn't the rivalry between schools that you see in other districts." Similarly, Carla de la Torre, English language learner coordinator and a former special education teacher for the district, remarked, "Special education never does its own thing; we are all responsible to know how to teach at higher levels of rigor and understand we teach all students." Coming together to solve what the DLT identified as the district's most pressing needs created new structures and ways of thinking that extended to all parts of the district, contributing to the development of shared experiences and a sense of community for staff, students, and families.

Superintendent Leadership

As in BCSC, the changes that led to sustainable improvements in Val Verde were promoted first by district leaders and then by school leaders, which included both principals and teachers. At the forefront of the improvement process was Michael McCormick, now serving as Val Verde's superintendent and in his 20th year of service with the district. Prior to becoming superintendent, McCormick served as assistant superintendent. In fact, he assumed leadership over instructional improvement when he held the position of assistant superintendent, engaging all parts of the district in designing and using data analysis protocols, an articulated instruction model (AIM), and a multi-tiered system of supports (MTSS).

Engaging all personnel in the district's efforts to increase the rigor of the curriculum aligned with standards meant working together to deliver instruction that supported deeper levels of learning for all students. It also meant that the district, led by McCormick, had to make expectations for collaborative learning clear; model collaborative learning at the central office level; create team structures at the school and classroom level to support data-informed collaborative learning and decision-making among personnel, and provide the time and resources needed (e.g., PD, coaching) to support personnel in continuously increasing the quality, relevance, and rigor of the instruction provided to all students in the district.

According to McCormick, "Breaking down isolated practice and raising the capacity of the entire system of 900 teachers through collaborative teaming is a substantial cost to the district, but one that is necessary for improving learning for all students." A frequent visitor to schools and classrooms, McCormick continues to identify effective instructional practices on a regular basis, capture demonstrations of such practices in the classroom, and share these demonstrations with other schools. Adept at the use of technology, McCormick takes advantage of social media to aid in system-wide diffusion of effective practice, support implementation and replication of such practices across the district, facilitate cross-team and cross-school visits to allow educators to observe effective practice, work with individual teachers who may need support with specific practices , and build the professional capital of the district (Fullan & Hargreaves, 2012).

Reducing isolation among program areas also continues to be a priority under McCormick's leadership. "We ask staff, 'what is your collaboration capital?' We have to increase collaboration and reduce competition by encouraging every staff member to share his or her best ideas. If we do that, all ships will rise," explained McCormick. Knudsvig noted, "We don't develop programs in isolation."

At his core, McCormick thrives on learning. The culture of inquiry established in the district—a culture of openness to feedback and using data as feedback to the system, monitoring the implementation of instructional strategies and its effects, and learning from implementation efforts—have allowed Val Verde to continue to improve on key indicators. Notably, the district has seen steady improvements since 2010: increases in student achievement overall; increases on early literacy benchmarks; improvements in attendance, PSAT and SAT participation, graduation, advanced placement (AP); and reductions in chronic absenteeism, dropout rates, and suspension and expulsion rates. In addition to receiving numerous awards, Val Verde has consistently been recognized nationally for its work to increase rigor while closing achievement gaps. In 2011, the district was recognized by the College Board as the *Advanced Placement District of the Year* for medium-sized districts, and more recently, was one of 130 school districts in the country to be included on the Gaston Caperton Opportunity Honor Roll[7] for demonstrating significant and consistent growth in the number of underrepresented and low-income students taking college-level courses and applying to attend college.

Under McCormick's leadership as superintendent, the district has sustained its focus on ensuring access to high-quality learning experiences and increasing depth of learning for all students. It has also enhanced its focus on ensuring that every student is well prepared for college or a career upon graduation through the integration of instructional technology in keeping with McCormick's belief that "technology is a force-multiplier." He explains, "Technology alone is not a silver bullet, but the effective introduction and integration of technology has exponentially increased the effectiveness of our pedagogy and helped us focus on what matters most—strong core instruction for all students."

Bloom Vernon Local School District

Bloom Vernon Local is a small district serving approximately 870 students in two buildings—a kindergarten through sixth grade elementary school and a Grades 7–12 junior/senior high school. Located in rural Appalachian Scioto County in an area often described as the Little Smokies, the village of South Webster (Ohio), where the district is located has higher than average unemployment and lower than average per capita personal income. Approximately 60% of the student population qualifies for free- or reduced-price lunches and many students live with family members who are unable to read.

The Character of the Change

District leaders credited the No Child Left Behind (NCLB) Act (2002) with causing them to look at student data and the quality of the instruction they were providing. Recounting feelings of personal embarrassment over the poor performance of groups of children, Heidi Holstein, former 4th/5th-grade intervention specialist, explained, "NCLB sent a clear call to action and made us realize that kids can do this; we just weren't set up to teach them what they needed [in order] to do well."

Teachers and administrators in both buildings began to focus on the data, on how children overall were learning across the district, and on the children who weren't achieving. Working with regional providers from the Ross-Pike Educational Service Center (ESC) and the State Support Team (SST) serving the district, Bloom Vernon staff gained experience and expertise in using a variety of relevant data (e.g., state assessment data, short-cycle assessment data, formative classroom assessment) circumspectly to identify the right systemic problems as well as to address the learning needs of individual children. They began to monitor the degree to which their actions were having desired effects. Eric Humston, director of the regional SST that worked with Bloom Vernon at the time, recalled, "Even more than the effective use of data, Bloom Vernon's practices led to a culture where every teacher takes responsibility for every student."

As a general rule, district staff tended to be resistant to accepting externally imposed programs, opting instead to use the data available to them to pinpoint areas of need, develop goals, and track progress. Focused goal setting in Bloom Vernon went hand-in-hand with effective data use and was driven by the district's newly adopted core values of high expectations, no excuses, and shared practice. For example, the district invested significant energy and resources into the instructional program at the Pre–K through first grade level and in family literacy initiatives with the immediate goal of increasing early literacy and the ultimate goal of improving the achievement of all students across the grade levels.

Several practices helped the district increase rigor in curricular content and consistency in instruction. Notably, leaders arranged weekly common planning times for teacher teams (i.e., grade-level teams at the elementary level and subject-/content-area teams at the junior/senior high level). They built these planning times into the schedule, supplementing the informal planning that was already taking place among teachers in the district and reinforcing the district's commitment to collaborative planning and decision-making. Leaders also used PD opportunities strategically. They devoted state-allotted waiver days to collaborative planning—supporting teachers' collaborative work to review data and discuss instructional strategies; and they ended the practice of offering a menu of PD offerings with minimal alignment to the district's focused goals.

Collaborative planning was also important at the district level: The DLT comprised of Superintendent Rick Carrington and the building administrators met monthly to review student data from grade-level and content-area teaching teams—data that had previously been submitted by teacher teams to their school principals. Members of the DLT used these data as a basis for discussing needs across the district and for monitoring progress. In addition to formal meetings, the superintendent and principals met informally over lunch on an almost-daily basis.

The strategies that the leaders used resulted in significant changes in the organizational culture of the district. Despite the demographics of the community they serve, Bloom Vernon personnel now have a "beat the odds" mentality. They no longer view the community as an impediment to students' learning but rather presume that the community's children and families have assets on which the district's educators can build.

Superintendent Leadership

Superintendent Rick Carrington's strong conviction that all children, no matter their circumstances, could become competent learners contributed to the development of a shared sense of purpose among Bloom Vernon personnel. He described the commitments underlying the district's more positive perspective: "I believe in the power of unification around purpose and ours is to help all kids learn at high levels. Our greatest challenge involves eliminating the mindset that because we're poor and rural, kids can't achieve."

Mobilizing staff to excel by "getting the right people in the right seats" exemplified Carrington's leadership approach and was evident in the administration's emphasis on building the capacity of all staff members to meet the instructional needs of all children. Holding high expectations for every child was a core and nonnegotiable commitment guiding all curricular and instructional practices as well as all personnel decisions.

Carrington's belief, shaped by close to 35 years of service in the district, was that "if you pay attention to the 'who,' you'll take care of most of the 'what.'" He regularly shared information on effective practices used by successful organizations and drew on Jim Collins' (2001) work on the flywheel effect (i.e., how some organizations have moved "from good to great" by preserving core values, while continuously making improvements through consistency, focus, and hard work) in making decisions about the employment, orientation, induction, and deployment of personnel.

In keeping with his commitment to collaborative planning and decision-making, Carrington involved teams of teachers in making hiring decisions. For example, in filling a fourth-grade teaching position, applicants might be interviewed by a six-to-eight-member team that would include the fourth-grade teachers, the counselor, and the principal to ensure, according to former 4th/5th-grade intervention specialist Holstein, that "the person selected is committed to kids first. We ask questions to find out if that person will go the extra mile for kids." Ranked in the bottom third of the county in terms of teacher pay (in a county that is itself among the poorest in the state), Bloom Vernon nevertheless seems to attract educators with genuine interest in working in the district, and there is little teacher turnover.

An unassuming and quiet man, Carrington had a high level of credibility among staff in the district during his tenure as superintendent. He continues, upon retirement from the district, to have the same high level of credibility among other superintendents in the region. In part, his credibility comes from the clarity of his vision. As he noted in the interview, improvements in district practice and performance came about by increasing focus; ensuring that new staff, students, and community members were carefully inducted into the district's core values, annual goal setting, and the sharing of effective practices across staff. According to Carrington, "We're not charismatic leaders and it's not about us. It's also not about programs. It's about avoiding minutiae, getting the right people, and keeping them focused on student learning."

INCLUSIVE LEADERSHIP: COMMONALITIES
ACROSS DISTRICT SUPERINTENDENTS

As exemplified by the three district vignettes included here, superintendents in the MYN districts tended to use a common set of leadership practices to initiate and sustain the four major strategies that resulted in significant improvements. We described these strategies in the discussion of themes above: focusing goals, using data well, monitoring improvement efforts, and fostering a culture of inquiry.

Here we turn attention to the leadership practices that the superintendents shared, and we also contextualize those practices within extant literature on inclusive leadership. These leadership practices involved managing the discourse, manipulating organizational structures, and mobilizing resources.

In addition to insights about these commonly used practices, another notable finding from the analysis of interviews was that all of the superintendents held strong beliefs about what inclusive leaders *were not*. In particular, they held the view that such leaders were not superstars: their leadership did not depend on "personality." Moreover, their success was not the consequence of a one-person effort, and it did not result from their ability to select one overarching ("silver bullet") approach to implementing change.

Managing the Discourse

Perhaps the most evident commonality in the practice of the superintendents of the MYN districts was their ability to manage discourse about the nature of the challenges their districts faced, the benefits their districts would realize as a result of implementing the improvement strategies, and the character of the changes that the improvement strategies implicated.

For instance, all of the superintendents talked about the change process in positive ways and, in doing so, refrained from painting either students or their families in a negative light. Regardless of the student population, these inclusive leaders promoted positive thinking among district and school staff. Rather than allowing staff to dwell on apparent deficiencies among students, families, or school conditions, such as high student poverty rates, community apathy, or lack of resources, these superintendents reframed apparent deficits as contextual problems that could be addressed by schools and communities working in league as partners.

Another related set of practices used by MYN district leaders involved their efforts to foster instructional discourse among all staff in order to reduce distractions and increase shared learning and instructional capacity. For example, McCormick and other Val Verde district leaders recognized that to develop the collective instructional capacity of the district, all personnel needed to be involved in the change process—that is, all of them needed to be talking in productive ways about instruction.

The practices these superintendents used to manage the discourse about improvement, inclusion, and social justice resembled those used by other leaders (mostly principals) in empirical studies documenting efforts to promote greater inclusivity in schools and districts. These practices included the following:

- communicating positive attitudes toward inclusive schooling (e.g., Kugelmass, 2006);
- articulating clear statements to stakeholder groups about the value of inclusiveness and the connection between inclusiveness and the district's strategic goals (e.g., Guzman, 1997; Hoppey & McLeskey, 2013; Lindqvist & Nilholm, 2014);
- modeling inclusiveness in actions relating to matters such as employment of personnel, and efforts to showcase student and staff accomplishments (e.g., Muijs et al., 2010; Ryan, 2010);
- challenging assumptions through critique and inquiry (e.g., Salisbury & McGregor, 2002);
- speaking out against school practices that did not work on behalf of inclusiveness (e.g., Leo & Barton, 2006); and
- encouraging productive conflict and effective conflict resolution (e.g., Rice, 2006).

Manipulating Organizational Structures

Superintendents in MYN districts also achieved increased inclusivity as well as higher achievement overall by changing the way personnel performed work—removing conditions that tended to sustain isolation and hierarchical power relations and replacing them with arrangements that enabled greater collaboration and sharing of leadership. Instituting and supporting collaborative structures (e.g., professional learning communities) and procedures (e.g., teacher-team analysis and interpretation of achievement data) were key practices among most of the superintendents. Promoting teacher leadership, especially leadership over instructional matters, was also a common practice.

Many related studies about inclusive leadership also pointed to the benefits of collaboration (e.g., Conrad & Brown, 2011; Harpell & Andrews, 2010; McMaster, 2013). In some cases, school leaders employed external consultants (e.g., instructional coaches) to stimulate dialog among teachers and provide support to teachers as they worked to expand their repertoire of effective instructional practices (e.g., Sperandio & Klerks, 2007). A related practice involved expansion of the responsibilities of a few effective teachers, giving them time during the school day and monetary compensation for providing instructional coaching to their colleagues (McGlynn & London, 2013). In other cases, collaboration took the form of co-planning and co-teaching with pairs or small groups of teachers sharing instructional decision-making, experimentation, and monitoring of results (e.g., Theoharis & O'Toole, 2011).

In general, these studies suggested that leaders who saw themselves as facilitators promoted collaboration more fully than those who held onto more traditional, authoritarian approaches to leadership (e.g., Smith & Leonard, 2005). As Smith and Leonard (2005) noted in their discussion of the inclusive leadership of principals,

> [School leaders] who empower teachers to collaborate and make decisions that are pertinent to successful inclusion will have greater success.... Principals who facilitate the development of the supportive behaviors of collaboration also will spawn behaviors that support school inclusion which, in turn, support the principal as facilitator. (p. 276)

Mobilizing Resources

Inclusive leaders also were intentional in directing resources to where they were needed to support the district change process. None of the MYN districts was affluent; all struggled in one way or another with the lack of needed resources. Superintendents and other central office leaders in MYN districts were nevertheless vigilant in finding resources to support their districts' improvement goals.

In many cases the resources with the greatest impact were those enabling teachers to participate in high-quality PD. Time for team meetings as well as more formal training activities was a resource that district leaders mentioned frequently. And most of the district leaders understood that the purchase of commercial curriculum materials would not be likely to motivate or sustain the district's desired improvements.

Related literature also points to the importance of giving teachers time to participate in PD linked directly to the instructional improvements they are working to make (e.g., Hoppey & McLeskey, 2013), and it positions collaborative inquiry as a high-leverage approach to PD because of its ability to foster cultural change as well as the expansion and improvement of instructional skills. In their description of a principal who had been successful in promoting inclusive practice, Leo and Barton (2006) commented,

> The principal promoted debate and discussion of contemporary research ideas. There was also a prevailing culture of challenge and debate on a range of issues which had served to build confidence and commitment to professional learning. This study demonstrates that the greater the involvement of senior leadership and teachers in professional learning, the greater the degree of organisational learning. (p. 177)

The Three Practices in Context

Not surprisingly considering their resonance with empirical findings about inclusive leaders, several of the leadership practices and change strategies used by the MYN superintendents fit well with the recommendations of authors who encourage school leaders to work on behalf of equity and social justice. Table 7.1, for example, shows how MYN superintendents' practices and their district strategies align with Skrla and associate's (2009) set of "equity oriented change agent" (EOCA) characteristics.

Interestingly, the MYN study also revealed the salience of two other senior leadership strategies and two other senior leadership practices. Notably, in

TABLE 7.1 Alignment between EOCA Characteristics and MYN Practices and Strategies

EOCA Characteristic	MYN Leadership Practice	MYN District Strategy
Demonstrates positive attitude toward equity	Manages the discourse on inclusivity	
Avoids demonization; maintains and assets perspective	Manages the discourse on inclusivity	
Initiates courageous conversations		Fosters a culture of inquiry
Demonstrates persistence		Focuses goals
Maintains a coherent focus		Focuses goals

addition to managing the discourse on inclusivity, MYN superintendents also created organizational arrangements that promoted collaboration and provided resources to support district-wide change. In this effort, they supported the use of two other strategies: using data well and monitoring improvement efforts. Arguably, efforts simply to manage discourse and maintain focus are insufficient to move a district from a less inclusive to a more inclusive set of practices.

INCLUSIVE LEADERSHIP: LINKS TO LITERATURE ON THE SUPERINTENDENCY

Much of the related literature that examines the practices used by school leaders to increase inclusivity focuses specifically on school principals. Fewer studies draw attention to the role of senior leaders (e.g., the superintendent and central office administrators) in initiating and sustaining inclusive practice. Studies of superintendents who frame district priorities around equity and social justice offer insights relevant to interpreting findings from MYN districts.

For example, Hatch and Roegman's (2012) study of superintendents who were working to improve equity in their districts showcased the role of collaboration as a key improvement strategy for superintendents themselves (e.g., through support networks with other superintendents) and for district personnel overall (e.g., through the use of instructional rounds). Self-reports and single-subject case studies of superintendents who have made significant changes district-wide often draw attention to their efforts to manage the discourse (e.g., core values, vision, and mission), maintain focus on instructional improvement, establish collaborative structures, use data well, and think systemically (e.g., Mullin & Keedy, 1998; Portis & Garcia, 2007).

Unlike these scattered and small-scale studies, Smith and Brazer's (2016) research on superintendents who reduced achievement gaps between students from minority and majority groups provided more substantive support for the leadership practices used by MYN superintendents and the strategies used in MYN districts. Of particular salience across the 13 superintendents in Smith and Brazer's study were strategies that allowed the district to gain and retain focus, use data well, monitor improvement efforts, and foster a culture of inquiry. Like the MYN superintendents featured in the vignettes presented in this chapter, all of the superintendents interviewed by Smith and Brazer fostered organizational learning by establishing a foundation for broader discourse focused on what the district wanted *all* students—regardless of race, disability, poverty, or first language—to experience (2016). Superintendents provided greater opportunities for all students by confronting low expectations and challenging assumptions; using data to surface important issues previously thought to be "undiscussable"; increasing curricular and instructional quality, consistency, and coherence; using collaborative structures such as professional learning communities to engage all staff in improving practice; and creating an inquiry mindset to promote double-loop learning (i.e., learning that leads to substantive change by addressing problems *and* their underlying causes).

While the mobilization of financial resources was cited as an important practice, the superintendents studied by Smith and Brazer (2016) identified as more important the development of personnel resources and stability (their own and the district's) in being able to reduce gaps between subgroups of students. "Their own longevity in the role was key because the longer they stayed in a stable situation, the greater influence they had through personnel decisions, relationships with their boards, and trust in their communities" (p. 66). These superintendents, like the MYN district superintendents, unified core work across the system by "moving from a district of schools to a school district" (p. 75).

SUMMARY

The MYN superintendents used inclusive leadership to change the organizational culture of the districts they served in significant ways, resulting in higher levels of learning for both students and adults across the system. Despite differences in district demographics and context, each superintendent made sure that the district prioritized its work by focusing on a limited number of goals related to instruction and student learning, used relevant data to inform instructional decision-making, monitored the district's improvement efforts, and fostered a culture of inquiry and collective learning that built trust and shared ownership for improvement on the part of personnel at all levels of the district.

Strategies, such as using data well, allowed the district, under the leadership of the superintendent, to surface critical issues and confront assumptions (e.g., belief that particular labels would prevent some students from being able to learn) that hindered system improvement on behalf of all groups of students. Each MYN superintendent managed the collective conversation about needed change by focusing the discussion of teachers, administrators, and other personnel on how to increase opportunities to learn—and learn at deeper levels—for all students in the district. They characterized differences among students as assets, not deficiencies, and focused on what the district could and should do to prepare each student for success.

The superintendents also decreased isolated practice by altering organizational structures, thereby "blurring" the lines between departments that traditionally operated in isolation. Breaking down isolated practice extended to teachers and other personnel through the development of collaborative learning structures (e.g., professional learning communities) that distributed leadership responsibilities and provided opportunities for principals, teachers, and related services personnel to learn from each other. Such structures also allowed teachers and other personnel to inform each other's instructional practice, and provided a mechanism for monitoring improvement efforts—aligned with the district's goals—at the classroom, school, and district level. Mobilizing and aligning resources (i.e., personnel, programmatic, financial, time) to meet the district's focused goals highlighted the importance of the stated priorities around instruction and student learning and supported meaningful implementation of strategies and actions to meet the goals.

Underlying the use of the superintendent strategies and practices described in this chapter was the strong commitment to providing equitable opportunities to learn for every student, a belief in the capacity of district personnel to teach every student at higher levels, the refusal to accept low expectations and poor performance, and the relentless pursuit of excellence in instruction that was sustained over time.

NOTES

1. Not surprisingly, these districts also had smaller-than-average achievement gaps between students from marginalized groups in general and other students (i.e., students who were not from marginalized groups).
2. The alignment between the team's interpretation and what has been reported in other empirical literature is discussed later in the chapter.
3. In Indiana, public school districts are called school corporations.
4. For more information, see https://www.smithsonianmag.com/arts-culture/by-design-110894174/
5. The Malcolm Baldrige National Quality Award, first awarded in 1988, includes education criteria for performance excellence, which can be found at www.nist.gov/baldrige/enter/education.cfm
6. For more information about UDL, go to www.cast.org/index.html and www.udlcenter.org.
7. See https://lp.collegeboard.org/gaston-caperton-opportunity-honor-roll

REFERENCES

Collins, J. (2001). *Good to great.* New York, NY: Harper Collins.

Conrad, D. A., & Brown, L. I. (2011) Fostering inclusive education: Principals' perspectives in Trinidad and Tobago. *International Journal of Inclusive Education, 15*(9), 1017–1029. doi:10.1080/13603110903490721

Fullan, M., & Hargreaves, A. (2012). Reviving teaching with 'professional capital.' *Education Week, 31*(33), 30–36.

Guzman, N. (1997). Leadership for successful inclusive schools: A study of principal behaviours. *Journal of Educational Administration, 35*(5), 439–450.

Harpell, J. V., & Andrews, J. J. W. (2010). Administrative leadership in the age of inclusion: Promoting best practices and teacher empowerment. *Journal of Educational Thought, 44*(2), 189–210.

Hatch, T., & Roegman, R. (2012). Out of isolation: Superintendents band together to improve instruction and equity in their districts. *Journal of Staff Development, 33*(6), 37–41.

Hoppey, D., & McLeskey, J. (2013). A case study of principal leadership in an effective inclusive school. *Journal of Special Education, 46*(4), 245–256. doi:10.1177/0022466910390507

Kugelmass, J. W. (2006). Sustaining cultures of inclusion: The value and limitation of cultural analyses. *European Journal of Psychology of Education, 31*(3), 279–292.

Leo, E., & Barton, L. (2006). Inclusion, diversity and leadership: Perspectives, possibilities, and contradictions. *Educational Management Administration & Leadership, 34*(2) 167–180.

Lindqvist, G., & Nilholm, C. (2014). Promoting inclusion? 'Inclusive' and effective head teachers' descriptions of their work. *European Journal of Special Needs Education, 29*(1), 74–90. http://dx.doi.org/10.1080/08856257.2013.8498455

McGlynn, C., & London, T. (2013). Leadership for inclusion: Conceptualising and enacting inclusion in integrated schools in a troubled society. *Research Papers in Education, 28*(2), 155–175. doi:10.1080/02671522.2011.600458

McMaster, C. (2013). Building inclusion from the ground up: A review of whole school re-culturing programmes for sustaining inclusive change. *International Journal of Whole Schooling, 9*(2), 1–24.

Muijs, D., Ainscow, M., Dyson, A., Raffo, C., Goldrick, S., Kerr, K., Lennie, C., & Miles, S. (2010). Leading under pressure: Leadership for social inclusion. *School Leadership & Management, 30*(2), 143–157. doi:10.1080/13632431003663198

Mullin, A. G., & Keedy, J. L. (1998). *Examining a superintendent's transformational leadership: From the model to successful practice.* Retrieved from http://eric.ed.gov/?id=ED421758 (ED 421758)

No Child Left Behind Act of 2001, P.L. 107-110, 20U.S.C.§6319 (2002).

Portis, C., & Garcia, M. W. (2007). Superintendent as change leader. *School Administrator, 64*(3), 18–26.

Rice, N. (2006). Opportunities lost, possibilities found: Shared leadership and inclusion in an urban high school. *Journal of Disability Policy Studies, 17*(2), 88–100.

Risen, C. (2005). By design. *Smithsonian Magazine, 36*(9), 1.

Rose, D. H., Gravel, J. W., & Gordon, D. T. (2014). Universal design for learning. In L. Florian (Ed.), *The SAGE handbook of special education* (2nd ed., 475–490). London, England: SAGE.

Rose, D. H., & Meyer, A. (2002). *Teaching every student in the digital age: Universal design for learning.* Alexandria, VA: ASCD.

Ryan, J. (2010). Establishing inclusion in a new school: The role of principal leadership. *Exceptionality Education International, 20*(2), 6–24.

Salisbury, C. L., & McGregor, G. (2002). The administrative climate and context of inclusive elementary schools. *Exceptional Children, 68*(2), 259–274.

Skrla, L., McKenzie, K., & Scheurich, J. (2009). *Using equity audits to create equitable and excellent schools.* Thousand Oaks, CA: Corwin.

Smith, R. G., & Brazer, S. D. (2016). *Striving for equity: District leadership for narrowing opportunity and achievement gaps.* Cambridge, MA: Harvard Education.

Smith, R., & Leonard, P. (2005). Collaboration for inclusion: Practitioner perspectives. *Equity & Excellence in Education, 38,* 269–279.

Sperandio, J., & Klerks, J. (2007). Leadership challenge: Blending inclusive special needs provision and reform of teaching methodology in a Dutch international school. *International Journal of Special Education, 22*(2), 140–149.

Theoharis, G., & O'Toole, J. (2011). Leading inclusive ELL: Social justice leadership for English language learners. *Educational Administration Quarterly, 47*(4), 646–688.

CHAPTER 8

LEADING FOR LEARNING

District Leaders as Networked Change Agents

Catherine McGregor
University of Victoria

Judy Halbert
Vancouver Island University

Linda Kaser
Vancouver Island University

There has been a tectonic shift in education over the past decade; *innovation* is the buzzword that represents both a desire and a demand for change. Certainly there is evidence that there are innovations present across educational systems around the world. The Organization for Economic Cooperation and Development (OECD) has devoted considerable time and resources to mapping this innovation, documenting the conditions that support it, and tracing the best practices that characterize exemplary jurisdictions (2013, 2015). Schools and school districts in British Columbia

The Contemporary Superintendent, pages 133–152
Copyright © 2019 by Information Age Publishing
All rights of reproduction in any form reserved.

(BC), Canada, have been identified as leading jurisdictions of innovation. In this chapter, we explore how a group of district leaders came together in a learning centered inquiry network in 2013 in order to begin a process of sharing and disseminating their learning. We describe the two primary features of their district level work and how it supports the development of innovation: first with investments in inquiry-based, networked learning systems and secondly, a focus on practices of learning centered leadership that accelerate change.

Before doing so, we also want to ground our story in the current school improvement literature, particularly theories which enable transformation and innovation. Three core themes will be addressed, including the power and nature of learning networks and learning centered leadership, the importance of inquiry mindedness, and what conditions accelerate and spread professional and student learning. We also provide background about our existing network of school superintendents in BC, who are taking these ideas and operationalizing them through an inquiry network/consortium devoted to enacting innovation to ensure success for all the learners they serve. A third purpose of our chapter is to extrapolate from this provincial case study how similar networks might accelerate a focus on learning at all levels in the system, and how leaders, particularly superintendents and district leaders, can be catalysts for learning centered educational reform.

EFFECTING CHANGE IN EDUCATIONAL JURISDICTIONS: KEY THEORIES AND CONCEPTS THAT INFORM INQUIRY-BASED LEARNING AND LEADERSHIP

For some time in BC, we have been convinced that learning centered leaders can create conditions that effect changes in schools and enable student success. Much of this work has focused in particular on the role that the school leader—the school principal and teacher (formal and informal leaders) can play in facilitating learning centered practice. As Robinson, Lloyd, and Rowe (2008) made evident, learning centered leaders can have powerful effects on learning cultures, particularly when they focus specifically on teaching and learning. Yet this focus is on the principal leader rather than the district leader. A focus on system leadership therefore expands attention to how learning can be supported and enhanced on the broader jurisdictional plane—the district or region.

There is some scholarship on system leadership; it makes evident the need for setting direction and developing an organization's capacity using processes that emphasize clarity, consistency, and continuity (Hopkins, 2011) or what Fullan and Quinn (2015) describes as coherence. As an actively innovating jurisdiction, we also believe that there are relational and contextual dynamics that seed and support greater levels of innovation and change. We start our discussion by addressing the question: What components really matter? It begins with professional inquiry as this is deeply embedded within and is central to our approach.

A Disciplined Approach to Professional Inquiry

Right from the outset with the inquiry networks, BC schools agreed to engage in an annual cycle of inquiry focused on changing student outcomes. Building on insights from the BC case studies and from the research in New Zealand on teacher professional learning, network principals collaborated with Helen Timperley to design a new approach to professional inquiry described as the spiral of inquiry (Timperley, Kaser, & Halbert, 2014).

There are several features that distinguish the spiral of inquiry from other action research approaches. The process always starts with a deep understanding of learning and the experiences of learners. It requires a collaborative approach by teams of educators. It builds on findings from Kimberley Schonert-Reichel and Shelley Hymel (2007), lead researchers on social emotional learning. The terminology used respects teacher judgment, their lived experiences, and their language. The spiral also draws from emerging understandings about frameworks for innovation and honours the findings from the school effectiveness and improvement literature, detailed in seminal publications such as the OECD (2010) *The nature of learning: Using Research to Inspire Practice.* This publication was built on consolidating the best of what is currently known about professional learning. The inquiry process also insists on incorporating indigenous learning perspectives (Williams & Tanaka, 2007). It is evidence informed at every stage through an emphasis on ongoing checking about student agency, their sense of belonging, and engagement in practices of self-regulation and metacognition (Hattie & Timperley, 2007).

The spiral of inquiry (Figure 8.1) involves six key stages of scan, focus, develop a hunch, engage in new professional learning, take new professional action, check that a big enough difference has been made and then reengage to consider what is next. Although the stages in the spiral overlap, paying attention to each aspect is critical in achieving the greatest benefit for all learners. At every stage, inquiry teams ask themselves: "What's going on for our learners?"; "How do we know?"; and "Why does this matter?"

The first two questions prompt educators to check constantly that learners are at the heart of what they do, and that all decisions are based on thoughtful evidence from direct observations and interviews in addition to more formal data sources. The third question helps to ground teams in the importance of the direction they are pursuing.

What's going on for our learners?
How do we know?
Why does this matter?

Figure 8.1   Spiral of inquiry.

Distributed Leadership

While inquiry is absolutely essential to our approach, there are strong connections between how one engages in professional inquiry and practices of distributed leadership. Spillane, Healey, Mesler Parise, and Kenney (2011) offers an important way for understanding why distributed leadership matters in the context of educational change and innovation: by focusing on distribution, we make evident the social contexts in which we engage in school improvement/innovation, and the iterative processes by which we create shared spaces in which leadership for learning is realized. This understanding moves beyond the typical ways of thinking about distribution as the sharing of tasks—the type of distribution that was once central to models of governance at the district level—but instead shifts towards understanding how we work collaboratively in teams at the district and school level and co-construct shared learning, thinking, and working spaces. In terms of our BC experience, districts routinely develop procedures and protocols that are centered around working with teams of formal and informal leaders, focusing not as much on the act of distribution but rather on how to support teams as they learn through professional inquiry together. In other words, professional inquiry has become embedded in the district's planning and operational focus, and it is inherently focused on creating learning teams; in this way, inquiry breeds distribution as a natural outcome of activity rather than something added on to the approach taken.

Routines and Tools

Spillane (2006) uses the terms "tools and routines" to describe how practices enable distribution, but this should not be interpreted simply as normalized/naturalized approaches or procedures for doing the work. He discusses that these processes or practices have embedded meanings that accrue over time within a community of practice. Professional inquiry can also be seen in this way. At one level, routines help us to approach our work efficiently because we know how to approach the task. Yet this is not their primary value. *Flexible routines* that vary to respond to local or unique contexts offer the capacity for emergent or creative approaches that can stretch across diverse settings and needs. But as our discussion of professional inquiry above made evident, these practices are much more than processes or routines, they carry with them strong moral intentions and purpose: with student learning always at the center, professional inquiry creates a professional commitment at the same time as it develops skills in investigation, data collection, and analysis. Professional inquiry is therefore a mutually reinforcing activity, developing the professional self and a moral commitment to advancing learning for all.

Ignition Processes

Another idea that resonates with our research group is what the authors of the McKinsey Report (Barber, Chijioke, & Mourshed, 2010) calls *ignition processes*; by this they means processes or strategies that deeply engage or motivate teachers and school leaders alike to commit to change processes. Ignition processes are important because they are more than just ways of systemically spreading innovation, but seek to accelerate its implementation. In the BC context, McGregor (2014) has described how existing professional learning networks (NOII/AESN) and relationally centered leaders create the dynamics of "catalytic affiliation"—a process that builds an interpersonal connection through a shared commitment to professional inquiry focused on making a difference for learners. It is this shared moral and professionally focused goal developed in an authentically focused, reciprocal model, which has provided a welcome contrast to top down models of change. When combined with professional learning routines embedded in moral purpose, catalytic affiliation offers a way of thinking about how innovation has spread so rapidly in the BC context.

Networking

Networking however, is also critically important to the ignition model we have found effective in our context. Networking enables strong interconnections among and between educators within the system, across and between different districts, schools, or regions. The emergence of social technologies have aided in the ease of these interconnections. For example, our superintendents' group regularly communicates by sharing documents via the web and then conduct synchronist conversations to discuss shared learning and points of analysis. We also have a blog through which we can share observations and learning, and are in the process of developing a website with both general availability and password protected features.

A network can also play an important social function by providing support to an individual or team who might be relatively isolated in their own setting. In a province as large as ours, this can be a very important way of maintaining a focus on inquiry as professional learning. As importantly, in working across such boundaries and spaces, actors who are networked in shared work draw upon external resources and organizations in developing and designing multilayered approaches in ways that enhance their learning or invite new ways to problem solve. Such networks extend the scope of thinking about educational goals beyond the typical classroom walls, potentially creating new partnerships between diverse actors who share the goal of enhancing student learning.

David Istance, the lead researcher of the Innovative Learning Environments study at the CERI and key contributor to the OECD publication *Schooling Redesigned* (2015) has coined the term the "meso" level, to illustrate the centrality of these networked partnerships as key to creating and growing innovation in schools. He describes these emergent educational spaces as "voluntary hybrids" that span broader spaces of learning, essentially bridging formal and nonformal learning environments. This idea of networked engagement across educational sites or jurisdictions creates opportunity for innovative thinking to thrive, because it offers a non-prescriptive, more flexible model that invites unique, emergent or creative solutions to be created by learning focused partners. It is this potential for acceleration of rich, interconnected and hybrid learning spaces that is particularly important.

As described here, learning networks have the capacity for diffusion (shared learning), acceleration (enhancing the reach of an initiative), and ignition processes (the growing of commitment across multiple school settings and between individuals and/or teams). They are powerful socially based, flexibly designed systems that can respond quickly to diverse contexts and needs. In sum, learning networks have the capacity to accelerate learning, among teachers, principals, and educational leaders as Bryk, Gomez, Grunow, and LeMahieu (2015) identified in their exploration of networked improvement communities (NIC). But it is district leaders with a network oriented, learning centered mindset who are able to envision and nurture networked, hybrid partnerships through their unique position as lead change agents—catalytic forces that create new or enhance existing learning pathways that is the goal of this chapter's discussion. I will return to these themes in the concluding sections of this chapter.

Adaptive Learning Systems

We want to end this initial framing of the work underway in BC by drawing upon Kramer, Parkhurst, and Vaidyanathan's (2009) description of how social agencies can be described as *adaptive learning systems*. An important part of this way of understanding is that systems can and do learn: not only do they assess their own goals and outcomes, but in sharing their approaches with one another, they can weave together complex ideas and approaches that inform much larger, more complex social problems. This idea of shared learning isn't new, but many school jurisdictions don't have the capacity to operate in this way. This is one of the powerful features of our school district consortium; we believe this network has really provided an important means of accelerating learning as we share progress and how problems are addressed. As the idea of distributed leadership and leadership routines, improvement networks, hybrid learning spaces, inquiry driven learning, and processes of acceleration and catalytic affiliation make evident, approaches to innovation in learning need to be shared so we can draw from others experiences, adapt and modify approaches that work, applying these flexible routines to our own unique contexts. With this principle as a starting point, in the next section we describe in some detail our own jurisdiction's approach and tease out those routines that matter, while drawing attention to their flexible features; we hope this approach will help other jurisdictions learn what might work for them.

THE BRITISH COLUMBIA CONSORTIUM

British Columbia is a large province, with 60 school districts, each with their own superintendent as the lead educator. These districts range in size from geographically immense areas with very small rurally based populations (such as Northerly Coastal[1] a district about 335,000 square kilometers in northern BC including the territories of three aboriginal nations), with a school population of about 4,500, to urban districts with large school populations (ranging between 18,000 and 70,000 students in each district). Student populations are diverse, and include many students from a range of ethnic and racial groups. An important policy and educational priority has been to better support aboriginal students across the province. A strong focus on equity and quality characterize the goals of all BC school jurisdictions.

British Columbia has a long history as a high performing system as measured by international measures such as PISA (Programme for International Student Assessment). And, like other western educational jurisdictions, there has been a long history of districts involved in school effectiveness (Edmonds, 1979) and later school improvement, with a shift towards thinking more about educational culture and how system wide implementation efforts could be supported (Sackney, 2007). More recently system change has been focused on the role leaders can play in dynamic, interactive systems, practices reflective of how complexity thinking now informs our work as educators. Indeed there is significant Canadian research literature that focuses on the ways in which leaders enable change and innovation (Fullan & Quinn, 2015; Kaser & Halbert, 2009; Leithwood, 2013) and how particular adaptive routines or learning focused frames, particularly learning networks, can be used as synergistic tools for innovation or change (Katz, Earl, & Ben Jaafar, 2009). An important catalyst in the BC context has been the existence of a province wide learning network, the Network of Innovation and Inquiry (NOII[2]). This grassroots voluntary organization of teachers and school leaders has informally supported teachers engaged in learning centered innovation at the school level for close to two decades. The co-directors of NOII also engaged individual school districts in professional development focused on inquiry and how a disciplined approach to inquiry might deepen school improvement efforts. It is this focus on innovation through inquiry, leadership, and learning that has set the stage for the emergence of what we describe in this article as a superintendent learning network (SLN) in the summer of 2015.

A group of 15 school districts met in May 2015 at a conference devoted to sharing stories of promising practice and impact connected to networked inquiry. The purpose of this meeting was to explore ways in which learning about the various ways districts are approaching inquiry might be accelerated through a cooperative approach. With the assistance of a researcher and the NOII principals, the group developed an inquiry plan that sought to answer the following questions:

1. In what ways do district strategic initiatives in professional inquiry act as catalysts for moving learning forward and enhancing student success?
2. What are the most effective approaches to supporting professional inquiry, reflection, and improvement in educational practice to enhance student success?

Drawing from successful innovation mapping methods used by the OECD, a questionnaire was developed. After exploring the OECD case study and its components, the group designed a data collection instrument adapted to fit the consortium's research questions; an ethics approval process was also initiated[3] Once this questionnaire was finalized, each district was asked to complete it within a period of 6 months. The researcher (first author) was asked to coordinate this work, and create data sets that could be used by the SLN consortium to analyze their successes and opportunities for action. The members of the consortium also prepared presentations highlighting their approaches to inquiry, demonstrating impacts and lessons learned. These were shared during 2 days in May 2016. Planning continued in the summer and fall of 2016, including the creation of a smaller working group devoted to providing ongoing communication between participating districts and district leaders; a primary focus has been to map preliminary findings to share at upcoming educational conferences in Canada and internationally.

WHAT HAS BEEN LEARNED?

The versatility and wide applicability of an inquiry approach as a means of supporting district level learning initiatives was found to be very significant for several reasons. First, the inquiry model provided a flexible framework that was used to develop and implement diverse activities and district priorities. For example, among the districts who participated in this study, inquiry was used as a way of promoting and supporting professional learning among teachers, but also as a means of engaging formal leadership teams in goal setting activities, or engaging all employees in district strategic planning. In each case, the inquiry model provided a means of exploring ideas, assumptions, and potential directions in a way that deeply engaged multiple participants in the activity, building collaborative teams while providing a model for enactment/action. It provided a pathway that was simple enough to describe and follow in early stages (scanning and developing a hunch or hypothesis) while also providing a structure for reviewing or revisiting progress over time. This is important because it provided a way of discussing modifications that emerged as a result of putting ideas into practice and reviewing their effectiveness. Another significant feature of the model that made it especially useful was how its continuous design/cyclical structure allowed for reentry or review points—this meant that the design or plan of a team or group was modified or revisited at multiple points in the cycle of implementation, emerging from new information or data becoming available. In some cases this meant districts described the processes of exploring an idea as "messy" or "difficult to muddle through," but because the structure and process encouraged ongoing sensemaking and correction based on what had to be learned, there was acceptance that over time, and with continued efforts, their work would pay off in impacts on student learning.

This shared goal and purpose created a stable platform from which to make progress, even when specific activities might be in flux.

Another aspect of this inquiry approach that is worth commenting upon is that it insists that teams work with known and proven educational research theories—hunches and hypothesis development come from exploring and drawing from proven techniques of student learning and engagement; for example, self regulation, social emotional learning models, formative assessment, and experiential/place based learning were foundations for planned actions. This builds the capacity of all practitioners to engage in research analysis, while ensuring suggested approaches are anchored in known, impactful measures of educational performance.

The Value of an Inquiry-Based Approach Among Districts: Three Examples

In this section we provide three examples to illustrate the points above. Firstly, we explore the case of a small school jurisdiction with a large Aboriginal student population. In this case, a district leadership team developed a core question to investigate: "Would creating a strategy map and accountability tool that carefully set out expectations for all employees enable us to meet our goal of all students reading by Grade 5?" This school jurisdiction was able to narrow the scope of their inquiry by looking at existing standardized test results to carefully map achievement gaps, particularly noting the differing expectations for Aboriginal learners. Having identified a particular focus, they then were able to conduct a detailed scan of the district and classroom learning environments, eventually identifying the importance of teacher and leader language. This led to a design focused on engaging teachers in examining language commonly used to describe Aboriginal learners, and how negative meanings were conveyed in their ongoing use. As the district leaders who reported on their work documented, this approach enabled them to "interrupt and disrupt" narratives of failure, replacing them with language and professional activity that was focused on student learning and success. Importantly, their inquiry was built upon educational research related to growth mind-sets (Dweck, 2006); this was important because it brought together local professional knowledge with external expertise, creating a stronger base and a pedagogical narrative that could both influence and persuade.

A second example will show another aspect of inquiry's value—developing a district wide shared commitment to learning—and a different level of implementation, this time, school by school. In this case a large urban district decided to implement their approach to inquiry by creating team leaders at the school level. They described these individuals as *coordinators of inquiry*; each coordinator was mandated to lead inquiry teams at the school level. Inquiry coordinators were given considerable opportunity to develop their skills in facilitating inquiry-based professional learning, but were also expected to work with teacher teams who would determine the focus of their professional inquiry. In other words, the teams develop their own priorities based on scanning their own learners within their individual school settings. Inquiry team leaders also met at the district level to share what each team was working on; this ensured the district could map the work of various teams, and provide a point of coordination through which to assess progress, provide supports and redefine the initiative so it better met local school level needs. These coordinators identified multiple examples of emergent innovation that were focused on enhancing different forms of learner success; in sharing these at the district level, it informed how other coordinators might support or guide innovation in another setting.

A second smaller urban district organized a similar approach at the district level but created what they described as *innovation coaches*—each coach trained in helping to develop other inquiry focused teacher teams. This school jurisdiction described this process as developing horizontal leadership—leaders across the district, each ready to engage and lead learning centered innovation through mentorship and shared inquiries. Over time, more teams were created; each year the model is expanded based on the interest of teachers and volunteers interested in taking on these instructional leadership roles. As the initiative matured, the district organized events using district resources to support sharing of inquiry initiatives between teams in regional groups. In this district the focus on learning helped elementary, middle, and secondary schools to better understand and integrate experiential and technology enhanced pedagogical practices. This example also illustrates the ways that acceleration of innovation occurs naturally as an outcome of ground-up forms of collaboration and team-based learning.

The third example comes from a small, rural district that sought to shift towards a more collaborative and distributed leadership culture district wide. The inquiry model was used to develop a template for schools to develop their own school growth plans. Lead teachers at the school level and school and district administrators with an interest and experience in inquiry were recruited to take a lead role in developing and implementing this approach. One important aspect of this approach was that schools were paired or partnered based on shared goals/interests: both school and district level leaders shared the task of facilitating the process of inquiry used to develop the growth plans. Importantly, growth plans were centrally focused on student learning and success. These growth plans, at their various stages of development were shared not only at the school level, but at the district level, during formally scheduled district meetings. The goal of this approach was to embed an inquiry-based approach to district level work, and to make evident how learning was necessary at every level of the organization.

As these examples illustrate, the core routine of inquiry is flexible enough to adapt to local circumstance, while also providing a structure that can be usefully used to organize and support diverse groups and group needs. This makes inquiry incredibly valuable to school districts whose goal is to implement innovation and to improve student learning. In essence, inquiry has become a foundational infrastructure for enabling and enhancing innovation. How these routines also broaden and enhance impacts is another key outcome, and one that will be revisited in our conclusion. A new, easily shareable resource that we believe can really help in accelerating the adoption of professional inquiry has just been published by Canadians for 21st Century Learning (C21). Entitled *The Spiral Playbook* (Kaser & Halbert, 2017), it offers another means of accelerating impact.

Yet while knowledge of the process is critically important, the leadership of district superintendents should not be overlooked; they provided the primary vision for structuring and resourcing the professional inquiry networks they initiated and guided. The importance of alignment—to student success and shared purpose will be discussed next.

The Power of Alignment

When districts shared their learning about inquiry and innovation in their own school districts there were a variety of themes that emerged, but perhaps the one that was described most consistently was the importance of alignment. Alignment was emphasized in several ways: one theme related to alignment of professional learning with planned activities and was about common language and messaging. Another take on alignment was about ensuring resources aligned to professional learning activities; still another emphasized the importance of aligning outcomes with impact measures so that a strong story could be told about the district's efforts. The final category of alignment was ensuring our activities and purposes related to inquiry were always centrally focused on student learning.

In general, the goal of alignment is to ensure that activities or events, processes or products are strategically considered through a lens that asks: "How does this fit our goal of enhancing student learning? Does it reflect our commitment to the principles of inquiry and learning as a district team?" Alignment didn't mean that all activities were common, but it did mean there was a clear coherence of purpose. As one district leader described, the goal is the "inspire, incite, and integrate" so that inquiry and learning centered practices are part of our school and district plans, and guide investments in time, resources and technology. Leaders at the district level are key to alignment measures; without this as a backbone to district work, the inquiry model would not have the level of professional impact across the jurisdiction.

Leadership for Learning: Catalytic Affiliation and Ignition Processes

As we noted in the literature reviewed for this chapter, leaders matter, and in the context of our story in this chapter, district superintendent leadership matters greatly. We know that district leaders can be important as mentors and guides for others who aspire to these roles, and while we acknowledge this as important work, we want to underline that district leaders need to put first their identities as learners themselves—openly and transparently—if they are going to truly ignite commitments to learning and accelerate the processes of innovation in their own educational jurisdictions. Honig (2012) talks about several things that district leaders need to do including: engaging in authentic, collaborative learning settings; modeling how one talks about oneself as a learner, including metacognition practices; engaging actively in reciprocal (nonhierarchical) examples of professional learning; making consistent and persistent commitment to learning; as well as prioritizing learning over administrative tasks.

The work of the superintendents in this consortium demonstrates the importance of learning centered leadership—but also its complexity. In general, joint, collaborative work, one of the central principles of professional learning, has been integrated in and become an indispensable part of the approaches taken by district superintendents in our study. This commitment to collaboration is firmly rooted in the approaches districts use to designing and implementing processes of inquiry, but are also embedded within their own formal activities at the district level. This commitment to principles of collaboration seems to anchor teachers' and school principals' commitments more fully and, is linked to creating cultural change at the district level. This is important for those already engaged with and focused on innovation and enhancing student learning. But an important observation is that collaboration isn't focused solely on those already engaged in inquiry work, but seeks to build connections so as to engage others not yet directly involved in change practices or inquiry-based teams. We think collaborative approaches and the inquiry model itself, with its emphasis on building teams and learning together, creates inviting pathways for others to join in, particularly among teachers or administrators who have been observing the work of early innovators and change agents from the edges. We have heard anecdotally from teachers that they have been drawn in by this "affiliative" approach, where they first see consistent commitment and engagement from district leaders, and then are drawn in by others they trust who are already engaged in inquiry work. Observations from mid-sized district leaders also reinforced this; you can, as a district leader, systematize or institutionalize certain activities or approaches, but for the change to become part of a district's culture, it needs to be taken up more widely by participants *in their own ways and these ways have as much value because of their diversity.* The best district leaders make space for this diversity.

Leaders then, build momentum and then accelerate change through relationally focused, professional inquiry. They also do this work by acknowledging the rich array and diversity of approaches, not focusing solely on one way forward. These observations were important points that emerged from our initial discussions as a learning network, and we hope to trace more fully in the next iteration of our shared inquiry work. If we can map growth in the numbers of teachers working in one and then in other related collaboration groups, we could create an acceleration model that will help us to show impacts more fully.

A Tool for Sharing Learning Across Multiple Jurisdictions

Before ending the discussion of our learning in our SLN consortium project, we want to briefly discuss another important benefit to district level practices of inquiry-based professional learning: adaptive integration (Bryk et al., 2015) and the spread of innovation across systems. How does district level professional inquiry accelerate learning among and between districts? One important observation we have made is that the common language of inquiry helps us to share what we are doing, and understand more deeply its potential application to other settings. With a common language of investigation, the process of sharing outcomes and implications becomes much simpler. With similar understandings about processes and goals, we can more easily understand the ways in which findings and outcomes can be translated or transferred from one jurisdiction to another. This has great value if we are to spread innovation among diverse educational regions.

Another feature of the professional inquiry model that is worth highlighting again is how it structures the inquiry process so that participants examine and draw from known educational research; in this way, it builds into the model the application of research to practice. *Adaptive integration* (Bryk et al., 2015) is key to acceleration efforts; in other words, new or promising practices needs to be integrated into multiple contexts so new improvement cycles will result in enhancing learning for all learners. At the district level, we believe our SLN network (which Bryk describes as Networked Improvement Communities or NICs) is key to ensuring the integration of improvement practices across multiple and differing jurisdictions. "It vital-izes a core belief that we can accomplish more together than even the best of us can accomplish alone" (p. 17).

SUMMARIZING OUR FINDINGS

In this chapter we have attempted to map out the work of our school dis-trict consortium and explain how our approach has enhanced innovation focused on student learning and student success. We think our approach can be mapped into a table that may help to see relationships between innovation infrastructures and accelerants (see Table 8.1). Infrastructure refers to those systems and supports that are institutionalized at the district level; accelerants are the conditions, practices, and principles what guide the work of innovation in the district.

While putting these items in distinct columns helps make evident all com-ponents of effective inquiry led innovation and provides a means of teasing out their various attributes or features, doing so tends to emphasize their independent features rather than they way they are interrelated and linked together in complex ways. As the earlier discussion of the inquiry projects taken on by district superintendents in our SLN consortium made evident, there are features that have been emphasized, such as the importance of the inquiry model or networks that support inquiry learning teams and shared learning, as well as principles such as alignment with overall purpos-es. Some other features such as the capacity for differentiation and the idea of emergent design are more subtle features of the inquiry model, but are just as important as they permit the acceleration of innovation in multiple sites, ensuring innovation is scaled to the jurisdictional level. However, we would like to end with a more detailed discussion of how and why we think this particular inquiry model has had so much success in the BC context. We hope this discussion will help other jurisdictions and superintendents,

TABLE 8.1 Innovation Infrastructure and Accelerants

Innovation Infrastructure	Accelerants
Inquiry model (Halbert & Kaser, 2013)	Catalytic affiliation & invitational approaches
Distributed/shared/collaborative leadership structures/teams	Relationality & culture of trust
Resources (time, money)	Shared commitment to learning centered professional practice
Networks	Alignment
Scheduled events	Capacity for differentiation & emergent design

who are themselves innovators and change agents, consider its fit with their own context and needs/interests.

Inquiry as a Routine That Is Embedded With Meaning and Moral Purpose

Why does the inquiry model accelerate innovation and improvement in BC school jurisdictions? Initially we think this comes from the consistent and clear description of the routine's purpose, and its explicit link to student learning, consistently and persistently. The repetition of the inquiry questions themselves and the continually reflection back on what's been done and its impact on learners helps with reinforcement. The visual representation of the model also emphasizes its cyclical nature, and this too adds to the feeling of the repetition as natural and necessary. However, the routine is also embedded with purpose: It is driven by a continually asked series of questions that puts learners and their success at the center of action.

Professional inquiry becomes deeply understood through use and collaboratively in practice. As noted above, we think that collaboration is an accelerant in the process of becoming a learning centered practitioner, which will assist in building district cultures devoted to innovation and deepened student learning. We have also emphasized that practices of relationality and shared purpose, both features of inquiry, help accelerate conditions for mutual trust. We have argued that only invitational models work in our jurisdiction; but we know that district leaders who model inquiry-based learning are catalysts who attract engagement from teachers, both mainstream and fringe. Sharing the work of inquiry is key here: it's not enough to talk about inquiry and who should do it, one must live it in practice by being part of teams who work to co-construct the path forward. So when teachers and leaders alike know that they are measuring their efforts to advance their learners' success; when they trace their activity against the goals of their inquiry project; when the plan they've developed is dog eared with use and posted in most, if not all classrooms; and when the rubric that documents how performance is measured becomes a reference point for teachers, district leaders, trustees, and community members, we know that we've created the conditions necessary for quality learning and have accelerated its advancement. It is the lived practice of inquiry minded, district superintendents and leaders that have set in place the opportunity to create an innovative jurisdiction; it is their commitment to working in learning teams, to having a strong moral purpose grounded in ensuring the success of all learners, to continuously model collaboratively engagement, to consistently map progress, that has given them the power to effect change.

WORK YET TO DO

Before concluding, we want to identify some goals and priorities we have set for ourselves as a part of our SLN network activity plan. Our initial examination of the cases we have collected and described in this chapter give us great hope that our work is having an important impact on student and teacher learning. Yet measuring impact and demonstrating its link to inquiry activities can be challenging. We have found some ways of measuring this work; for example, in one rural jurisdiction video narratives have been created that deeply explore the structures, processes, and impacts of inquiry on teacher learning. These short videos have had considerable impact on practitioners and leaders alike who see themselves in these stories of learning and inquiry. Another district has created a website for sharing and communicating impacts. Such stories provide important evidence to stakeholders about the work we are doing and communicates how it values students and their learning. We also have districts in our consortium that have mapped changes in student confidence and success using pre and post measures designed to show the effectiveness of particular approaches. These measures help us to know we are making a difference for learners, and provides important models that can be shared with other districts who are part of our consortium, so we can better describe our impacts while linking them to interventions and approaches taken through our inquiry projects. Another innovative measure several districts have started to use is a rubric designed by a district Aboriginal leader. The purpose of this rubric was to more consistently identify growth in levels of knowledge and commitment to the integration of Aboriginal knowledge and pedagogies into classroom practices; it is a self reflective tool that is being used to measure leader and teacher learning. Another rubric related to tracing progress in inquiry practice is being piloted in one district.

These are all good exemplars of evaluation measures being designed to show our progress and impact, each customized to fit inquiry work within a district. Yet we know there is a need to more systematically define and capture our impacts. To deliver on this outcome, the consortium members met in 2017 to review and summarize the features of their inquiry work; a reflective inquiry guide was developed and has been piloted in several districts. Several rounds of revisions have been undertaken and the consortium has plans for making this framework more widely available to superintendents and teams across Canada.

CONCLUSIONS

We started out and ended this chapter with a discussion about the two primary features of BC's innovative school jurisdictions—investments in inquiry-based, networked learning systems and secondly, a focus on practices of learning centered leadership that accelerate change. However, as researchers who work with these incredible district leaders, we felt it would be respectful to end this chapter with some of their words. We hope as you read these quotes you will see how inquiry has inspired their approaches to learning and leading, and in particular, how inquiry is essential in the transformation of schools.

> Through an inquiry approach, the school growth planning process has now become a natural, ongoing process rather than an event that occurs once or twice a year. But this process is not just limited to the growth planning process. The spirals of inquiry model is beginning to be embedded as part of the culture of our district and applied on a continual basis to support the ongoing improvement of student achievement. (Superintendent 1)

> Over the past 3 years, our district has been focusing attention on the "Why," "What," and "How" of transforming learning: why we are engaging in transforming learning, what are the components of the transforming learning process, and how we will engage in the transformation process. For us, the "How" is collaborative inquiry. At the district level, we have been fostering a culture of being curious, asking questions, and going deeper. District innovation grants and professional learning opportunities are framed around inquiry questions and ongoing learning, action, and reflection. Our collaborative learning has been further enhanced through supporting our school administrators in bringing to life the spiral of inquiry process in their daily work in schools. Inquiry is truly a way of being and learning, not an event or initiative. The transformation is underway. (Superintendent 2)

> From a systems perspective, the positive impact of inquiry to our ability to move forward as a district is undeniable. It is now part of who we are and how we investigate possibilities for our students. We have designated time for school and district teams to use the inquiry process to develop and implement school learning plans and the district's strategic plan. Using inquiry is part of our district culture and has resulted in innovative approaches to instruction and school programming options. Inquiry as a way of learning and teaching supports our core value of curiosity. There is so much more cohesiveness and alignment in our district that has resulted from a systems approach to inquiry. The collaborative inquiry reflects increased meaning for classroom teachers and an increased buy-in. I am very excited to follow this deeper and forward for the good of students. (Superintendent 3)

> Our work as a consortium of network leaders has been vital. Connecting with one another with intentionality and focus through the spiral of inquiry, sharing rich practices of the impact of inquiry in our own contexts, and then reaching deeper to learn from one another and act as critical friends to one another's practice, has proven a crucial revitalization of the work in our school district. We have a singular focus: to enhance learning for all learners—students and professional learners. The work of the inquiring districts

collaborative has provided us a responsive learning community from which to deepen our impact for the good of all. (Superintendent 4)

We hope you are as inspired by these words and commitments to action as we have been as partners in our mutual learning journeys.

ACKNOWLEDGMENTS

The authors of this chapter gratefully acknowledge the contributions made by a group of dedicated BC school superintendents; their insights and thoughtful discussion were essential to constructing the framework that was used in this writing chapter.

NOTES

1. All district names are pseudonyms.
2. NOII and AESN are acronyms for two networks that were initially founded by two co-authors of this chapter, Drs. Halbert and Kaser. For more information, visit https://www.noii.ca
3. Ethical approval was granted by the University of Victoria in the Fall of 2015. Each district consented to participate in this data collection. A copy of the data collection instrument is available via the authors.

REFERENCES

Barber, M., Chijioke, C., & Mourshed, M. (2010). *Education: How the World's most improved school systems keep getting better.* London, England: McKinsey & Company.

Bryk, A., Gomez, L., Grunow, A., & LeMahieu, P. (2015). *Learning to improve: How American's schools can get better at getting better.* Cambridge, MA: Harvard Education Press.

Dweck, C. (2006). *Mindsets: The new psychology of success.* New York, NY: Random House.

Edmonds, R. R. (1979). Effective schools for the urban poor. *Educational Leadership, 37*, 15–27.

Fullan, M., & Quinn, J. (2015). *Coherence: The right drivers in action for schools, districts, and systems.* Thousand Oaks, CA: Corwin Press.

Halbert, J., & Kaser, L. (2013). *Spirals of inquiry: For equity and quality.* Vancouver, BC: BCPVPA.

Hattie, J., & Timperley, H. (2007) The power of feedback. *Review of Educational research, 77*, 81–112. doi:10.3102/003465430298487

Honig, M. (2012). District central office leadership as teaching: How central office administrator support principals' development as instructional leaders. *Educational Administration Quarterly, 48,*(4) 733–774.

Hopkins, D. (2011). Realizing the potential of system leadership. In J. Robertson & H. Timperley (Eds.), *Leadership and learning* (pp. 86–99). London, England: SAGE. Kaser, L., & Halbert, J. (2009). *Leadership Mindsets.* New York, NY: Routledge.

Kaser, L., & Halbert, J. (2017). *The spiral playbook: Leading with an inquiring mindset in school systems and schools.* C21 Canada. Retrieved from www.http:c21canada.org/playbook

Katz, S., Earl, L., & Ben Jaafar, S. (2009). *Building and connecting learning communities. The power of networks for school improvement.* Thousand Oaks, CA: Corwin Press.

Kramer, M., Parkhurst, M., & Vaidyanathan, L. (2009). *Breakthroughs in shared measurement and social impact.* Boston, MA: FSG Social Impact Advisors. Retrieved from http://www.socialimpactexchange.org/sites/www.socialimpactexchange.org/files/Breakthroughs%20in%20Shared%20Measurement.pdf

Leithwood, K. (2013). *Strong districts & their leadership.* Oakville, Canada: Ontario Ministry of Education. Retrieved from http://www.ontariodirectors.ca/downloads/Strong%20Districts-2.pdf

McGregor, C. (2014). Disrupting colonial mindsets: The power of learning networks. *In Education, 19*(3). Retrieved from https://ineducation.ca/ineducation/article/view/136/622

Organization for Economic Cooperation and Development. (2013). *Innovative Learning Environments.* Paris, France: Author.

Organization for Economic Cooperation and Development. (2015). *Schooling Redesigned.* Paris, France: Author.

Robinson, V. M., Lloyd, C. A., & Rowe, K. J. (2008). The impact of leadership on student outcomes: An analysis of the differential effects of leadership types. *Educational Administration Quarterly, 44*(5), 635–674.

Sachney, L. (2007). A history of the school effectiveness and improvement movement in Canada over the last 25 years. In T. Townsend (Ed), *International handbook of school effectiveness and improvement* (pp. 167–182). Dordrecht, The Netherlands: Springer.

Schonert-Reichl, K. A., & Hymel, S. (2007). Educating the heart as well as the mind: Why social and emotional learning is critical for students' school and life success. *Education Canada, 47,* 20–25.

Spillane, J. (2006). *Distributed leadership.* San Francisco, CA: Jossey-Bass.

Spillane, J., Healey, K., Mesler Parise, L., & Kenney, A. (2011). A distributed perspective on learning leadership. In J. Robertson & Helen Timperley (Eds.), *Leadership and Learning* (pp. 159–171). Thousand Oaks, CA: SAGE.

Timperley, H., Kaser, L., & Halbert, J. (2014, April). *A framework for transforming learning in schools: Innovation and the spiral of inquiry* (Seminar Series Paper No. 234). East Melbourne, Australia: Centre for Strategic Education.

Williams, L., & Tanaka, M. (2007). Schalay'nung Sxwey'ga: Emerging cross-cultural pedagogy in the academy. *Educational Insights, 11*(3). Retrieved from http://einsights.ogpr.educ.ubc.ca/v11n03/pdfs/williams.pdf

CHAPTER 9

SOME "CENTRAL" ISSUES IN CREATING PROFESSIONAL LEARNING COMMUNITIES

A Superintendent's Perspective

Jesus "Chuey" Abrego
University of Texas Rio Grande Valley

Jamie Lopez
University of Texas Rio Grande Valley

Today's public schools are faced with many challenges, increased accountability for student scores, changing demographics, including the increase of English Language Learners (ELLs) and competition for resources (Rubin, Abrego, & Sutterby, 2015). In order to address these and other educational issues, school districts and superintendents are implementing a professional learning community (PLC) framework (Abrego & Pankake, 2011; Hipp & Huffman, 2010a; Supovitz, 2006).

How *does* a superintendent go about implementing a PLC across an entire school district? What are specific challenges that superintendents face

The Contemporary Superintendent, pages 153–167
Copyright © 2019 by Information Age Publishing
All rights of reproduction in any form reserved.

during change reform? How does the organization learn how to become a PLC? Whether we begin to examine implementation from the perspective of a small or large school district, may not necessarily be the lens through which we begin our discussion, instead the premise for this chapter involves taking a closer look at specific actions and processes applied by one superintendent (Lopez, 2015) to influence the planning and implementation of a district wide PLC through central office.

In this chapter, we argue that in order to successfully implement and sustain a PLC across a district, specific central office day-to-day work will require attention. As Abrego & Pankake (2011) point out in their study of a district wide PLC, "it is process, not programs, that sustain the dimensions of a professional learning community across a district" (pp. 9–10). Thus, the chapter will reveal one superintendent's process to influence the breadth and depth of PLC implementation by focusing on the following central office issues: the creation of key positions, professional development, and implementation of structural changes.

District wide implementation of a PLC requires a systemic approach (Abrego & Pankake, 2011; Lopez, 2015; Ostmeyer, 2003). It involves moving from a philosophical stance about issues toward creating and implementing tools and strategies based on the needs of the district and campuses. Pankake and Abrego (2011) state that

> creating an organization with leadership as a systemic characteristic is a challenging but worthy effort. A major component for accomplishing this effort is to build the leadership capacity of individuals within the organization. (p. 4)

The purpose of this chapter is to elaborate on implications for district leaders as they think about how to engage in PLC work. That is, the everyday work of building a PLC. Professional learning community work is defined as the activities that aid in the development of a PLC (Nelson, 2009). There is growing evidence that specific PLC work requires that all professional members of the organization participate in the PLC (Abrego & Pankake, 2011; Hord & Roussin, 2013; Lopez, 2015; Pruitt, 2013). The chapter will share voices from the field that carried out PLC work.

CHALLENGES IN IMPLEMENTING A PLC

What role should central office play with regards to educational reform? Should the role of central office and the superintendent focus on compliance or continuous improvement? Researchers and practitioners alike have come to realize that both are two sides of the same coin. Since national and state funding are both tied to some degree to compliance, school districts and superintendents are obligated to meet compliance regulations or face consequences.

In addition, school districts and superintendents are faced with recent changes in national and state legislation as well as with enormous challenges stemming from high stakes testing and lack of appropriate funding for teaching and learning.

Just as challenging, are the internal disruptors found within a district. It's important to reflect on what resistance a superintendent will face and how he or she will resolve that resistance. Additionally, in most cases, the superintendent is not directly responsible for the daily monitoring of implementation; he or she is dependent on the work of various individuals (Pankake, 1998). Thus, in light of these challenges, what role does a district play, and more specifically, its superintendent, in developing capacity of its district staff to implement PLCs? And, what role does district leadership play in adult learning in order to build capacity?

IMPLEMENTING THE PLC FRAMEWORK DISTRICT WIDE: REVIEW OF LITERATURE

What is a district wide PLC? A review of the literature found limited empirical evidence (Abrego & Pankake, 2011; Ostmeyer, 2003; Stoll & Louis, 2007; Wells and Feun, 2007) examining PLC work at the district level. Fullan (2005) proposed a shift from the culture of the school to a larger focus of the culture of the district. Fullan suggested proposing PLCs in a larger perspective since a fair amount of research has been conducted at the campus level. Therefore, he noted limited or no research exists at the district level where all or most of the high schools have established PLCs.

Given the success of campus PLCs (Hipp & Huffman, 2010a), more and more districts are attempting to implement the model of PLCs district wide (Abrego & Pankake, 2011; Hord & Sommers, 2008; Lopez, 2015). According to Horton and Martin (2013), the role and support of district central office administration—the superintendent, school board and central office plays a key role in the implementation of a district wide PLC.

For the purposes of this chapter, Hord's (1997) dimensions of a PLC were used as a lens through which to study the district. Hord's original work stems from her 5-year study conducted by Southwest Educational Development Laboratory (SEDL). Hord's five dimensions of a PLC consist of the following:

1. *Supportive and shared leadership* requires the collegial and facilitative participation of the principal who shares leadership by inviting staff input and action in decision-making.

2. *Shared values and vision* include an unwavering commitment to student learning that is consistently articulated and referenced in staff's work.
3. *Collective learning and application of learning* requires that school staff at all levels are engaged in the processes that collectively seek new knowledge among staff and application of the learning solutions that address students' needs.
4. *Shared personal practice* involves the review of a teacher's behavior by colleagues and includes feedback and assistance activity to support individual and community improvement.
5. *Supportive conditions* include physical conditions and human capacities that encourage and sustain a collegial atmosphere and collective learning (Hord, 2004, p. 7)

In their earlier work, Hipp and Huffman (2010b) identified two types of conditions or settings necessary to build effective PLCs; they include structures and relationships. According to Hipp & Huffman, structures refers to the systems used to allow members of the organization to come together to work and learn without discounting their personal time (Hipp & Huffman, 2010b). While, relationships refer to the creation of a culture of trust, respect, and inclusiveness to better develop the community of learners (Hipp & Huffman, 2010b). These dimensions do not operate separately and in isolation but are interwoven; each dimension influences the others (Hipp & Huffman, 2010c).

A Select Summary of Central Office Studies and Professional Learning Communities

Eaker and Keating (2009) and Drago-Severson (2012) identify district leadership as a critical factor in making a difference across a district but more important stress the role of central office in adult learning. Eaker and Keating (2009) elaborate on their findings from White River School District in Buckley, Washington. In their study,

> the district embraced the assumptions that adult behavior can best be impacted by deep learning and that the goal of deep learning can best be accomplished by doing the work of a professional learning community. (p. 51)

In her study of three urban school districts, Honig (2012) focused on central office staff specifically devoted to working with principals one-on-one to strengthen their capacity for instructional leadership. The study focused on staff or senior management that reported directly to the superintendent's cabinet or comparable group. Honig (2012), claims that over the past decade more and more central offices are involved in a shift from traditional roles of compliance to a more "intensive job-embedded support led by executive-level staff—those reporting directly to superintendents, deputy superintendent, or the equivalent—work intensively with principals to strengthen their instructional leadership" (p. 734).

Furthermore, Lopez's (2015) research work followed a school district along the U.S. Mexico border that claimed to be implementing a PLC district wide. He identified the following findings and role of central office: (a) PLC work influenced the development of Hord's five dimensions of a PLC to varying degrees, (b) the district is at the implementation phase of the change process, (c) the superintendent played a key role in PLC implementation through his understanding and use of a change model, and (d) archival data noted changes in student achievement scores throughout PLC implementation. Overall, the findings suggest that the implementation of structural changes influenced the development of a culture of learning and collaboration in the district.

Ostmeyer's (2003) work of a district wide PLC, also provides findings about how the superintendent influenced the district development toward a PLC by implementing job role behavior changes in teachers, principals, and central office administrators. In addition, the superintendent developed a collaborative working environment by restructuring central office and hiring new staff members (pp. 250–251).

Abrego and Pankake's (2011) follow-up case study of Ostmeyer's work within the same school district provided a keen insight as to the types of PLC work required for implementation and sustainability of a district wide PLC (10-year period). This particular study revisited an established district wide PLC. The study concluded that the district had sustained it's district wide PLC over time. Abrego and Pankake (2011), found

> the factors that enhanced and promoted the sustainability of a professional learning community from a district-wide perspective included the initiation and implementation of district-wide staff development in the form of continuous improvement (Baldrige Model for Excellence) which helps address issues of trust, collegiality, and communication within the district. Thus the processes—the physical, tangible end-products that staff use on a daily basis in their workplace; the creation and implementation of a data-driven decision-making matrix; the use of continuous improvement planning and management tools; and the creation and use of a score card, for example—have allowed the district to operate from the view that, in order to continue to move forward toward increased student achievement, the district requires the use of very specific tools and resources for all staff in order to move the district forward. It is process, not programs, that makes a positive difference at

Western Crossing ISD in sustaining the dimensions of a Professional Learning Community. (pp. 9–10)

ROLE AND SUPPORT OF DISTRICT CENTRAL OFFICE PLAYS KEY ROLE: VOICES FROM THE FIELD

What follows are excerpts from interviews from a study (Lopez, 2015) that explored the role and influence of a school superintendent as he implemented a district wide PLC located along the U.S.–Mexico border. The case study examined what dimensions of a PLC (Hord, 2004; Hord & Sommers, 2008) were evident, how the superintendent approached the change process with a community of teachers and administrators, and the PLCs influence on student achievement.

Numerous researchers and practitioners (DuFour, DuFour, & Eaker, 2008; Hipp & Huffman, 2010c; Huffman & Hipp, 2003) affirmed "it is impossible for a school or district to develop the capacity to function as a professional learning community without undergoing profound cultural shifts" (p. 91). Furthermore, they contended that the work of developing PLCs is not just adopting or implementing new initiatives—it is the challenge of reculturing or the challenge of impacting an organization's habits, expectations, and beliefs that constitute the norm (DuFour et al., 2008).

District superintendents play an integral role in change efforts (Horton & Martin, 2013). One of their major roles is to communicate priorities effectively and in agreement with district staff (Hurley, 2006). In our particular case study, the superintendent sets the stage by introducing the concept of PLCs to his school board, what follows is one board member's perspective about PLCs:

> When our new superintendent came (superintendent's name] and he began talking about professional learning communities and PLCs. I think that frankly, all of the board members were wondering just what is the superintendent talking about. So I made a concerted effort to visit, to be in the room when some of them [discussion] were taking place. So my perspective is influenced by those visits and what I heard. We now talk about it so openly and frequently.... My perspective of it is that it is a very intentional effort to involve individuals from various levels and give me/them the opportunity to work together. (School Board Member 1)

The superintendent discusses his plan to introduce PLCs to the district in light of the change process. During his interview, the superintendent indicated having previous experience in district-wide PLC implementation in different districts.

I guess on PLCs, the concept of a Professional Learning Community, one of the things was my background in (previous school district). Let me start off with (previous school district). I was the Assistant Superintendent for the (previous school district) Learning Community so that in itself, the concept of PLC's was ingrained. That was something that we did so we have a system of implementation of a Professional Learning Community...What that was, it was much targeted, it was very systemic, and it was something that we enjoyed. I was only there a year or a year and a half. Then I was in previous school district, we began the concept, and we became more structured in our approach. In other words, everywhere I have been, we have been in a situation where we were moving into more structure, more assistance, and a more system of support from the central office. (Superintendent)

Additional expectations are shared by the superintendent, in terms of the role of PLCs within the school district and how staff operate with that context.

At the district level all divisions and departments operate as PLCs according to the superintendent. So our divisions, even our division leaders, lead their employees or our essential office staff, through Professional Learning Communities. Our deputy superintendent for transformation leads through a PLC concept.

As mentioned earlier, the superintendent in this case study had contextual experience in the change process and with implementing PLCs. He used these important experiences to guide implementation and the district's decision-making process. During the interview, the superintendent goes on to mention that he has a background on change theory as a result of his doctoral work. The following is an excerpt from the interview.

On change, one of the things again and I have referenced Kotter, I believe why transformation efforts fail is seminal work for me with regards to what and how transformation should occur. So I used that quite a bit. I learned that obviously at the (university) when I was working on my doctorate at (university) in 1999 to 2001. (Superintendent)

Thus, the superintendent had a foundation in change theory and experience in district-wide PLC implementation at the central office level in two previous districts. According to Evans, Thornton, and Usinger (2012) when district leaders have a working background in change theory, the change efforts will be more successful.

In addition, to having previous experience with the change process and PLCs, he was deliberate about operationalizing a plan by initially executing an entry plan for the district. Basically, the superintendent conducted his own central office research through open-ended interviews with key central office administrators, principals, and school board trustees; and found that while the district had established a culture of pride, it had over time also created a climate in which different schools represented a fragmented system, which encouraged campuses and central office to act independently from each other. In the interview, the superintendent stated the following on this topic:

> I could tell we had several independent school districts within our own school district. Which again there is nothing wrong with that. If the data is consistent throughout the entire organization, I believe that a pocket of excellence is not something to be very proud of. I would rather be proud and that is what we are striving for [as] a system. (Superintendent)

In this particular case study, the superintendent applied an entry plan (strategy) to help him understand the context of what was happening across the district and then used it as a starting point to initiate district wide change. His plan to introduce change was informed by stakeholders.

A District Leaders Approach to Change

Talbert (2010) suggests that even if leaders have a research-based approach to PLC implementation, their approaches can differ. Talbert outlined two strategies—*bureaucratic strategy* and *professional strategy*. First, a bureaucratic strategy encompasses a mandate approach driven by directives, implementation checklists, and sanctions to leverage change (Talbert, 2010). Second, a professional strategy links change to leader modeling, use of decision making structures, and feedback to engender change (Talbert, 2010). The superintendent SCISD, employed a *professional strategy*. The following excerpt presents the superintendent's approach to moving staff through change:

> But when you come to a district like SCISD, one of the things that we realized is that and we continue to realize let us make sure that everyone is ready. Let us make sure that they are prepared. Let us make sure that we have done the things that we need to do for successful implementation and fidelity to that implementation. I can tell you it has taken us a while. It has taken us a while, some people might say too long. I think we are right at the right speed. (Superintendent)

The superintendent believed in creating the conditions for change by presenting a case for change rather than by issuing directives to staff, even if it meant that change would take longer to initiate. In the interview, the superintendent acknowledged the change process for the district had taken a long time to develop. This aligns with Fullan (2007) who noted that for change to become ingrained in the existing culture—can take from 5 to 8 years. The SCISD was in the sixth year of PLC work. Nevertheless, the superintendent's focus was on setting up sustainable structures to ensure changes were entrenched in the district's culture rather than rapidly moving through superficial change efforts. In his interview, he stated, "I do not believe in a pocket of excellence. What we are working for is a system of excellence" (Superintendent).

The Role of Central office in PLC Implementation

Horton and Martin (2013) contend that support for PLC implementation at the district level is essential in successful development of a PLC. Building the capacity for change in a school district begins when central office administrators create a space to review research and engage in conversations on change (Hurley, 2006). More precisely, Horton and Martin (2013) asserted that district leaders must be willing to work diligently to develop a clear and focused understanding for change to occur. Data collected in this study indicated that central office administrators played a key role in the development of the PLC. The superintendent intended to have central office administrators serve as a resource group that assisted in building capacity at all levels of the district. The superintendent stated:

> I can tell you though that if we do not coach from the central office, if we do not assist in our system support to monitor our PLC progress, there will be those that are still prone to say "Well, maybe common collaborative planning time is not as important" or "The development of norms in a certain grade level might be left to chance there as well" when in fact it has to be highly, highly functionalized throughout the entire campus. But by that campus, by each area, by all campuses so our job as providing in the central office, *systems of support* is also assessed where we are at each individual campus in their PLC development. (Superintendent)

Central office administrators acknowledged in their interviews that the district implemented a structure to create a line of support from the classroom to central office. The district created two separate but overlapping categories of support positions; one for learning and one for leadership.

The assistant superintendent for curriculum and instruction had responsibility for overseeing the learning category. This category worked with the facilitators at the elementary and middle schools and the LASER (Leader's Achieving Superior Educational Results) teams at the comprehensive high schools. In the interview, the assistant superintendent for curriculum and instruction said:

All those things that deal with what we say the learning side of the house, that's my responsibility, and the leading side of the house, think of a Venn-diagram, that is (deputy superintendent for transformation), that side, that's the leading side and I'm on the learning side. And so we work together in concert to make sure that we hit the leaders, all the principals etc., and then also on the learning side together. (Central Office 2)

In terms of coaching staff, this was the assistant superintendent's comment:

We actually sent them to smart-coaching training this year so that can really work to support the teachers, so literally like a coach; they're on the teachers side: I'm here to help you do better, I'm gonna work with you, I'm gonna teach you, I'm gonna be on the sidelines, I'm gonna help you desegregate data; all of those things as opposed to being evaluative like (formal teacher evaluation tool). (Central Office 2)

Data collected for this study demonstrated a clear line of communication and collaboration in the learning category. The line goes from the classroom teacher, to the central office coordinator, to the assistant superintendent for curriculum and instruction, and finally to the superintendent. Interview data indicated that communication and collaboration occurred during PLC meetings. The role of central office administrators is to plan, coordinate, and present at these meetings. The assistant superintendent for curriculum and instruction said that every PLC meeting included a learning portion. The intent of this practice is to build capacity.

So we spend the whole day on topics that pertain to other things in the district too but we focus a lot on that learning piece so if we have a benchmark exam, we call them district curriculum assessments right now. If we do that, then those results also get fed up line so that even the superintendent knows where are we at, how are we doing, what do we need to do to adjust and then we work together on that to execute whatever plans we come up with. (Central Office 2)

The leading category is similar in approach except this line of communication and collaboration goes from the classroom, to principals, to central office, to deputy superintendent, and finally to the superintendent. The central office administrator in charge of this category is the deputy superintendent of transformation and learning, and collaboration happens at their designated PLC meetings. Principal 3 cited in interview:

Now, a principal's meeting always has a learning piece ... the board meeting is the smallest portion of the principal meeting now. It's like here's the information you could have gotten in minutes on the internet, so now let's go into the learning piece, the cooperative learning, the development of PLCs ... they're constantly training, the staff development is embedded, the sharing of knowledge, it's just a whole different purpose [for the] meeting. (Principal 3)

DuFour et al. (2008) states that it is imperative for central office to create a clear line of communication to ensure that initiatives are verbalized effectively and in one voice. The voices from the field shared in this chapter included staff that had served under two superintendents—the previous and current superintendent. All interviewees met specific criteria. Thus participants were able to share their perspectives regarding change over time across two distinct superintendents.

CONCLUSIONS: ACTIVITIES AND STRATEGIES FOR IMPLEMENTING A PLC DISTRICT WIDE

The district in this study was found to be an emerging PLC. In short, as each of Hord's dimensions of a PLC was analyzed against the district culture and climate, the district was found to be at the beginning stages of implementation. Several particular areas or findings were identified as important to any district leadership team but especially for a superintendent interested in implementing a district wide PLC.

As mentioned earlier, there were "central issues" or central office issues that stood out from the study. These can be described as specific central office day-to-day work, which influences the implementation and sustainability of a district wide PLC. The central issues included the creation of key positions, professional development, and implementation of structural changes. Table 9.1 outlines the key positions created by the district. The key positions in the district were created to provide support to personnel. The new positions included the following: deputy superintendent, associate principal, facilitator, and director for staff development.

With regards to the term structure, for the purposes of this study, Hipp and Huffman, define structures in the following manner, it "includes

TABLE 9.1 Positions Created		
Position Name	**Assignment**	**Role Description**
Deputy Superintendent	CO	Oversees all transformation efforts across the district
Associate Principal	HS	Teacher Coach
Facilitator	MS and Elem.	Teacher Coach
Director for Staff Development	CO	Coordinates staff development for the district

Note: Central Office (CO); High Schools (HS); Middle School (MS); Elementary (Elem.)

TABLE 9.2 Type of Change/Structure	
Tool and/or Structure	**Type of Change**
Site Based Decision Making Committees	Structural
PLC Meetings	Structural
District Exec Improvement Com (DEIC)	Structural
Extravaganza	Structural
Additional Support Personnel	Structural
All Collaborative Team Meetings	Structural
System of Support	Structural
Surveys	Structural
OHI (Organizational Health Inventory)	Structural
PLC Agenda	Structural
Assistant Principal Academies	Structural
Principal's Institute	Structural

systems (i.e., communication and technology) and resources (i.e., personnel, facilities, time, fiscal, and materials) to enable staff to meet and examine practices and student outcomes (2010c, p. 13). Twelve structural changes were either introduced or modified. See Table 9.2 for the different tools or structures imbedded into the district.

The district implemented a variety of structures to promote teacher and administrator collaboration, improve conversations, promote staff learning, and promote the use of data to inform decisions.

Another major finding, included professional development, specifically, job-embedded professional development took place via collaborative team meetings, which were populated by different interest groups from across the district. Professional learning also took place within structural supports—such as PLC meetings, assistant principal academies and so forth. See Table 9.3 for additional examples of where learning took place.

It is important to note that even though meeting times were scheduled for professionals to collaborate across the district, Talbert shares that getting together does not ensure the right type of conversations happen (2010). Thus, the district approached this issue by repurposing collaborative meetings and structuring conversations.

The superintendent's intentional leadership to develop key positions, job-embedded professional development and structural supports that encouraged collaboration, shared personal practice, and shared leadership were crucial steps in the implementation and sustainability of a PLC.

In summary, a specific number of key themes surfaced from the research: (a) PLC work influenced the development of Hord's 5 dimensions of a PLC to varying degrees, (b) the district is at the implementation phase of the

TABLE 9.3   SCISD Collaborative Team Meetings

Name	Assignment	Meeting Time	Description
South Central Learning Community (SCLC)	Central Office	Monthly	Collaborative Structure to build capacity in Central Office and Campus Administrators
Counselor Meetings	Central Office	Monthly	Central Office Contact person organizes meetings for district wide collaboration
Librarian Meetings	Central Office	Monthly	Central Office Contact person organizes meetings for district wide collaboration
Principal Meetings	Central Office	Monthly	Central Office Contact person organizes meetings for district wide collaboration
Grade Level Meetings (PLC Time)	Campus	Varies	Campus Level Collaborative Structure
LASER Team	High Schools	Varies	Assist in collaborative efforts at High Schools

Note: Leader's Achieving Superior Educational Results (LASER) teams consist of a member from each department at the comprehensive high schools. LASER teams include up to 15 members that meet daily and monthly with district support staff to collaborate.

change process, (c) the superintendent played a key role in PLC implementation through his understanding and use of a change model, and (d) archival data noted changes in student achievement scores throughout PLC implementation. Overall, the findings suggest that the implementation of structural changes influenced the development of a culture of learning and collaboration in the district.

PLCs are not an improvement program, but rather a structure for schools to improve staff by building capacity for learning and change (Hord, 2004; Tongeri & Anderson, 2003). Central office, principals, teachers, and other professional staff in schools and districts with established PLCs put learning first before achievement and testing, and student achievement improves as a consequence (Stoll & Louis, 2007). It is process, not programs, that makes a positive difference in sustaining the dimensions of a PLC (Abrego & Pankake, 2011).

REFERENCES

Abrego, J., & Pankake, A. M. (2011). The district-wide sustainability of a professional learning community during leadership changes at the superintendency level. *Adminisitrative Issues Journal, 1*(1), 3–13.

Drago-Severson, E. (2012). *Helping educators grow: Strategies and practices for leadership development.* Cambridge, MA: Harvard Education.

DuFour, R., DuFour, R. B., & Eaker, R. E. (2008). *Revisiting professional learning communities at work: New insights for improving schools.* Bloomington, IN: Solution Tree.

Eaker, R., & Keating, J. (2009) Deeply embedded, fully committed. *National Staff Development Council, 30*(5), 50–55.

Evans, L. M., Thornton, B., & Usinger, J. (2012). Theoretical frameworks to guide school improvement. *NASSP Bulletin, 96*(2), 154–171. doi:10.1177/01926365 12444714

Fullan, M. (2005). Professional learning communities writ large. In R. DuFour, R. E. Eaker, & R. B. DuFour (Eds.), *On common ground: The power of professional learning communities* (pp. 209–223). Bloomington, IN: National Educational Service.

Fullan, M. (2007). *The new meaning of educational change.* New York, NY: Teachers College Press.

Hipp, K. K., & Huffman, J. B. (2010a). *Demystifying professional learning communities: School leadership at its best.* Lanham, MD: Rowman & Littlefield Education.

Hipp, K. K., & Huffman, J. B. (2010b). Demystifying the concept of professional learning communities. In K. K. Hipp & J. B. Huffman (Eds.), *Demystifying professional learning communities: School leadership at its best.* Lanham, MD: Rowman & Littlefield Education.

Hipp, K. K., & Huffman, J. B. (2010c). Methodology and conceptual framework. In J. B. Huffman & K. K. Hipp (Eds.), *Demystifying professional learning communities: School leadership at its best* (pp. 23–28). Lanham, MD: Rowman & Littlefield Education.

Honig, M. I. (2012). District central office leadership as teaching: How central office administrators support principals' development as instructional leaders. *Educational Administration Quarterly, 48*(4), 733–774.

Hord, S. M. (1997). *Professional learning communities communities of continuous inquiry and improvement.* Austin, TX: Southwest Educational Development Laboratory.

Hord, S. M. (Ed.). (2004). *Learning together, leading together: Changing schools through professional learning communities.* New York, NY: Teachers College Columbia.

Hord, S. M., & Roussin, J. L. (2013). *Implementing change through learning: Concerns-based concepts, tools, and strategies for guiding change.* Thousand Oaks, CA: Corwin.

Hord, S. M., & Sommers, W. A. (2008). *Leading professional learning communities: Voices from research and practice.* Thousand Oaks, CA: Corwin Press.

Horton, J., & Martin, B. N. (2013). The role of the district administration within professional learning communities. *International Journal of Leadership in Education, 16*(1), 55–70.

Huffman, J. B., & Hipp, K. K. (2003). *Reculturing schools as professional learning communities.* Landham, MD: Scarecrow Education.

Hurley, B. (2006). Learning on the job: The education of a school board president in shared leadership. *Yearbook of the National Society for Study of Education, 105*(1), 107–198.

Lopez, J. (2015). *Professional learning communities and school culture: A case study in district-wide implementation of a PLC* (Doctoral dissertation). University of

Texas, Brownsville, TX. Retrieved from https://utrgv-ir.tdl.org/utrgv-ir/handle/2152.6/693?show=full

Nelson, T. (2009). Teachers' collaborative inquiry and professional growth: Should we be optimistic? *Science Education, 93*(3), 548–580. doi:10.1002/sce.20302

Ostmeyer, C. J. (2003). Professional learning community characteristics: A study from a district perspective (Doctoral dissertation). Texas A&M University, Commerce, TX. Available from ProQuest Information and Learning Company. (UMI No. 3094635)

Pankake, A. M. (1998). *Implementation: Making things happen.* Larchmont, NY: Eye of Education.

Pankake, A., & Abrego, J. (2012). Building capacity: The foundation of developing others. In A. Pankake and E. Murakami-Ramalho (Eds.), *Educational leaders encouraging the intellectual and professional capacity of others* (pp. 3–23). Charlotte, NC: Information Age.

Pruitt, M. E. (2013). *Central office administrators' perceptions of the professional learning community process.* Denton, TX: UNT Digital Library. Retrieved from http://digital.library.unt.edu/ark:/67531/metadc283851/

Rubin, R., Abrego, M. H., & Sutterby, J. A. (2015). *Less is more in elementary schools: Strategies for thriving in a high-stakes environment.* New York, NY: Routledge.

Stoll, L., & Louis, K. S. (2007). Professional learning communities: Elaborating new approaches. In L. Stoll & K. S. Louis (Eds.), *Professional learning communities: Divergence, depth and dilemmas.* New York, NY: Open University Press.

Supovitz, J. A. (2006). *The case for district-based reform: Leading, building, and sustaining school improvement.* Cambridge, MA: Harvard Education Press.

Talbert, J. E. (2010). Professional learning communities at the crossroads: How systems hinder or engender change. In A. Hargreaves, A. Lieberman, M. Fullan & D. Hopkins (Eds.), *Second international handbook of educational change* (Vol. 23, pp. 555–571). New York, NY: Springer.

Tongeri, W., & Anderson, S. E. (2003). *Beyond islands of excellence: What district can do to improve instruction and achievement in all schools.* Washington, DC: Learning First Alliance. Retrieved from http://files.eric.ed.gov/fulltext/ED475875.pdf

Wells, C., & Feun, L. (2007). Implementing of learning community principles: A study of six high schools. *NASSP Bulletin, 91*(2), 141–160.

X CHROMOSOME IN A Y-DOMINANT WORLD

What Could Possibly Go Wrong?

Barbara Qualls
Stephen F. Austin State University

Let her sleep
For when she wakes
She will move mountains.

—Napoleon Bonaparte

Who would have thought that Napoleon was a closet feminist? Today, there are so many legal and social protections for different classes of people that it is difficult to imagine that discrimination of just about any kind could slide by unnoticed. Indeed, Title IX is a strong shield against discrimination on the basis of sex, but *all* civil rights law can be invoked in fighting the good fight for women. Even though there is a wealth of statutory law, judicial action, and changing sociopolitical attitudes, there still remains both hard and soft sex discrimination when women dare to lead.

A surface level consideration of the business of education would seem to render it fertile ground for women and leadership. After all, a huge majority of teachers are women. Most leadership positions in education presume

The Contemporary Superintendent, pages 169–179
Copyright © 2019 by Information Age Publishing
All rights of reproduction in any form reserved.

and require teaching experience, which also requires education licensure. Thus, the leadership candidate pool should be proportionally skewed with women members. Because public school is a branch of government and controlled by governmental labor law, salary schedules and employment benefits programs are designed in compliance with nondiscriminatory law. With all those advantages, why is it even a point of discussion about difficulties women face in *educational* leadership positions?

For an entirely different set of reasons and sociological phenomena, the fields of higher education research and think-tank institutional research, like public school, also have more women practitioners than men. While there is compelling empirical evidence that women are, indeed, discriminated against in public school leadership acquisition, there also is a lot written about it, in part because there are women researchers who notice and care. This chapter will first examine some generally held positions concerning women in the CEO (superintendent) position in schools. Next, the voices of women who actually hold superintendent positions will speak through some selected qualitative research. Last, the political role of the superintendent, regardless of sex, will be considered, with some application about how execution of the role may be approached differently by women. In each section, the specific experiences of the writer will be used as a filter for the examination.

I consider the 14 years that I served as superintendent of three different Texas school districts to be the culmination of a public school career that few women get to experience. My family was not poor, but education was not highly prized and I was not encouraged to pursue even college, much less graduate degrees and male-dominant leadership positions. As a result, I can see now that the social upheaval of the 1960s and early 1970s was probably more influential than any other factor in making me believe that I could do or be most anything I wanted. That is why I chose a male-dominant teaching field and did not hesitate to continue into equally male-dominant public school administration. My own reflection on sex discrimination—and actually being aware of experiencing it—did not occur until the superintendent years. My superintendent leadership career included three different schools. The first was a small rural district that struggled with financial challenges. The second was a small but growing very wealthy district in an outer suburb of a metropolitan area. The third was a large district, also in an outer suburb of another metropolitan area, but with a strong community identity so that it operates in the manner of a small independent city.

WOMEN IN LEADERSHIP POSITIONS

The numerical disparity between female and male superintendents is undeniable, but why that disparity exists has many different explanations. Shepard

(2000) believes that women "may be their own worst enemies" in that women tend to appear to accept discrimination or negative attitudes without sufficiently robust rebuttal. She describes a pattern of discrimination and negative attitudes toward women in leadership positions held by the individuals who have the power to select or promote women for leadership. While not exactly "blaming the victim," Shepard contends that women fail to persist or present a strong enough effort to overcome that discrimination. Another area identified as a barrier is the socialization/gender role pattern traditionally held by women. A basic example of this barrier might be something as simple as golf clubs, hunting groups, men's sports teams, and an overall pattern of male grouping that includes formal membership, as well as mutual interests and goals. Women and girls' groups are generally less formal and more fluid. That argument may be oversimplified but does hold some promise for explaining the difference between the socialization patterns of men and women, when either men or women aspire to leadership roles.

In addition to these barriers for women superintendents, Shepard cited what she observed as lack of aspiration or motivation among women, lack of networks or support systems that are as strong as those of men, and finally, an absence of persistence to overcome barriers. Actually, Shepard's work tends to fall into two main areas: There is embedded discrimination against women in educational leadership caused by attitudes of both men and women, but women do not push against those attitudes with enough vigor to cause transformative change. An entirely different way of looking at women's experiences as superintendents is that they just prepare for leadership in a different way from men, and that the women's way may be better.

The AASA (American Association of School Administrators) conducts periodic studies about the state of the superintendency. Attention to the state of women in the superintendency generated a seven-point set of reasons posited by Thomas Glass (2000) about why the numerical disparity between male and female superintendents exists. Each of the points is a generality and individual superintendents probably have singular back stories, but his conclusions are generalizable and are based on extensive nationwide data from the turn of the twentieth century:

1. *Women are not in positions that normally lead to the superintendency* (p. 28). Glass' argument has to do with the prevalence of men as high school principals, women as elementary principals. Another compelling observation (not made by Glass) is the path to leadership that frequently comes through successful athletic coaching positions.

2. *Women are not gaining superintendent's credentials in preparation programs* (p. 29). Glass no doubt found this to be true, but it is likely that the intervening years have erased this argument.

3. *Women are not as experienced or interested in district-wide fiscal manage-ment as men* (p. 29). One possible explanation is that women who "like" math or numbers become private sector accountants or math teachers.

4. *Women are not interested in the superintendency for personal reasons* (p. 29). Because women are still most frequently primary caregivers for children, Glass' argument has face validity.

5. *School boards are reluctant to hire women superintendents* (p. 30). There will be discussion of the male-dominated school board system later, but Glass' work underscored boards' prejudice against women as inferior managers of fiscal, safety, and construction systems.

6. *Women enter the field of education for different purposes than men* (p. 31). The option of upward mobility for women in education is not a *new* concept, but it is more likely that women enter education in order to teach, and the aspiration for leadership comes later.

7. *Women enter education administration too late* (p. 31). The traditional career path includes classroom teacher, assistant principal, princi-pal, and central office position. If any of these stops along the way are extended, there may not be sufficient time to pursue a superin-tendent position.

While all seven of the Glass (2000) points are frequently cited, refuted, and discussed by education leadership practitioners, there are other reasons that may be equally important (Kelsey, Allen, Coke, & Ballard, 2014). These include the inability or unwillingness to relocate, absence of training for the school boards that hire superintendents, and the "glass ceiling effect" (Dana & Bourisaw, 2006). Ten years after Shepard's work and Glass's seven points, Brunner and Kim (2010) concluded that women superintendents had better academic preparation than their male counterparts and that the career arcs of women were more varied than those of men, a point which contributed to the better preparation exhibited by women. Better and more varied preparation may not be enough to actually get hired, though. Dana and Bourisaw (2006) concluded that embedded sexism in hiring practices exists both in boards and in search firms. Although there are scattered examples of diversity, elected boards and search firms are heavily White/male dominant. Unless there is a calculated effort to avoid stereotypical hiring, it is likely that both boards and search firms gravitate toward White/male superintendent candidates.

My Own Back Story on Leadership Positions

While all the research findings and observations make clear sense to me and I am acquainted with other women who could be the poster girls for the kinds of discrimination described, I did not experience overt discrimination in the preparation process, in the career arc leading to the superintendency, or in the hiring process. That may be because I chose a male-dominant teaching field—high school band director—and started my entire public school career with an I-am-the-only-one-of-my-kind attitude. Indeed, I met my first "other" female high school band director 3 years after I started teaching. During academic preparation, there were more women than men in my doctoral and superintendent program. Attrition was high, though, and more women than men dropped out. By the time of graduation, the male/female numbers were equal. For a unique set of reasons, I did not face discrimination in hiring, but I am keenly aware of many women who did. The single identification I found with the set of points from Glass was the last one—starting an administration career late. Because my teaching career was enormously rewarding and generated a higher salary than classroom teaching, I chose to stay in it for a longer period of time than most educators who aspire to leadership roles. Once into administration, though, I moved quickly in the field and also continued to serve for several years past the traditional retirement age.

WHAT DO WOMEN SUPERINTENDENTS SAY ABOUT DISCRIMINATION OR SEXISM?

Practitioners from every civil rights protected class are fair game for research study. Because discrimination against women is frequently couched in sexual predation or limited career mobility, women superintendents are "heard" clearly in the literature, though perhaps less so by political and legislative change makers. In fact, there is a name for the circular process of identifying, studying, recommending, then repeating the cycle again and again: echo chamber effect. However, there is always the chance that the collective voices of women superintendents will join with the research and lead to transformation. Kelsey et al. (2014) asked twenty Texas female superintendents to describe their experience, using open-ended questions. The respondents were representative of a range of ages, years of experience, school size, and career path. The first question was about preparation for the superintendency, networking and identification. Most of the respondents indicated that the idea of being a superintendent came well into their career, not as an initial goal. They formed networks and found collegial identification through somewhat formal routes, such as regional service centers and professional organizations. Other trend answers included the importance of staying current in the field and practicing servant leadership. The second question was about helping other women in leadership. Although there was more variation in the second set of answers than the first, all respondents felt a deep responsibility to help younger women. The most frequently mentioned methods to do so were by serving as a role model and by offering women on their staffs opportunities for decision-making and leadership practice. The third and final set of questions was about balancing between career and family. The common ground answer was that a supportive spouse and/or waiting to begin their superintendency until their children were older were important factors in their success. A significant number of respondents mentioned the importance of their faith. All the respondents reported that even though the conversation about the need for women in leadership has been in play for over 50 years, that stereotypes, the "good old boy" system, and conflict with the goals of their school system all continued to be barriers for women both in acquiring a superintendent position and in succeeding once hired.

An earlier Texas-based study (Dobie & Hummel, 2001) had revealed similar results—that women superintendents are academically well prepared, are influenced by their faith, and believe in the importance of a good mentor. One significant difference, though, and one that offers some evidence that the "message" about capable women superintendents is achieving an audience outside the echo chamber, is that Dobie and Hummel's participants in 2001 were either silent about (or denied) having personal ambition to rise in the leadership ranks and were likewise silent (or denied) having experienced gender bias. By the time Kelsey et al. conducted their work in 2014, there was also evidence that the highly gender-specific categories of Glass and Dobie and Hummel's silent or denying women superintendents were diminishing.

While women superintendents generally are well prepared, collaborative, and perhaps are spiritual, they still encounter some performance barriers that may not plague men. One of those is having a comfortable relationship with power. Certainly, raw power is less pervasive than observers might assume—superintendents respond to a wide spectrum of stakeholders, all of whom claim slices of the power that may appear to rest with the superintendent. Katz (2006) studied women superintendents in several states and found that the respondents are both reluctant and uncharacteristically at a loss for words in discussing power. Clearly, to achieve both longevity and success, a woman superintendent must have more than a casual relationship with the use of power, but equally clearly, that usage appears to be intuitive. One respondent said that if "you're in this position for the power, you're deluded because you don't have any." Further into her response, she clarified that sometimes the position and title are confused with actual power. A pervasive finding for Katz was that her respondents felt that shared power or delegated power helped to increase their own sphere of influence. While the women respondents had some difficulty in articulating a clear definition of power, they did recognize its existence, as well as the necessity of managing power and the way others in their organizations viewed their use of it.

It has been mentioned several times by researchers that women superintendents, while being quite verbal and sophisticated communicators, are silent in some areas and have difficulty in articulation in others. Skrla, Reyes, and Scheurich (2000) found another area where that reticence is evident: the silence of the school administration profession concerning sexism and discrimination toward women superintendents. Her methodology for examination of this phenomena was a very focused interview of three former superintendents. "Former" was an intentional, not convenience, consideration because all three participants said that their answers were considerably different than they would have been as a practicing superintendent. In general, the duality of their roles surfaced frequently. For example, they all agreed that there were many cases where board members or staff members behaved toward them in a manner that would never have happened had they been a man. Other examples centered on doubt about their capacity, interest or ability—simply because they were women. Concrete examples of those were situations such as questioning decisions about areas traditionally not considered areas of strength for women: finance, construction, politics, security. The duality was exhibited in another way: expectation of femininity and male-type toughness at the same time. The examples given were generally about the frustration of trying to meet both kinds of expectation. If they behaved in a decisive, responsible manner that indicated being in charge, that attitude was interpreted as unfeminine. They felt that the same behavior in a man would be praised. Similarly, attempts to build consensus was interpreted as indecision and absence of leadership.

As former superintendents, the respondents spoke freely, but acknowledged that during their time in the position, they were complicit in personal silence on the topic of sex discrimination. They offered reasons for that silence such as wanting to be "better than that" or "above that," but admitted that their silence may also have been because they simply did not want to confront the issue. In addition to personal silence, there was also silence from the preparation programs that they had used to acquire academic training and silence from the professional organizations on which they were dependent for identity, collegial experiences, and professional support. Not surprisingly, when given opportunity to suggest solutions to the problems of sexism and silence, the respondents said that the issues should be discussed and examined by the preparation programs and professional organizations.

My Own Back Story on Discrimination or Sexism

I definitely experienced sexism in all three schools where I served as superintendent. In the first school, the in-place male administrative staff members were very hostile, both due to simple sexism as well as because two of the three had applied for the top job themselves. I sometimes suspected that I was hired so that the board would not have to make a choice between the two hometown men. In addition, the board was heavily skewed with male members. There were frequent events of attempted physical intimidation such as refusal to sit so that they were always taller than me, requests for coffee or some other chore that put me in a subservient role. In the second school, the sexism was overt, but was intellectual and, at least, based on political and values differences. The community and board were extremely conservative and my progressive liberal politics, while not militant, were known. The third school had two male board members who had singular and personal issues with me that *might* not have happened with a man. One had an ongoing personal and business conflict with city government and wanted to exploit the political weight of the school district in that battle, and expected me to be his spokesperson for that effort. Another board member was a former district employee who had expected a salary increase that did not happen, so came to the board with a personal grudge. In all three schools, the initial board that hired me was a different group than the board with which I had conflict. As will be examined later, a truly board-savvy superintendent will continue to build new relationships as board membership fluctuates. Unfortunately, my experience did not allow that to happen as the new membership and the resulting hostility was predicated on political decisions made by the old membership.

SUPERINTENDENT–BOARD RELATIONSHIP: IT *IS* DIFFERENT FOR WOMEN

Skrla's (Skrla, Reyes, & Scheurich, 2000) silent preparation programs and professional organizations are often equally silent on the general topic of Superintendent–Board relationships. There are shelves and shelves of material about collaboration, teamwork, empowerment, and even how to dissolve the relationship, but not so much about how to mend broken ones. As a rule, how-to material is generated by organizations that represent either superintendents or boards, and that affiliation colors the direction of the material produced. One example is the Texas Association of School Board's Team of Eight Training. While it sounds good and *is* good when there is no fundamental conflict, the reality is that the "team of eight" is made up of seven elected, unpaid non-educators and one appointed, salaried professional. The seven choose, pay, evaluate, retain, or terminate the one. That is not a team. Maeroff (2010) had an interesting position: that the encroachment of federal regulations, NCLB, Title programs, state law, finance restrictions, licensure and employment policy, and judicial activism at all levels, has dissolved the capacity for meaningful governance at the local level. Exponential growth in the involvement of state and federal government in decision-making in schools, including serious intrusions of judicial action, have changed the way local school boards function. Members who originally sought their public service position in order to impact within a narrow personal political plank—often to lower taxes, pass a bond, fire a coach, name a school—are often disappointed to find that the capacity to push through their intent is severely curtailed by actual rules of law that are not commonly known in the community. Some boards start with a level of dysfunctionality, simply because of that disconnect between members' intent and capacity. Maeroff (2010) uses the explanation of the "mirage of local control" to describe the position of modern board: prestigious in a symbolic way, disappointing to those who had hoped to accomplish a narrow goal. That disconnect between expectation and reality may contribute to the fragility of the board–superintendent bond. An extension of that might be that with the narrowing of real authority of the local school board for decision-making, there is a tendency for boards to focus too much energy or attention on an area they *do* still manage—the superintendent.

That is a glass half-empty approach, though. It is possible to forge a positive and productive relationship between superintendent and board. Thompson (2014) found that there is a significant difference in perceptions of board presidents and superintendents concerning their working relationship and that of the board. Although Thompson did not factor the sex of the superintendent, he still found differences in superintendent–board perceptions. In the population studied, there was also a significant difference between the educational level and experience level of the board president and their superintendents. Thompson did not try to draw inferences based on that variable, but rather pointed out its existence. He also found that there frequently is a reluctance to deal with board–superintendent conflict in the spirit of solving relationship problems.

Skrla's (Skrla et al., 2000) respondents who found silent professional organizations concerning superintendent role issues did not credit Paul Houston and Doug Eadie for their efforts to define, advise, and inform the general area of superintendent–board relationships. While she is correct that there is little help specifically geared for the problems faced by women superintendents, it is safe to assume that both Houston and Eadie hold the belief that their advice, if followed, is effective for male or female, any ethnicity, any age. Both Houston, a former executive director of the American Association of School Administrators, and Eadie, a national board-CEO consultant and contributor to the *American School Board Journal,* gear their essays on advice for their constituents. That advice is universal and is not sex-specific, but if followed scrupulously by board and by superintendents, conflict caused by sex differences would be minimized.

Being an effective public school superintendent is a precarious job (Houston & Eadie, 2002), regardless of gender, but being a woman adds another layer of challenge. Houston and Eadie refer to the relationship between a superintendent and their board as a "precious but fragile bond" and that the holders of both the board member positions and superintendent are ambitious, high-achieving, strong-willed Type A personalities, thus making it likely that the "precious but fragile bond" can erode quickly when under planned or undermanaged.

Even with an evolving definition of local control, there is great capacity to do more if the superintendent and board can find appropriate common ground. Effective superintendents may be described by what they are not: not defensive, not operating in damage control, not bemoaning meddlesome board members (Eadie, 2009). It is essential to recognize the innate conflict between the board's ends-focused work and the superintendent's means-focused function. Indeed, finding the fulcrum point in expectation, responsibility, and collaboration should open a new opportunity for achievement rarely recognized in modern board–superintendent relationships.

My Own Back Story on Superintendent–Board Relationship

While I certainly have less than pleasant memories of skirmishes with individual board members, the relationships with the board presidents that I dealt with were almost all exceptionally strong. In fact, several times, the relationship became a friendship that may have seemed exclusionary to other board members. While very rewarding at the time, if I had the same experience to do again, I would probably wait until the president left board membership to allow the personal friendship to develop. I definitely agree with Maeroff's (2010) conclusion that federal and state restrictions make local control something of a mirage. For that reason, it takes a very special, humble, and open individual with a strong servant-leadership orientation to be a successful and happy board member. Since those qualities and characteristics are never seen as campaign planks or slogans on yard signs for board member candidates in elections, it is safe to assume that the inherent conflict between boards and superintendents will likely continue, but with care and mutual effort, a productive relationship can be formed. And researchers will continue to have material.

REFERENCES

Brunner, C. C., & Kim, Y. L. (2010). Are women prepared to be school superintendents? An essay on the myths and misunderstandings. *Journal of Research on Leadership Education, 5*(8), 276–309.

Dana, J. A., & Bourisaw, D. M. (2006). *Women in the superintendency: Discarded leadership.* Lanham, MD: Rowman & Littlefield Education.

Dobie, D. F., & Hummel, B. (2001). Successful women superintendents in a gender-biased profession. *Equity & Excellence in Education, 34*(2), 22–28.

Eadie, D. (2009). The partnership tango. *American School Board Journal, 196*(12), 42–43.

Glass, T. E. (2000). Where are all the women superintendents? AASA's latest study of the profession suggests seven reasons why female members still lag in top district posts. *The School Administrator, 57*(6), 28–32.

Houston, P., & Eadie, D. (2002). The board-savvy superintendent. Lanham, MD: Scarecrow Press.

Katz, S. J. (2006). Influencing others: Women superintendents speak (reluctantly) about power. *Journal of Women in Educational Leadership, 4*(2), 103–111.

Kelsey, C., Allen, K., Coke, K., & Ballard, G. (2014). Lean in and lift up: Female superintendents share their career path choices. *Journal of Case Studies in Education, 7,* 1–11.

Maeroff, G. (2010). School boards in America: A flawed exercise in democracy. New York, NY: Palgrave Macmillan.

Shepard, I. S. (2000). Barriers to women entering administration: Do they still exist? Is there the will to overcome? In A. Pankake, G. Scroth, & C. Funk (Eds.), *Women as school executives: the complete picture* (pp. 176–184). Austin, Texas: Texas Council of Women School Executives.

Skrla, L., Reyes, P., & Scheurich, J. J. (2000). Sexism, silence, and solution: Women superintendents speak up and out. *Educational Administration Quarterly, 36*(1), 44–75.

Thompson, R. (2014). The superintendent and school board relationship: Functioning as a group. *International Journal of Organizational Innovation, 7*(1), 69–77.

CHAPTER 11

LIKE FATHER, LIKE SON

Superintendents Mentoring for Success Through Fictive Kinship Community

Rhonda Baynes Jeffries
University of South Carolina

J. R. Falor Green
Fairfield County School District
Winnsboro, SC

I hope you grow up to become that everythin' you can be
That's all I wanted for you, young'n, like father, like son
But in the end I hope you only turn out better than me
I hope you know I love you, young'n, like father, like son
—Taylor, Smith, and Best (2005)

Contrary to popular misconceptions about Black fathers and their relationships with their sons; the preceding lyrics commemorate the birth of
gangsta rapper and actor Jayceon Taylor's (The Game) son and signify his
hopes that mirror most parents' dreams for their children. The salient literature suggests that Black fathers are not positively engaged with their sons
due to multiple obstacles and that there are ways to create more impactful

The Contemporary Superintendent, pages 181–196
Copyright © 2019 by Information Age Publishing
All rights of reproduction in any form reserved.

connections between Black fathers and sons (Caldwell et al., 2014; Coates & Phares, 2014; Perry, Harmon, & Leeper, 2012). Furthermore, this research presents evidence that interaction with fathers/father figures improves Black males' academic and social experience in schools.

A significant number of factors influence the achievement gap among Black males as the systemic inequalities existing among home, school, and community life for this demographic group of students converges (Lofton & Davis, 2015). Fragmentation of the Black family unit is noteworthy considering Black children are more likely than their racial contemporaries to live in a family arrangement that does not include two parents (Vespa, Lewis, & Kreider, 2013). Academic performance for Black males presented lower for on-time graduation rates at 47% compared to 78% for White males (Schott Foundation for Public Education, 2010); and the achievement gap for Grade 12 reading and math is wider in 2015 than in 1992 for Black students compared to White students (Kena et al., 2016). Furthermore, home based risk factors contributing to the persistence of low achievement among Black males may not be easily eliminated, but can certainly be addressed with proven interventions constructed around creating positive and caring communities within schools (Fantuzzoa, LeBoeufa, Rouseb, & Chenc, 2012). School-based communities that rely on the notion of fictive kinship broaden opportunities for Black male students to build relationships with individuals who may mentor and are invested in their success in and beyond their educational experiences.

These social catastrophes including institutional racism and the school to prison pipeline are among the specific factors that impede many Black fathers from assuming a more active and engaged role in their son's lives. Regardless of race, many fathers tend to rely on mothers/mother figures to enact the primary role of caregiver, manage educational pursuits, and troubleshoot for their children (Kim & Hill, 2015). Allen and White-Smith (2014) examined the persistent culture in schools that supports a pipeline to prison for Black males that was nationally identified in the historical Children's Defense Fund (1975) study on school suspension. Studies of this nature noted in particular the attitudes and dispositions of classroom and administrative educators having a large impact on the perpetuation of this damaging cultural practice. Additionally, these studies highlight the disproportionate rate at which Black males who live in lower socioeconomic households are the most frequently targeted individuals suffering at the hands of practices that channel students away from schools into punitive settings. After 40 years of exploring this phenomenon, the problem persists and existing school structures and relationships appear ineffective at providing relief.

The historical dissolution of the Black family in the United States as a result of chattel bondage required the institutionalization of fictive kinship relations. Chatters, Taylor, and Jayakody (1994) reviewed the development of fictive kin associations in the African American community and noted the significance of this relationship structure to augment missing links and resources that exist in Black families and communities. Likewise, the systemic criminalization of Black males in schools through suspensions and expulsions demands the use of alternative structures and relationships to address the divide between Black males' educational needs and what they actually receive. The exclusion of Black male educators as role models in the school setting is exacerbated by the unreasonably high rate of incarceration experienced by Black fathers. While Black males may not or cannot perform fatherhood using a traditional White male model, Black fathers often ensure the well-being of their children by accessing kinship networks with extended family or non-family individuals who receive the honor and fulfill the expectations of blood related family members (Roy & Vesely, 2009).

The theoretical frameworks for this study include critical race theory to deconstruct the achievement gap phenomenon among Black males (Delgado & Stefancic, 2001; Price, 2010; Zuberi, 2011); and theories of fictive kinship to understand the significance of superintendents who sanctioned communities in schools as a means of reform (Cook, 2010; Stack, 1974). Focused on providing collective support to encourage Black males to meet high expectations, superintendents in this study developed Bow Tie Clubs at high schools in each superintendent's district. The Bow Tie Club concept, based on the work of Benjamin Mays, includes the mission that each participating Black male will be: (a) well read, (b) well spoken, (c) well dressed, (d) well traveled, and (e) well balanced. The clubs provide the structure and resources to enable Black male educators in leadership positions to design a replicable program that advocates on behalf of their students' academic and complimentary nonacademic needs. Understanding that the level of support needed to close the achievement gap does not occur through any other school programming, the responsibility ultimately resides with the chief instructional leader, the school superintendent.

This chapter explores the impact that school district superintendents may have on creating and sustaining school-community based environments that harness the power of parental influence for Black males. The guiding research question explored the theoretical and practical responses of Black male superintendents in the state of South Carolina to the persistent achievement gap experienced by Black male students. The study examined the impact of Black male superintendents' experiences in the creation of programs that garner resources intended to bolster the academic performance of Black male students in particular. The study's outcomes suggest that Black male superintendents bring a unique level of understanding to this influential leadership position. In the case of the study participants, their personal and professional perspectives give them unique insight to assist with the development of effective strategies for addressing the academic needs of Black male students and reducing the level of jeopardy in which our current society places them.

CONTEXTUALIZING COMPLIMENTARY COMMUNITIES FOR BLACK MALES

Howard (2013) thoroughly reviewed the state of education for Black male students and effectively deconstructed the institutional, as opposed to individual, deficits that negatively impact Black male academic success. The call for a paradigm shift in this study converges on the precept that despite statistical outcome measures indicating failure and negative cultural perceptions that govern the daily treatment of Black male students in schools, they are capable of succeeding on a large scale given appropriate supports. Appropriate supports need to include what Bourdieu (1977) defined as cultural capital. This term indicates the overall cultural practices including beliefs, behaviors, preferences, experiences, verbal patterns, and formal and informal knowledge that is generationally shared among families and close associations (Macleod, 2008). With the preponderance of Black males to live in homes where gendered knowledge may not be readily available, alternative models of support are critical to successfully close the achievement gap that persists among Black male students.

A comparative study of Black fathers in South Africa and the United States demonstrated that individuals functioning in kinship roles were able to provide culturally appropriate supports to young Black males who were living without the traditional father figure in their homes. The similarities between the two settings, including racial discrimination, high levels of incarceration, health disparities, and economic disenfranchisement provide a compelling argument for the replication of fictive kinship networks to sustain Black males who are overwhelmingly victimized by institutional injustices (Madhavan & Roy, 2012). African-centered methods are a compelling basis for a Black male mentoring program founded on the concept of umoja, the Swahili term for unity. Watson, Washington, and Stepteau-Watson (2015) noted promising school and community based initiative created to stimulate positive self-esteem, increase academic achievement, and destroy the school to prison pipeline. An intensive curriculum teaches traditional African drumming, introduces African art, and uses African based communication styles to engage young Black males in a mentoring experience with which they identify.

The impact of kinship roles in mentoring programs cannot be underestimated and were shown to have a strong relationship with grade outcomes for Black students in under resourced schools. Convincing data from the research of Biggs, Musewe, and Harvey (2014) reported higher grades in mathematics, reading, and science for middles school students who interacted with comprehensive mentoring programs that included academic and social supports as compared to programs solely focused on academic achievement. The research collectively indicates a significant relationship between mentoring programs that effectively address the needs of students in and out of the school setting.

Complementary associations between district superintendents and school personnel may prove critical in addressing the needs of Black males. According to Ellis, Rowley, Nellum, and Smith (2015) positive perceptions about race were strong predictors of Black males' success in school. When Black male students were not associated with detrimental stereotypes, they lived up to the belief that others professed about them. This research advocates for strong mentoring programs designed and administered by educators who understand the barriers typically experienced by Black males and the most effective ways to overcome them to achieve academic success.

METHODS

This chapter utilized individual interviews and focus group interactions to determine and produce the data set for this research project. The participants were initially chosen as the premier source of valid perspectives to explore the strategies specifically considered effective by Black male superintendents who have targeted the amelioration of Black male underachievement in their districts. School superintendents are viewed as having high stakes investment in the overall achievement of students in a district and the individual held responsible for academic failure. What makes this participant group unique is the cultural struggles experienced by Black male superintendents who report feelings of fear that highlighting disaggregated data that reveals the achievement gap that rest with Black male students at its widest point may spark public discord in their districts or even result in the termination of their appointments (Sherman & Grogan, 2003). This sample of superintendents were willing to share their efforts to rise above the fear and risk their professional security to challenge the general complacency that produced and preserves Black male underachievement.

There is a high concentration of Black superintendents in the participants' state with 25% of districts in the state employing a Black district leader in comparison to Black superintendent representation at 2.5% nationwide. In a state with a total of 10 Black male superintendents, four from this group were purposively selected to participate in the study. Representing

TABLE 11.1 Overview of the Participants				
Participant	District Facilities	Student Enrollment	Student Demographics	Unique Dimensions
Superintendent District One	28 elementary 9 middle 8 distinct centers 7 secondary	22,695	73% Black 19% White 8% Other	Largest district led by Black male
Superintendent District Two	2 elementary 2 middle 1 secondary	1,636	68% Black 29% White 3% Latin@	Achievement Gap success
Superintendent District Three	8 elementary 3 middle 3 distinct centers 2 secondary	9,178	40% Black 47% White 9% Latin@ 1% Asian 2% Other	Majority White district
Superintendent District Four	7 elementary 3 middle 5 distinct centers 1 secondary	7,154	55% Black 32% White 5% Latin@ 3% Asian 3% Other	Excellent Report Card Rating

diverse districts in terms of geographical area in the state, number of student personnel, and demographic composition, the participants contributed unique perspectives to the research questions. Table 11.1 shows an overview of the participants.

The interview protocol was designed in response to the literature and focus group interactions. Open-ended questions were followed up with specific queries intended to prompt clarity of understanding regarding the administrators' perspectives. All formal interviews were conducted at the participants' offices and were arranged in advance. Each participant was assured reasonable measures of confidentiality.

Case study design was used to collect a structured set of data from multiple sources that converge around thematic points of reference aligned with the research questions under investigation (Merriam, 2009). The data were analyzed using a constant comparative method and thematic concepts associated with Black male superintendents' theories and responses to the Black male underachievement confirmed established knowledge from the extant literature. Limitations of this study include parameter of selecting superintendents from only one state and the size of the sample population within that state which limits the overall potential participants available for a study of this design. Nevertheless, the limited sample size provided diversity across the participant pool which expands the scope of variables influencing the participants' beliefs and behaviors.

PERSPECTIVE ON BLACK FATHERS/FATHER FIGURES:
SUPERINTENDENTS THEORIZE

It's about time we have a father to son
Sit down let me tell you 'bout your fatherless sons
How they grew to be men and father they sons

—Carter (2000)

The prevailing idea that Black fathers are not present is a duplicitous one that acknowledges the reality of social circumstances that may render them physically absent but dismisses the psychological impact of their presence toward the well-being of their children. Furthermore, the idea that community members impact Black children through encounters in schools, churches, and other settings was lost during desegregation. One superintendent discussed the impact of Black male role models and figures that influenced the experiences of male students when he was in school compared to now:

> Mr. Doe was the male teacher at our elementary school and he helped you understand that you needed to be disciplined. If you weren't, you went down to his class, he had a leather strap, he took that strap and tore your butt up, and you went back and tried to sit down. Well, we did not have out of school and in school suspension during this era. You went down to his room, got what you needed and came on back to class.

The frustration over the general lack of Black males in the school system that might function as a surrogate father figure was repeated by other participants. Superintendents noted the importance of these individuals, but thematically found their presence missing:

> The lack of African American male role models in our educational institutions continues to exist today. In far too many instances, our educational institutions fail to provide African American boys with African American male role models. Many of these boys fail to develop authentic, trusting relationships with any education professionals. This inevitably impedes their ability to form a sense of connection, and belonging in the educational setting.

The absence of Black males in educational settings is exacerbated by the increased absence of Black males and fathers in particular for young male students whose behavior may reflect their internal frustration with having no individuals with whom they can readily identify. Another superintendent reiterated the impact of this phenomenon:

> I didn't have any African American male teachers. We did have one African American male PE assistant. That was one of the shortcomings that I had growing up. I did not have anyone that I could go to in the academic realm.

Desegregation was cited as an historical landmark event that complicated life for Black male students in myriad ways. While the mandated policy forced Black males to assume a heavy burden of responsibility regarding integration as expressed by one superintendent who was encouraged to become one of the first Black students to integrate a White school: "In this life you give a service for the space that you occupy. If I don't do anything else, and I'm sure I probably will, but that was my service. That was my sacrifice." The social implications of community and kinship what once exited and thrived for Black males began to unravel:

> The role models (lawyers, business people, teachers, principals, policemen, bankers, etc.) lived across the street and in the neighborhood. I can remember 25 doctors that lived in my neighborhood at that time. During segregation, Blacks did not have access to equal housing and could not move to the suburbs. I could see them every day. I was inspired by their accomplishments, which made me want to achieve. Role models did not have to drive in from the suburbs to spend an hour or two a week with me. Today many of our Black male students live in communities where there are no resident role models. In many areas they don't see working males.

The two parent family with a father present was repeatedly noted as a core of strength for young males who were unlikely to find the support they needed in schools and the surrounding community, especially after *Brown v. Board* (1954) and sociocultural shifts that grew from the civil rights movement. This superintendent's parents possessed little formal education; however both individuals were invested in his access to education and his related academic success:

> My daddy had a third grade education and my mamma had a sixth grade education. But you knew you were going to school, and you were going every day. And if there were a chance to go to college, you were going to be there.

Another superintendent noted the encouragement provided by his parents that predictably supported his success. He suggested that his father was an integral part of his ability to focus on his educational goals and realize his dreams:

> I learned a lot from him. That's why I have so much respect for him now, even in his absence. He really pushed me. I dare say that I would not have done anything, not much of anything at least, if he had not pushed that way.

The influence of a father/father figure was thematically credited as the necessary support for young Black males to experience success. At this junction, the superintendent participants noted:

A lot of them just don't have the two-parent family. Now I say that because I know what a difference it made for me. If you just stop to think, you've got grandparents raising these Black boys, a mother maybe or sometimes an aunt or other relative.

One superintendent who was raised by his grandmother with the assistance of uncles, community members, coaches, and church family reflected on his experience without his father being engaged in his education and his life:

Children born to single mothers are probably one of the biggest situations that need to be addressed in the African American community. When fathers don't get involved, it has an impact on black boys. I played sports all the way through school and never had a male figure since my father was not involved. It had an impact on me. I never said anything to anyone. But when we were out there playing, other kids had their fathers there. We never had that.

Feelings of disappointment and even abandonment are often experienced by young Black males who struggle to negotiate their place in the world that is increasingly hostile to their existence. It is imperative that the absence of Black fathers be mitigated with initiatives that supplement this critical need.

PERSPECTIVES ON FICTIVE KIN RELATIONSHIPS AND RESPONSIBILITIES: SUPERINTENDENTS RESPOND

Your dreams ain't easy; you just stick by your plan
Go from boys to men; you must act like a man
When it gets hard, y'all; you just grab what you know
Stand up tall and don't you fall
—Archer (1994, Track 1)

While the Black Lives Matter movement is a more recent response to a widespread assault that has overwhelming targeted Black males; Black men were well aware prior to this movement of the social conditions that presented the need for community solidarity. The Black Men United lyrics (Archer, 1994) quoted here suggest that the mid-1990s were troubled times to the degree that over 25 Black male recording artists and groups collaborated on this track to create a message of encouragement and support. Shortly thereafter, the first Million Man March on Washington, DC was organized to present to society an adjusted view of Black males, organize Black men around a campaign for mutual support, and design self-preservation strategies to combat low wages, high levels of incarceration, alternative functioning families, and other societal problems plaguing the Black community.

Efforts of this nature are not new and continue to be a critical aspect of building a fictive kinship network across Black communities. One superintendent described the difficulties and apprehension that Black males who take up this mantle often experience:

> You've got to go beyond fear. What are you going to feel like at the end of the day? Are you going to feel like you did a service? Are you going to feel like you're just sitting up there? I guess you have to ask yourself that question. I know some people say, "Man, hey, I just got here. I don't want to get run out of town before I settle down."

Another participant questioned the commitment of schools districts in general to proactively address the lack of academic achievement among Black male students. His frustration is likely born from his realization that there is no one else willing to reliably focus on this glaring problem other than the few like himself who have taken this mission on as a personal act of service:

> I'm not exactly sure how we are going to turn it around, other than to give back. I'm talking about some serious giving back. It can't be lip service, because I hear a lot of that. People talk about what needs to be done. The charities have their thing, the fraternities, boys and girls club, but I don't see the consistent commitment. How serious are we about changing the condition of young black males? I don't know.

Systemic inequities and racism were offered by one superintendent as the reason why Black male students are not achieving at levels similar to their demographic contemporaries. He reiterated the absence of Black male leaders that consistently function as role models and interact with Black male students in the school system as reason district leaders need to accept the challenge for change:

> I think the system is stacked against them. Like I said earlier, every group other than African American males has someone that they can emulate. We have African American female teachers that African American females can relate to. We have white male teachers, white female teachers, but very seldom do you see an African American male teacher.

Aside from the school system, the larger community was cited as another space where society has failed young Black males. One superintendent acknowledged the outlying Black male students that have father/father figures and refuse to optimize their resources, and others that have limited paternal family support and manage to succeed despite distractions. Nevertheless, a large portion of Black male students experience frustration and need this essential component to mature and thrive. His response to the influence of a male figure is evident in the following comment:

> Some of these young boys don't even know their fathers. I think that it takes a man to raise a boy, and the absence of one, whether it's the father or a significant other male, has a tremendous impact.

Because these superintendents are convinced that positive male interactions are instrumental to addressing the academic performance of Black male students, they have committed to establishing and sustaining inclusive mentoring programs in their districts. Their efforts have been successful because they garnered commitments from men in their district's communities to lead, guide and function as father figures for young Black males that need positive supports in their lives. One superintendent led the development of the Bow Tie Clubs mentoring program described as follows:

> Bow Tie Clubs have been established in several of the district schools that provide young men with guidance in what is referred to as the "Five Wells." All activities support the perspective that young men should be Well Read, Well Traveled, Well Dressed, Well Spoken, and Well Balanced. At the time of the interview, two of the mentoring groups were on a field study to [nationally recognized, predominantly Black, men's college in the southeast U.S.] and tours were scheduled for visits to a predominantly White research institution in the southeast U.S. and a small, predominantly Black coeducational liberal arts college.

He elaborated on the significance of these specific types of experiences in the development of positive self-esteem among young Black males who might envision opportunities to transform themselves through education:

> I feel like it's important for those boys to understand and experience college life. They need to see it. The two most essential components stressed in the mentoring initiatives are respect and effort. Young men are constantly reminded that a part of this journey from boyhood to manhood involves respecting themselves and others. In addition, they owe it to themselves to always do their best.

Another superintendent describes this mentoring effort aimed at bolstering the outlook for young Black males as such:

> The Bow Tie Club mentoring group was established for young boys in grades 9–12. Many of these young men were experiencing behavioral or academic difficulties. In addition to others goals, this initiative [was intended to] reduce the number of students that elected to leave school before earning their

diploma. This is one of several mentoring initiatives occurring in his district and while [it is impossible to conclude that] this mentoring efforts alone resulted in these improvements, the dropout rate has reduced from 7% to 1% and the graduation rate has improved from 66% to 82%. The performance of all subgroups has improved, but the performance of the African American males has been the most significant.

These data suggest that the achievement gap experienced by Black males will persist until their academic success rises to the top of school districts' goals and objectives for improvement. Furthermore, school district board members are culpable for the outcomes of this besieged group of students by either supporting superintendents that take up the mantle for positive change or by threatening their livelihoods if they subvert the dominant paradigm. This superintendent described the tenuous relationship between activist superintendents and school board members when these achievement goals are confronted:

> I've asked several board members, if we want to improve the performance of this district, we have got to tackle it for everyone. Once we look at the students that are performing at the very lowest, that's the group we've got to target. If we don't spend some extra time and resources on the lowest performing subgroup, how can the district improve? Right now the lowest performing subgroup is African American males. I look forward to the day that the lowest performing subgroup is not the African American male. Then we can focus our attention somewhere else.

It is indisputable that Black male academic achievement in unacceptably low and current instructional strategies are not producing appreciable improvements. The data reported in this study suggest on a small scale that initiatives designed to focus on this demographic subgroup can address the cycle of failure that schools are experiencing with Black male students. Furthermore, these efforts must be viewed as complimentary to the overall school performance so that district leaders are not reprimanded but rather rewarded for institutionalizing supports to cure an educational ill that has pervaded nearly every U.S. social institution.

DISCUSSION AND CONCLUSIONS

> *School districts are ultimately defined by average student performance, not the performance of individual subgroups. The reality is that a Blue Ribbon School, in which African American males significantly lag behind that of other subgroups, is still a Blue Ribbon School. School and district administration, school boards, and the community celebrate them just as vigorously.*
>
> —Black male superintendent

No school should be celebrated that consistently fails to produce success for a minority of its students regardless of the schools' ability to achieve high outcomes for the majority of its students. It is a statistical atrocity to resist the disaggregation of data in order to obscure the failure of many schools to support the academic success of Black male students. Detractors of initiatives intended to level the playing field for all students suggest that efforts of this nature ignore the mandate described in most school districts' mission statements to treat students with equal opportunities. In fact, the last thing Black male students need is equal opportunities or the same treatment that every other student receives. These types of policies precisely cultivate the attitudes and behaviors that sustain schools' failure among young Black males.

There was consensus among the participant superintendents on the theory that disintegration of the family unit and the perceived and actual absence of Black fathers has hampered the success of Black male students. Moderated structures and supports for many young Black males are the result of the devaluation of the normative, traditional family in Black communities. The sporadic presence or full absence of fathers in the lives of Black male students effect behavior negatively which often translates into loss of interest in school and school related activities. Despite these home based challenges that result in diminished academic focus, Black male superintendents did not perceive this variable as the only aspect of this problem that warrants change. They did not accept these challenges as the sole reason for failure and they assumed the position that if family and home are the primary reasons for poor academic performance among Black male students; then the remedy is to create these networks through fictive kinship alliances that provide the structure and support so sorely needed.

Mentoring programs exist in the districts of each participant superintendent. The participants' collaboration to develop the Bow Tie club initiative assures that young Black males who need additional support that might be typically found in the traditional family structure, have access to these invaluable relationships. These clubs, exclusively comprised of male students and staffed by male mentors, expand opportunities for club members to dialogue and interact with positive males about topics and issues that young men may only be comfortable discussing with other men. While each Bow Tie Club has the freedom to structure activities tailored to the particular needs of their students, typical meeting frequency is two to three times per month. Members receive bow ties and basic instructions on how to wear this accessory is provided. Additionally, the members are required to wear their ties at Bow Tie Club meetings and functions, providing for many of the members an opportunity to dress in professional attire for the first time in many years or ever. Surprisingly, an adjustment of this small nature is powerful enough to impact their self-esteem and generate positive behaviors and related school outcomes.

Other activities experienced by club members include selected group readings such as poetry and biographies about significant Black male figures in history. This aspect of the Bow Time Club curriculum addresses literacy gaps that are prevalent for these students. Content for selected reading typically focuses on the relevance of dedication and determination in academic preparation. Life skills are another important aspect of the curriculum, and topics include navigating the space between boyhood and manhood, understanding responsible and safe sex, and exploring the duties encompassed in the role of fatherhood. Academically and culturally oriented outings in neighboring cities that some of the students have never travelled to are additional components of the club curricula. Ultimately, club members must acknowledge that respect is earned when given and they are asked to prioritize this position. Integrity, attention to civic duty, and empathy for one's school and home community are essential features displayed through the behavior of the men they will become.

As the incidence of young Black males living in single mother and nontraditional family arrangements rises, initiatives like the Bow Tie Clubs are needed more than ever. Gender exclusive initiatives have proven effective measures for addressing the specific needs of Black males (Mitchell & Stewart, 2013) and programs aimed at improving outcomes for Black male students are definitively more effective when they are theoretically grounded, culturally responsive, and designed to impact a broad range of needs including academic achievement, economic advancement, mental and physical well-being, and social interaction requirements (Belgrave & Brevard, 2015). Regardless of the defensible knowledge base on effective mentoring programs, it is undeniable that more culturally appropriate programs based on the scholarly literature are needed. Mentoring programs of this type are critical for the academic, social, and economic advancement of young Black males.

REFERENCES

Allen, Q., & White-Smith, K. A. (2014). "Just as bad as prisons": The challenge of dismantling the school-to-prison pipeline through teacher and community education. *Equity & Excellence in Education, 47*(4), 445–460.

Archer, M. (1994). U will know [Recorded by Black Men United]. On Jason's Lyric Soundtrack [CD]. New York, NY: Mercury Records.

Belgrave, F. Z., & Brevard, J. K. (2015). *African American boys: Identity, culture, and development.* New York, NY: Springer.

Biggs, S. A., Musewe, L. O., & Harvey, J. P. (2014). Mentoring and academic performance of Black and under-resourced urban middle grade students. *Negro Educational Review, 65*(1–4), 64–86.

Bourdieu, P. (1977). Cultural reproduction and social reproduction. In J. Karabel & A. H. Halsey (Eds.), *Power and Ideology in Education* (pp. 487–511). New York, NY: Oxford.

Brown v. Board of Education, 347 U.S. 483 (1954).

Caldwell, C. H., Antonakos, C. L., Assari, S., Kruger, D., DeLoney, E. H, & Njai, R. (2014). Pathways to prevention: Improving nonresident African American fathers' parenting skills and behaviors to reduce sons' aggression. *Child Development, 85*(1), 308–325.

Carter, S. (2000). Where have you been? [Recorded by JayZ & Beanie Sigel]. On The Dynasty: Roc La Familia [CD]. New York, NY: Roc-A-Fella Records.

Chatters, L. M., Taylor, R. J., & Jayakody, R. (1994). Fictive kinship relations in black extended families. *Journal of Comparative Family Studies, 25*(3), 297–312.

Children's Defense Fund. (1975). *School suspensions: Are they helping children?* Cambridge, MA: Washington Research Project.

Coates, E. E., & Phares, V. (2014). Predictors of paternal involvement among nonresidential, Black fathers from low-income neighborhoods. *Psychology of Men & Masculinity, 15*(2), 138–151.

Cook, D. A. (2010). Disrupted but not destroyed: Fictive-kinship networks among Black educators in post-Katrina New Orleans. *Southern Anthropologist, 35*(2), 1–25.

Delgado, R., & Stefancic, J. (2001). *Critical race theory: An introduction.* New York, NY: New York University Press.

Ellis, J. M., Rowley, L. E., Nellum, C. J., & Smith, C. D. (2015). From alienation to efficacy: An examination of racial identity and racial academic stereotypes among Black male adolescents. *Urban Education.* doi:10.1177/0042085915602538

Fantuzzoa, J., LeBoeufa, W., Rouseb, H., & Chenc, C. (2012). Academic achievement of African American boys: A city-wide, community-based investigation of risk and resilience. *Journal of School Psychology, 50*(5), 559–579.

Howard, T. C. (2013). How does it feel to be a problem? Black male students, schools, and learning in enhancing the knowledge base to disrupt deficit frameworks. *Review of Research in Education, 37*(1), 54–86. doi:10.3102/0091732X12462985

Kena, G., Hussar W., McFarland J., de Brey C., Musu-Gillette, L., Wang, X.,...Dunlop Velez, E. (2016). The Condition of Education 2016 (NCES 2016-144). U.S. Department of Education, National Center for Education Statistics. Washington, DC. Retrieved from https://nces.ed.gov/pubsearch/pubsinfo.asp?pubid=2016144

Kim, S., & Hill, N. E. (2015). Including fathers in the picture: A meta-analysis of parental involvement and students' academic achievement. *Journal of Educational Psychology, 107*(4), 919–934.

Lofton, R., & Davis, J. E. (2015). Toward a Black habitus: African Americans navigating systemic inequalities within home, school, and community. *The Journal of Negro Education, 84*(3), 214–230.

MacLeod, J. (2008). *Ain't no makin' it: Aspirations and attainment in a low-income neighborhood.* Boulder, CO: Westview.

Madhavan, S., & Roy, K. (2012). Securing fatherhood through kin work: A comparison of Black low-income fathers and families in South Africa and the United States. *Journal of Family Issues, 33*(6), 801–822.

Merriam, S. (2009). *Qualitative research: A guide to design and implementation.* San Francisco, CA: Jossey-Bass.

Mitchell, A. B., & Stewart, J. B. (2013). *Sex Roles, 69*(7), 382–392. doi:10.1007/s11199-011-0074-6

Perry, A., Harmon, D., & Leeper, J. (2012). Resident Black fathers' involvement: A comparative analysis of married and unwed, cohabitating fathers. *Journal of Family Issues, 33*(6), 695–714.

Price, P. L. (2010). At the crossroads: Critical race theory and critical geographies of race. *Progress in Human Geography, 34*(2), 147–174.

Roy, K., & Vesely, C. (2009). Caring for "the family's child": Social capital and kin networks of young low-income African American fathers. In R. Coles & C. Green (Eds.), *The myth of the missing Black father* (pp. 215–240). New York, NY: Columbia University Press.

Schott Foundation for Public Education. (2010). Yes We Can: The Schott 50 state report on public education and Black males. Cambridge, MA: Author.

Sherman, W. H., & Grogan, M. (2003). Superintendents' responses to the achievement gap: An ethical critique. *International Journal of Leadership in Education, 6*(3), 223–237.

Stack, C. B. (1974) All our kin: Strategies for survival in a Black community (1st ed.). New York, NY: Harper & Row.

Taylor, J., Smith, T., & Best, A. (2005). Like father, like son [Recorded by The Game & Busta Rhymes]. On the documentary [CD]. New York, NY: Buckwild.

Vespa, J., Lewis, J., & Kreider, R. (2013). America's families and living arrangements: 2012. U.S. Department of Commerce Economics and Statistics Administration. U.S. Census Bureau.

Watson, J., Washington, G., & Stepteau-Watson, D. (2015). Umoja: A culturally specific approach to mentoring young African American males. *Child and Adolescent Social Work Journal, 32*(1), 81–90.

Zuberi, T. (2011). Critical race theory of society. *Connecticut Law Review, 43*(5), 1573–1591.

CHAPTER 12

THE SUPERINTENDENCY

The Cost of Making a Difference—
The Personal Toll

Dennis G. Parsons
University of Calgary

Jim Brandon
University of Calgary

Sharon Friesen
University of Calgary

Michele Jacobsen
University of Calgary

This chapter originated as part of a research study, *The Impact of the Office of Superintendent of Schools on the Personal Lives of Superintendents* (Parsons, 2016). Parsons used a qualitative case-study methodology involving six participant superintendents in semi-structured interviews, two from each of western, Atlantic, and northern Canada. The findings revealed work lives

The Contemporary Superintendent, pages 197–223

significantly impacted personal and family life. Regardless of location or size of school district, all participants described an all-consuming work life: rampant with political agendas, conflict, public scrutiny, unreasonable expectations, and one where technology has left superintendents more exposed to the whims of the disenfranchised. They were clearly hindered across all selected jurisdictions by troublesome and disruptive elements present in their work role. The evidence is so compelling it calls into question the current system of elected school board governance and forces consideration of how the system can better support school superintendents. This chapter specifically explores the personal cost to superintendents who must navigate within this hindered system and the prevalence of the personal toll on superintendents across different jurisdictions. The chapter concludes with some advice to superintendents and with research findings.

PURPOSE AND RESEARCH QUESTIONS

The purpose of this study was to gain deeper understanding of the superintendent work life through a focused investigation of how the office of superintendent impacts the personal and family lives of superintendents (Parsons, 2016). The primary research question was:

> Do the work lives of superintendents serving in the K–12 public education system have an impact upon their personal and family lives, and if so how, and to what extent?

The following sub-questions assisted in answering the primary research question:

1. What is the nature of the work carried out by superintendents in selected jurisdictions across Canada?
2. What elements in the work lives of superintendents have the greatest impact on their personal lives?
3. Are the impacts on the personal lives of superintendents similar or different when looking across different jurisdictions?

CONCEPTUAL FRAMEWORK

A conceptual framework (Figure 12.1) was developed to guide this inquiry and to help frame the literature review (Parsons, 2016). The conceptual framework constituted a significant overarching element in the inquiry, and was the model for the research and investigation.

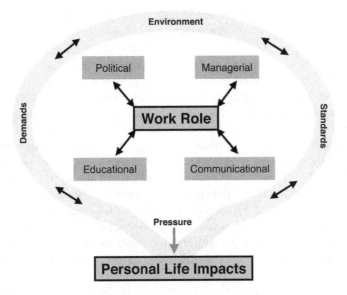

Figure 12.1 Work role and personal life impacts.

As the CEO to the board and as the chief education officer within his or her respective school district, the superintendent is ultimately responsible for all the district's activities (Edwards, 2007). This great leadership challenge is something superintendents of education share with CEOs across other organizations. Porter and Nohria (2010) explored the veracities of being a CEO. While their work delved into the leadership realities of CEOs in general, their findings were applied directly to the school superintendent as a CEO and helped provide a practical framework for this inquiry.

A total of five themes were identified and applied from Porter and Nohria (2010). First, while many CEOs including school superintendents have previously held leadership positions, they are often surprised by how much more demanding the job is compared to previous positions. Porter and Nohria argued this feeling stemmed from the new range and intensity of responsibilities, which included the many demands that emanated from external constituencies such as board members and politicians. Second, another reality of being a CEO is the inherent limit to power. According to Porter and Nohria, while CEOs may have the authority to make broad unilateral decisions, doing so can have unintended negative consequences. Knowing when and how to utilize the power that comes with one's appointment as CEO is significant. Third, like other CEOs, another challenge for superintendents is ensuring he or she has the right information. Porter and Nohria observed that while it is fairly easy for CEOs to access information, ensuring it is reliable is very difficult: "CEO's get cut off from the informal channels in the organization. Information that is presented to the CEO is typically formal, extensively processed and synthesized. Also, information is rarely presented to the CEO without some underlying agenda" (p. 439). Thus, like all CEOs, superintendents constantly struggle to seek out information to get a true picture of what is happening in their organization. Fourth, the reality of being superintendent, or any CEO, is that "every word and action are followed and scrutinized closely—both inside and outside the organization" (p. 440). This explains why, at times, even the most innocent remark can have unintended consequence. This atmosphere where people hang off of every word or action adds another layer of complexity and possible tension to the work of the superintendent. Finally, Porter and Nohria asserted that CEOs including superintendents are expected to be "agents of change." However, like other CEOs, superintendents learn quickly that making changes is not a simple matter. Superintendents, like CEOs in other organizations, "inherit people, resources, capabilities, strategies, cultures, processes . . . all of which limit their ability to act as if they had a blank sheet of paper" (p. 442).

The conceptual framework (see Figure 12.1) depicts the work role of the superintendent, one that appears to be more and more demanding and indefinitely more complex. Superintendents are increasingly being asked to balance a multitude of political, managerial, educational, and communicational demands in an environment that is more diverse, is resounding with calls for reform, has fewer resources and has new standards of accountability. Within this unique leadership position the superintendent serves as the chief executive officer to the board of trustees thereby assuming all responsibilities that extend from the board as a corporate body; he or she also serves as the chief education officer and therefore responsible for all operational decisions as well as the operational performance of the district. While there is considerable authority vested in the office of superintendent, the research of Porter and Nohria (2010) outlining the reality of being a CEO, provides insight into the balancing act that appears to be the work life of the superintendent.

METHODS AND DATA SOURCES

The design for this research was case study, which Yin (2009) defined as "an empirical inquiry that investigates a contemporary phenomenon within its real-life context" (p. 18). Merriam (2009) concluded, "The single most defining characteristic of case study research lies in delimiting the object of study, the case" (p. 40). A case study is a detailed investigation of a bounded system where "bounded means that the case is separated for research in terms of time, place or some physical boundaries" (Creswell, 2012, p. 465). In Parsons' (2016) case, the phenomenon being investigated was the superintendent's role and specifically how work life within the role impacted the superintendent's personal and family life. What bounds this case and constitutes this case study's unit of analysis is all participants are superintendents, they are Canadian, their roles lie within the K–12 public education system and all have 5 or more years of experience in the role.

A purposeful sampling strategy was employed to gain insight and understanding; about the phenomenon under study (Merriam, 1998, 2009). The process and criteria for selecting the interview sample of six superintendents was relatively simple. Prospective participants were informed of the study, that it would utilize purposeful sampling, semi-structured interviews and case-study methodology to help ascertain, comprehend, and advance insight into the work life through possible impacts of the work on their personal and family lives. Participants needed to have served as superintendent for a minimum of five or more years in a school district. The total of six participant superintendents were selected on the basis of engaging a male and a female superintendent, from different jurisdictions in each of western, Atlantic and northern Canada. In Parsons' (2016) study, it did not matter if the superintendent served in an urban, semi-urban, or rural district. The diversity regarding location of jurisdiction and district size was by design. If the phenomenon under study were present, these elements would help reveal its prevalence, nature and extent across the selected jurisdictions.

Participant Profiles

Considering the importance of participants in case study research, some understanding of the participants involved in the Parsons (2016) study is deemed helpful in providing perspective on participant commentary and the research findings:

Don
Don was the superintendent of schools in a geographically large western jurisdiction consisting of both suburban and rural schools. He had been in the superintendency for 9 years with the vast majority of that time spent in the same school jurisdiction. A career educator with approximately 30 years' experience in public education, Don worked as a teacher prior to taking up positions at district office. According to Don, the thing that helped him most in preparing for the superintendency was working as an assistant superintendent in a jurisdiction where there was a clear focus on succession planning.

Lee
Lee also served in a western jurisdiction and had been superintendent for 5 years in a predominately large urban setting. Prior to becoming

superintendent, Lee worked as a teacher, assistant principal, principal, direc- tor of special education, and an assistant deputy superintendent. She possessed a master's degree and had completed coursework towards her doctorate.

Lee had worked in public education for more than 30 years. She consid- ered herself a teacher, first and foremost, and stated she brought her love for the interaction between teacher and student with her to the office of superintendent. She said "it stayed and became part of the purpose of what I thought I should be doing as a superintendent" (Lee).

Scott

Scott, was the superintendent of schools in a geographically large Atlan- tic Canadian jurisdiction consisting of urban, suburban, and rural schools. A career educator, he had approximately 16 years in senior district level leadership positions but, due to much provincial reorganization and con- solidation, that time was spread over both the assistant superintendent and superintendent positions. Prior to these positions, Scott was a teacher who came to district office as a program specialist and worked extensively on the program side; this positioned him to move into the assistant superintendent's role when he first came to district office. Like Lee, Scott possessed a master's degree and had completed some work towards his doctorate in education.

Lynn

At the time of the study, Lynn had 19 years at district office, 11 of those years in the position of superintendent in three large Atlantic Canada school jurisdictions. Regarding her first superintendent position, Lynn said, "The superintendency was not something I aspired to do or become, but I was encouraged to put my application forward as a candidate for the position" (Lynn). At that time, she was in the position of assistant director, responsible for programming in the school district. Lynn stated, in that position, in her particular province, she was responsible for school develop- ment, student services, and curriculum delivery. As well, she had completed a number of years as manager of human resources, which expanded her background a little broader than most, especially with regard to working with collective agreements and employees. In addition to her district level experience, Lynn had extensive experience at the school level. She had been a teacher, a department head, a vice principal of a K–12 school, prin- cipal of an aboriginal school and a senior high school, and she had been a program specialist. Lynn said, "I knew the district well and I was encour- aged to apply" (Lynn).

Marie

Marie, was the superintendent of schools in a geographically northern jurisdiction consisting of primarily suburban and some rural schools. She had been in central office for the last 15 years, serving for 9 years as assistant superintendent and the last 6 years as the superintendent of schools. Prior to moving to central office, Marie worked in the same jurisdiction as a classroom teacher across multiple grades, then as an assistant principal and principal respectively in two different schools. A career educator with over 30 years' experience in public education, Marie stated what helped her most in gaining the superintendency was her diverse experience across all grade levels, which assisted in "understand[ing] the scope of all our schools."

Mark

A career educator and administrator, Mark had over 40 years of service as a teacher, principal, assistant superintendent, and the last 18 years as superintendent. The last 10 of those superintendent years were spent in a northern jurisdiction. Mark believed the key to his success was helping the board develop a strategic plan and getting buy-in from staff so the entire district was pulling in the same direction.

MAKING A DIFFERENCE

All six participant superintendents identified, "making a difference for students" as the single most important reward they received from their work as 21st Century superintendents. It did not seem to matter if the jurisdiction of the participant superintendent was located in western, Atlantic, or northern Canada—all participants took great joy and satisfaction in seeing their work benefit students and they had no difficulty conveying their delight over the satisfaction they received from helping students succeed. This finding is in keeping with the literature review. Specifically, this finding supports the mid-decade study by Glass and Franceschini (2007), who concluded, "[the] superintendent's motivation for entering the superintendency was to serve the community more than themselves" (p. 46). This finding is also in alignment with the Lowe's (2015) study on resilience in leadership, which was shared in a November 3, 2015 interview with the president of the College of Alberta School Superintendents (CASS) president, Barry Litun. President Litun recounted how the study documented that 95% of survey respondents derived a sense of accomplishment from their work (Litun, 2015).

This altruistic motive is evident in the data from our participant superintendents across the different geographic locations. Don illustrated it when he said "every day, his mind [is] going a hundred miles an hour about things that could be done to help benefit kids and families." In a similar way, Lynn demonstrated an altruistic motive when she spoke of student success as "the critical work we do." Likewise, Scott spoke of the rich reward he felt in having helped shape his district's intense focus on students and their well-being. Marie echoed a similar view when she discussed, "If it's not making a difference in the classroom, there is no point in doing it." Lee also expressed an altruistic motive when she spoke of the role of public education in society and of the larger responsibility she felt in her role as superintendent. Finally, Mark illustrated unselfish motives when he spoke of his biggest reward being one of seeing the big improvement in student academic results.

THE COST OF MAKING A DIFFERENCE: THE PERSONAL TOLL

The work of superintendents to make a difference for students was not without its challenges and many of those challenges, according to the data, exacted a huge personal toll on the lives of participant superintendents and their families.

The primary purpose of Parsons' (2016) study was to gain a deeper understanding of how the work lives of superintendents impacted their personal and family lives, thereby providing the reader with another window through which to view and understand the work life of the superintendent. Going into the study, Parsons (2016) assumed he would learn a lot about what elements in the work lives of superintendents had the greatest impact on the personal lives of incumbents and recently retired superintendents. This was indeed the case. The findings provided rich evidence that the participant superintendents' professional lives were so demanding and all-encompassing that superintendent roles literally dominated and frequently choked out or made almost impossible their personal and family lives. It is true the literature on the superintendency tells the story of a demanding job. To name a few, Pettigrew (2000) described the "stamina" required, Short and Scribner (2002) discussed the complexity of this leadership position, and Sovine (2009) conversed on how the superintendency was the most visible and influential leadership position in the business of education. However, what seems to be missing in the literature is a detailed investigation of the personal toll the superintendent's job has on superintendents and their personal lives. What follows is a detailed look at the personal toll on participant superintendents as they worked to make a difference for the students entrusted to their care.

The Never-Ending Job: 24/7

In a relatively recent article, Kisch (2012) focused explicitly on the question, "With the expectations of public education performance never higher, how is it possible to be 'on duty' 24/7 and to be present everywhere the community seems to demand?" (p. 43). In our investigation, it was very clear from all six of the participant superintendents that they worked around the clock and consciously used the term "24/7" to describe the work demands they had to cope with in the fulfillment of their duties as superintendents. The interview with CASS president Litun also revealed the unpublished study's finding that, on a weekly basis, to keep up with their work demands 95% of respondents took work home with them and close to 40% were working 16 or more additional hours per week (Lowe, 2015). The Lowe study interpreted this finding "as a major source of work-family/personal life interference" (p. 17). Specifically, in response to the question of the 24/7 nature of the job, Lowe (2015) stated,

> It is interesting to note that teacher workload has received significant attention (and appropriately so), however, it is disappointing that [many organizations] have been mute on this topic for senior administrators... It is morally, and ethically, and psychologically wrong to keep asking fewer senior administrators to do more. (p. 38)

In Parsons' (2016) study, all participants described the nature of the work as constant, all consuming, and unpredictable. From a jurisdiction perspective, in western Canada, Don described how he "gave everyone but his own family his time" and how he was more or less "in the background while his wife raised their family." Lee described life in the superintendency as really living in the middle between government officials, the board of trustees, students, parents and the broader community. She said, "When you agree to be a superintendent you are a superintendent 24 hours a day, 7 days a week." She also spoke of "sleeping with one eye open" because the job was there 24/7.

In Atlantic Canada, Scott described working 60 to 80 hours a week, being on call 24/7 and the strain this placed on his family. He described how the superintendency, which he described as functioning at the juncture of operations and governance, is so intertwined with all aspects of the work that while chunks of work get completed the work with students, parents, staff, government, the community, the board, facilities, human resources, budgets, strategic planning, bussing, food services, collective agreements, media, and in many other areas is simply a never-ending quest that keeps the superintendent jumping from one area or crisis to another. Also in Atlantic Canada, Lynn described working 14- to 16-hour days and how she tried to protect her weekends but discovered it was virtually impossible because her time was not her own.

In a similar way, Marie in her northern jurisdiction described the time requirements of the job as simply "enormous" and how this impacted her personal and family life. She also discussed the personal cost she was expected to pay to achieve the community visibility the board wanted. Also from a northern jurisdiction, Mark described how he had to work outside of normal hours and how he often missed dinner with his family even though he and his family enjoyed sitting down together for dinner. He made a direct link between his 24/7 work life and his failed marriage; he said, "My ex-wife and my kids will tell you that" (Scott).

All participant superintendents viewed working 24/7 as connected with their dual responsibility of chief executive officer to the board and chief education officer in the district. The duties were varied and far reaching including: night meetings, responding to serious incidents, speaking engagements, unscheduled meetings, human resource issues, political agendas, and many more. The demanding 24/7 nature of the job as described by participants is certainly in keeping with one of Porter and Nohria's (2010) realities of being a CEO, as discussed in Parsons' (2016) conceptual framework. His study clearly supports findings expressed in the research literature, such as Jonsson (2008) who found superintendents often work 80-hour weeks, Antonucci (2013) who found the work role of the superintendent is an all-consuming profession and possibly "overwhelming." It also supports researchers like Kisch's (2012) who asserted the role requires the superintendent to be on duty 24/7.

It is noteworthy that there were no significant differences in the responses between male and female superintendents regarding work demands (Parsons, 2016). Both males and females spoke of the 24/7 nature of the job using similar terminology and illustrations to tell their story. Unlike Crowley and Elster's (2012) contention regarding the dark side for women in the workplace, no gender differences were apparent in the data collected. The closest any participants came to this line of thinking was when Lynn, a female superintendent in Atlantic Canada, spoke of the inordinate number of nights she had to be out of town that she had no personal life. However, she did not connect this to her gender, and certainly acknowledged that male superintendents were away at the same meetings.

Public Scrutiny: My Life, Everybody's Business

The level of public scrutiny evident in the data as experienced by all participant superintendents was in keeping with the fourth reality of Parsons' (2016) conceptual framework. Porter and Nohria (2010) discuss how one reality of being a CEO is that "every word and action are followed and scrutinized closely—both inside and outside the organization" (p. 440). The reality that superintendents live under intense public scrutiny has been documented in the literature. Konnert and Augenstein (1990) stated: "When one accepts the superintendency s/he moves into the fishbowl. One now becomes a big fish in a small pond" (p. 215). Other researchers like Blumberg (1985) found many superintendents believed their communities treated them as if they were "public property." More recently Jensen (2011) reported on how "visibility in the community is always important to the success of a superintendent" (p. 14). However, participants in Parsons' (2016) study did not speak in terms of a constructive sense of visibility in their communities. Instead, all spoke of excessive public scrutiny, lack of privacy, and being held to a different standard, which affected their work, their lives and the lives of their families.

The life-altering impact that resulted from the high level of public scrutiny can be seen in the comments made by participants. Don spoke of "having to retreat to the middle of nowhere to help restore and rebuild himself"; while Lee shared how she knew she was "constantly watched," and how she "had no idea she would become such a public presence and warrant such public scrutiny of her life outside of her work." In Atlantic Canada, Scott spoke of intrusion and interference in all aspects of his life. He said, "It was difficult to carry out daily routines without having some encroachment or interference." Also in Atlantic Canada, Lynn spoke of how "in her jurisdiction the media were relentless" and often left her feeling "publically brutalized." In the northern jurisdictions, like Lee, Marie spoke of being "constantly watched" and left feeling like she needed to give up some of her friends; and Mark talked about being in the public eye and giving up certain aspects of his life. He said, "It seemed everyone knew what I did or did not do. I quickly realized I was always in the public's eye."

It is clear, based on the overwhelming nature of the data collected, that Parsons (2016) study supports the "fishbowl" nature of life in the superintendency. However, he was surprised by the strength and consistency of the data across the selected Canadian jurisdictions. Given that most of the research literature on the superintendency is primarily U.S. based, and given the importance of this unique leadership position to public education in Canada, it is evident to us that more study is urgently needed by researchers on other Canadian jurisdictions. This call for more research needs to determine if and whether the level and nature of public scrutiny being experienced by superintendents in Canada is so intrusive and disabling that it is leaving superintendents, as Lynn stated, "Feeling publically brutalized."

Social Media: Public Flogging, Private Response

As if the high level of public scrutiny being experienced by participant superintendents in Canada wasn't enough for superintendents to contend with, enter social media. As a relatively new phenomenon, it certainly is part of the public scrutiny discussion and could have been discussed above.

However given some of the unique challenges it presents for superintendents, it warrants its own focus.

All participant superintendents from all selected jurisdictions spoke of the urgent challenges presented by social media. In particular, 100% of participants spoke of the ease with which any person can bypass established channels and go directly to the minister of education or the premier on almost any issue. Don succinctly captured this new reality when he commented, "Normal protocols no longer apply everyone has access to everyone." While this new reality is having an impact on all organizations to varying degrees, based on the commentary from all participants, it is easy to see how social media has dramatically changed the educational landscape for superintendents. Scott spoke to one aspect of this change when he described how "in recent years, society and in particular governments react to what is trending on social media not what is coming through normal [work] channels." He also said, "There is no demarcation between the personal and the professional in the work role of the superintendent any more."

Probably the most profound change for superintendents, and a concern shared by all participants, was how superintendents are now subjected to public ridicule, mockery and scorn at the push of a button during all hours of the day and night, and they are almost powerless to do anything about it. Certainly they cannot respond through social media, as they are professionals who must act professionally. The frustration of superintendents, who discussed trying to respond privately to damaging public accusations posted openly on social media, was troubling.

There can be little doubt that social media technology is yet another pervasive form of public scrutiny that enables the disgruntled to rant and rave anonymously and often attack individual superintendents and or their school districts in very damaging ways. It appears, based on the strength of the data, that the public scrutiny superintendents must endure has reached an all-new level. The lack of privacy for superintendents and their families, the damaging public commentary being posted and the lack of conventions governing what is off limits is taking a huge personal toll on superintendents. Research to determine if social media is impacting attrition among superintendents and how to function in this new reality is certainly needed.

Health and Well-Being: The Need for Balance

As discussed in the section on 24/7, the 21st century superintendency is an all-consuming profession. This view is reflected in the literature with researchers like Hodgkinson and Montenegro (1999) describing the job of the local school superintendent as "one of the most difficult chief executive undertakings in America today" (p. 1). In our Canadian context, Pettigrew

(2000) documented the constant struggle of a superintendent to preserve his personal life from the constant demands of his work that wanted to consume his evenings and weekends. In the interview with president Litun, it was evident that many of the 361 assistant superintendents and superintendents surveyed in the Lowe (2015) study were struggling with health and well-being (B. Litun, personal communication, November 3, 2015).

In the Lowe (2015) study, health and well-being outcomes were benchmarked using Statistics Canada's Canadian Community Health Survey (CCHS) in which survey respondents were compared to groups such as professional occupations in education, management occupations, the employed workforce, and the adult population. President Litun also shared how the CASS survey participants rated their general health below the CCHS benchmark group. Only 18% of respondents perceived their health to be excellent, compared with 30% in professional occupations in education. When it came to perceived mental health, members gave much lower self-ratings than the benchmark groups. Only 23% of CASS members who answered this question rated their mental health as excellent, compared with 76% to 82% of the benchmarked groups.

The data gathered in Parsons' (2016) inquiry are certainly in keeping with work life pressures of the superintendency as discussed in the conceptual framework and with the research literature. While it warrants more study, the data collected from all six participants in the Parsons' study paints a picture similar to that of the Lowe (2015) study. This worrisome picture is portrayed in participant comments. Don spoke of his poor physical health and openly regretted the missed time and events with his family.

> As I look back on it now, I really wish that I'd spent more time with my family. It is the regret that I feel over missed time with my family and missed events that is for me the most problematic part of being a superintendent.

Scott spoke of one set of "puppet strings," "micro-management," and how his reputation and credibility were constantly on the line. The situation was so severe he openly worried over his physical and mental health. He said.

> There is a personal and family cost to working like this and it threatens the well-being of my family and I.

Lynn and Mark both openly described how work encroached upon their personal and family lives to such a degree that they made connections between their failed marriages and their work. Mark captured his lost marital relationship as if the stress and headaches were not bad enough the overwhelming number of hours required to do the job meant I was almost never home. This was the leading reason why my marriage failed and why my wife and I got divorced.

Marie, Lee, and Lynn also lost their marriages while serving in the superintendency. While they did not draw a direct line between their failed marriages and their work, they certainly discussed how a lack of work-life/ personal-life balance was most likely a factor. Marie also discussed how her demanding work life makes it very difficult to meet someone. In total, four of the six (66%) participating superintendents were divorced; two marriages were still intact, though one participant had been living apart from his spouse for almost two years due to reorganization in the workplace.

Across all the selected jurisdictions within Canada, superintendents told a similar story. It was a story of life out-of-balance due to the demands of their office. It was a story where their personal needs got pushed to the background because superintendents, with their 24/7 work demands, did not have the time or the energy to attend to other important aspects of their lives. These important aspects frequently involved their relationships with their spouse as well as their physical and mental health. Based on the data it would appear that, in the superintendency, finding a balance between personal and professional life is necessary and key to overall well-being. More research and discussion regarding how best to support and help superintendents achieve this needed balance may be key to future success of the education system.

Stress and Burnout: Serious Concerns

Stress and the possibility of burnout are also serious concerns that appeared in the data as having an impact on the work lives of superintendents and, most likely, their personal and family lives. Houston (2007) spoke of the transformation in the superintendency from a relatively straightforward responsibility to now being a complex maze of legislation, politics, and community activism. The complexity and pressures on 21st century superintendents take a toll both on the individuals holding that office and on their personal lives. Glass and Franceschini (2007) documented in a mid-decade study that approximately 60% of American superintendents were suffering from either considerable stress or very great stress. Their work over 3 decades showed a marked increase in the levels of stress being experienced by superintendents over that period of time. Some of the suggested causes for this increase in work-place stress involved negative media, difficult board relations, conflicting community demands, and limited resources.

In Parsons' (2016) study, all six participant superintendents from different geographic regions told their stories involving high levels of work-role stress. The nature and extent of the stress being experienced was revealed in what they shared. All participants spoke of stress associated with: political agendas, numerous conflicts, the 24/7 nature of the job, and multiple diverse demands. In addition to these common stressors, each participant identified other stressors.

From the western jurisdictions, Don spoke of stress caused by the "moral dilemma" he felt in not having the resources to meet the diverse needs of students; while Lee shared how it was the huge "time commitment" and the "larger responsibilities of her office" that kept her up at night. In Atlantic Canada, Scott spoke of the stress resulting from "micro-management," "voracious appetite for more with less," "social media," and from being physically separated from his wife and children due to his work. Lynn shared how she felt incredible stress from "loss of privacy," and "being publically brutalized by the media." In the selected northern jurisdictions, Mark spoke of "many sleepless nights, tension headaches, high blood pressure, and how he and Tylenol 3 are best friends." Marie related how she was stressed over the many "overwhelming demands" and "dwindling resources."

The Lowe (2015) study revealed that only 1 in 10 survey respondents reported little or no stress in their lives as compared to 1 in 5 for the benchmark groups. Approximately 50% of survey respondents said their lives were "quite a bit stressful" or "extremely stressful," which is also above the benchmarks. Work was also overwhelmingly the main source of stress in respondent's lives, with workload being the most frequently mentioned type of work-related stressor (Lowe, 2015). In addition to the high level of stress being experienced on a daily or weekly basis, between 11% and 42% of respondents experienced a range of symptoms associated with burnout (Lowe, 2015).

Based on the data from Parsons' (2016) study along with the Lowe (2015) study, it appears the research supports the view in the literature that superintendents are experiencing high levels of stress. Since there is no switch to turn off stress when superintendents are away from their work, if they are ever away from their work, it seems appropriate to conclude the personal and family lives of superintendents are being impacted by the high levels of work-related stress. As stated in the literature, while stress is not necessarily a negative component of the superintendency, it can become a disabling condition affecting behaviour, judgment, and performance. It is extremely important that proper coping mechanisms are put in place to reduce the potentially negative effects of stress. When Parsons (2016) contemplated the data in his study, such as the high rate of marital failure, he could not help but wonder if Canadian superintendents are getting the support they need to deal with the high levels of stress in their work environment?

IMPACTS ACROSS JURISDICTIONS?

Anticipating the Role

To determine whether the impacts on the personal lives of superintendents were similar or different when looking across different jurisdictions, it was necessary to establish what superintendents anticipated the role would involve prior to becoming a superintendent. This understanding would afford a perspective from which to compare and contrast experiences across jurisdictions and across geographic regions.

The data revealed how participant superintendents anticipated a work role with long hours of work, difficult decisions, stress, conflicts, media scrutiny, travel, and that there would be family life impacts from this leadership position. However, in great detail, what the data truly revealed was that 100% of participant superintendents did not anticipate the gravity or the extent of the many life-altering elements in their work lives on their personal and family lives. Don most likely captured this reality the best when he commented:

> The distance between the assistant superintendent's chair and the superintendent's chair, there's a chasm between those two chairs... [and] you have no concept of the difference between the two until you actually live it.

This stark reality of having to live the role to know its impacts was further brought to life by other participants in their comments. For example, when Lee stated,

> The whole context of the world changed... I anticipated difficulties, but the gravity and the extent of so many conflicts and the resulting far-reaching nature of the media scrutiny caused my whole life to become more and more difficult. This was simply beyond anything I anticipated.

Mark's comments that the superintendency was a "lonely place," and "he did not know who to confide in or trust" also drove home the isolation and inherent vulnerability of the position.

This overriding perspective in the data that, regardless of jurisdiction or geographic regions, superintendents were genuinely taken aback and possibly shocked by the pervasive impact their work lives had on their personal lives affords great insight into the role of superintendents across the selected jurisdictions. The similarity in superintendent perspectives across the selected jurisdictions possibly equates to a changing society and/or to a lack of preparedness going into the role. Further study would help in our understanding of why the impact of the work in the office of superintendent on the personal lives of superintendents and their families was so challenging and at times devastating.

Actual Experience in the Role: A Changing Society

The superintendent is the primary agent or representative between the board, the school district, and society in general. As such and as revealed in the Parsons (2016) inquiry, the participant superintendents had to contend with a multitude of issues and concerns. In this regard, all participants spoke of a changing society and, while we have already touched previously on some elements, a closer look at this phenomenon and how the changing work of superintendents is impacting their personal and family lives is warranted.

Don shared how he felt he entered the superintendency with his "eyes wide open" from being mentored for the position of superintendent as part of a transition plan in his district; yet he related how the politicization of education, the me-generation's sense of entitlement, and the pervasive use of social media meant the superintendency became "such a different job." Lee's comments concurred with Don's. She too recognized the superintendency as having become a different job over her 5-year tenure as superintendent. In fact for Lee, the societal changes were so significant, and the reduction in resources and the increase in diverse demands so great, she called for less division and duplication in the system and said,

> What the system needs is a more unified well-funded public education system where diverse needs are met within the system as opposed to across different systems.

This type of call for change reflects a perspective in the data that our public education system is under such intense strain from societal changes, new technologies, limited resources, and the many diverse demands that significant restructuring with a focus on optimization not on duplication is necessary.

In the selected Atlantic jurisdictions, Scott echoed similar thoughts when he spoke of the changing nature of the world around him. In particular, Scott spoke of "micro-management" and "blatant political interference" coupled with the incredible use of "social media" as being responsible for transforming the world of the superintendent into something unrecognizable. He described the enormous effort it took to continually operationalize the system after each heavy-handed consolidation. Also in Atlantic Canada, Lynn spoke of how easy it is for parents today to challenge the system and how different this is from when she first became a superintendent. According to Lynn, one illustration of our changed society is how a reporter will now call her and say, "I noticed on Facebook...," which suggests Facebook is now being used as a source of news; or when staff members expect to be away from work simply because "that is what they want and therefore expect."

In the selected northern jurisdictions, Marie and Mark spoke along similar lines to their southern colleagues when they spoke of a changing society. Marie focused on concerns regarding entitlement, reduced resources, loss of privacy, the extraordinary use of social media, and others. Mark related his experience pertaining to more and more parents operating on both extreme ends of the spectrum. He shared how parents in his jurisdiction are either abdicating their responsibilities through saying "it was the district's or the school's responsibility if their child was not attending school" or "hovering" so close to protect their kids that staff were unable to do their jobs.

It is evident that the changing nature of society, the media, and the impact they are having on the work lives of superintendents is worthy of further study. This point can be seen in the Lowe (2015) study and was acknowledged by CASS president Litun when he spoke of the six risks of a psychologically healthy workplace as revealed by the study. Four of the identified risks pertained to "expectations," "job demands," "workload management," and "work life/personal life balance," all of which figured strongly in Parsons (2016).

A Paradox for Superintendents: A Cry for Change

Within the literature it was clearly evident that, over the last number of years, there has been an incredible focus on reform and restructuring within the education system. One element of this movement saw a significant push towards standards of practice, which linked school system leadership to student learning. This development was certainly supported by reputable researchers: such as Leithwood (2008, 2010, 2011); Louis, Leithwood, Anderson, and Wahlstrom (2010); Friesen and Lock (2010); Marzano and Walters (2009); and Sheppard, Brown, and Dibbon (2009). They argued in pointed contrast to the notion of the "blob"—that school system leaders can make a difference. There is little doubt that the work of these researchers added significant weight to the primary premise of *The Alberta Framework for School System Success* (Brandon, Hanna, Morrow, Rhyason, & Schmold, 2013) that system leadership does have a significant role to play in improving student learning.

These new standards of practice were evident in Parsons (2016) study. As stated previously, all six participant superintendents identified "making a difference for students" as the single most important reward they received from their work as 21st century superintendents. Yet, it was baffling to learn from the Lowe (2015) study on assistant superintendents and superintendents in the province of Alberta that

> 62% of respondents at risk of leaving their current jobs for another employer were ages 45 to 54, the age group that school jurisdictions would be drawing on to fill the most senior positions being vacated through retirements. (Lowe, 2015, p. 5)

In Parsons (2016), all participant-superintendents were educators; they came up through the K–12 system, aspired to the superintendency for altruistic reasons, and received great satisfaction from their stated goals of making a difference for students. Why then are so many superintendents contemplating leaving their jobs for other employment? During the course of the interviews, Parsons (2016) explored independently with each participant superintendent the aspect of their job they would change to protect and enhance their personal and family lives. The responses to this prompt proved interesting and provided insight into the work lives of superintendents, and to motive(s) that superintendents might have for possibly leaving their position.

In the western jurisdictions, Don, who has been in the superintendency for 8 years, spoke of the stressful nature of the superintendency, in particular he spoke of the "24/7 role of the superintendent," "the loss of privacy," the "divisive politics," and "lack of resources," among others. He described how as a superintendent he went repeatedly to his own "internal well." He made the point that you can only draw from your own internal resources for so long before you have to replenish. If he could make one change he would "institute an enforced system of sabbatical leaves" that would enable him to go away and come back refreshed and invigorated. Like Don, Lee also shared how she had to so frequently deal with the divisive politics surrounding the board, nasty in fighting, trustees with single agendas, and multiple conflicts that it was virtually impossible to focus on the real purpose of educating students. She felt the impact of the divisive politics so strongly that she said,

> If I could change one aspect of my job as superintendent to enhance my personal and family life I would get rid of school boards . . . if they were abolished, then I could probably do the job I was hired to do and in the process take pressure off of my personal and family life.

In Atlantic Canada, Scott was similar in his response to his western counterparts. He was quick to say in order to safeguard and protect his personal and family life, he would eliminate the blatant political interference and micro-management that caused him so much anxiety and stress in his role as superintendent. Also in Atlantic Canada, Lynn focused in on the need for support and appropriate resourcing. She interestingly questioned why school boards, who are supposed to be in the governance realm, could not "meet quarterly" like other large corporations thereby freeing up much of the evening and weekend time the board now takes in the superintendent's schedule. This was yet another call for structural change.

In the selected northern jurisdictions, Marie and Mark independently called for changes that would reduce the enormous draw on the time required to fulfill their duties as superintendent. For Marie this translated into either receiving "additional resources" or "lowering expectations by taking certain elements off the plate." Her suggestions were directly aimed at freeing up time, which she could spend with her family in the evenings and on weekends. Like Marie, Mark also called for more resources: "If he had additional resources it would take a lot of worry and stress off his plate and enable him to spend more quality time with his family."

The responses from participants illustrated a significant paradox surrounding superintendents and our public education system. The literature review clearly revealed how the push for reform towards standards of practice was intended to link school system leadership to student learning. That linkage was evident in Parsons' (2016) study when all six participants (100%) viewed student success as "the work" and articulated this focus by independently and unanimously naming student success as the most significant aspect of their leadership role.

Parsons (2016) also revealed how superintendents are struggling with their very demanding leadership role that is being made more burdensome by a lack of support, political interference, micro-management, and numerous conflicts. Sadly, these elements that are extraneous to the core business of education are consuming superintendents' time, causing untold stress and, undoubtedly, impacting their personal and family lives. Despite the geographic and regulatory differences that separated selected jurisdictions in western, Atlantic, and northern Canada, all participants identified these elements and appeared to be engaged in a struggle to protect their personal and family lives from similar job-related aspects of the superintendency.

This apparent paradox involving superintendents in Canada wanting to do what the research deems they should do but finding they are being hindered by political interference, micro-management, and numerous conflicts, needs further study. Based on the evidence, it is likely safe to connect the reason for those planning on leaving the superintendency to the mounting frustration that comes from a strong desire to serve students, but being confounded by a multitude of extraneous elements present in the work. We believe further study will help to determine how best to address the identified issues and allow superintendents to focus on the true work of leading school systems rather than of dealing with the multitude of extraneous items now consuming their time.

A Possible Preparation Gap

Parsons (2016) did not set out to examine superintendent preparation programs or whether superintendents were adequately prepared for the job. That is to say, the question of preparation was not the focus of his inquiry. The focus was on deeper understanding of the work lives of superintendents by studying how the work role impacted their personal lives and the lives of their families. In this regard, participants were asked, and did speak to, how preparation might help in safeguarding their personal and family lives. In the exploration of this question, participants spoke of their pathway to and their experience in the superintendency. Without exception, this involved commentary from all participants that might indicate a possible preparation or readiness gap.

Three of the participants, namely Don, Marie, and Lynn, spoke of how they were specifically mentored for the role of superintendent; but it was Don who put the mentoring in perspective when he said, "There is a chasm between the assistant superintendent's chair and the superintendent's chair." This chasm is so great and, given the uniqueness of the office and the weight of responsibility it carries, accordingly Don, Marie, and Lynn all spoke of having to "walk-the-walk"; in other words, "learn the ropes as they went." Lee spoke of how "life experiences" served to prepare her for the superintendency and how the mentoring she received from her provincial superintendent's association was not successful because "her assigned mentor was not familiar with the type of system Lee was responsible for." Each of the two remaining participants, Scott and Mark, both shared they were not prepared for the role. Scott was explicit when he commented:

> I wasn't adequately prepared for . . . the pressure of certain situations, the conflict, the dynamics amongst and between board members, the dynamics of dealing with the department, staff dynamics around unions and strikes, the detailed complexities of finance and so many other situations.

Mark spoke of being a "hands-on type of person" that did not know how to delegate in ways that would support his office. Consequently, Mark shared how he was seldom home because he did not have the required supports in place to assist him with the work.

It was clear from the data, superintendents who had received mentoring as part of their pathway or transition into the superintendency valued it. It was also clear that there seemed to be something lacking in the readiness of superintendents to assume the role. All participants seemed to indicate they would have benefited from programs that philosophically followed a case-study or scenario-based approach in preparing them for the superintendency. From direct or indirect reference in the data, this finding parallels Orr's (2006) findings; superintendents in his study indicated their graduate programs were most effective when they integrated theory and practice.

The superintendent participants in Parsons' (2016) study identified the need for more hands-on case-study preparation infused into their educational programs. The underlying belief seemed to be that it would be beneficial for post-secondary institutions to take core questions surrounding key elements in the superintendency and to develop a case study or scenario-based preparation program. Even with such preparation, a superintendent would still have to learn the actual job on the job, however, at least he or she would have a rich background of scenario-type hypothetical situations to draw from that hopefully would complement and enable his/her practical experience.

Finding Balance: Advice to New Superintendents

All participant superintendents in Parsons (2016) openly discussed how their work lives dominated and, in many ways, impacted their personal and family lives. Five of the six participants (83%) advised incoming superintendents to take control in order to build a work-life/personal-life balance. Among the five superintendent participants who offered this type of advice: two spoke of putting in place structures and systems that would enable distributed leadership, two others spoke of simply taking control so the job did not dominate their lives, and one participant spoke of deliberately putting aside blocks of time for self and family as a way to achieve work-life/personal-life balance. The sixth participant felt one could not separate the work of the superintendent from one's personal life and accepted life out-of-balance as the personal cost of being a superintendent.

Across the selected jurisdictions, it appears the effect the superintendent's work life has on his/her personal life and family is similar and can be described in a broad way as "life out-of-balance." This finding is in keeping with the literature, for example, the work of researchers like Pettigrew (2000) who spoke of the superintendent's struggle to preserve his/her personal life from the constant demands of the work role. The work of other researchers like Schlechty (2002), Murphy (1994), and Antonucci (2013), who all found the role of the superintendent, whether in a small or large district, a difficult one. This finding is also in keeping with Porter and Nohria (2010) and the conceptual framework upon which Parsons' (2016) study was based.

The advice of Parsons' (2016) participants was reflective of their personal experiences in the superintendency across selected jurisdictions. The commonality of their experiences and the advice offered is cause for concern. It would appear that superintendents need help in mitigating the serious impact of their work lives on their personal lives. Unless such help is forthcoming, those serving in this unique leadership position, and their families, will most likely continue to experience impacts. How to help superintendents achieve greater work-life/personal-life balance is a topic that warrants further investigation and action.

SUMMARY

The purpose of this chapter was to build a more holistic understanding of the impact the superintendent's work life has on his/her personal life, by providing analysis, synthesis, and interpretative insights into the research findings. While adhering to Parsons (2016) conceptual framework, the challenge was to make sense of the data in order to see and understand the connecting patterns and themes when compared and contrasted to issues raised by the research literature. The implications of these findings were intended to enrich our understanding of the work role of superintendents in the public school system by examining how the work lives of participant superintendents in selected jurisdictions impacted their personal and family lives.

The work life experiences of participant superintendents serving in selected jurisdictions in western, Atlantic and northern Canada depict a story of concern. Certainly, the discussion illustrates the demanding nature of the superintendent's work and the many ways it spills over into their personal lives. The discussion and analysis advanced in relation to the research findings also suggest that, while superintendents aspire to the superintendency for primarily altruistic reasons, their demanding work lives take an incredible toll on their personal and family lives.

Parsons (2016) Findings

The findings of this inquiry provide greater insight and understanding into the work lives of superintendents in western, Atlantic and northern Canada. Parsons' (2016) findings show that, while education in Canada falls under provincial jurisdiction, the experience of superintendents appears to be similar across provincial jurisdictions. Explicitly stated, conclusions apply across all the selected jurisdictions (western, Atlantic and northern Canada) and are as follows:

1. All six participant superintendents (100%) identified "making a difference for students" as the single most important reward they

received from their work as 21st century superintendents. The altruistic motives of serving students and communities were the major motivators for these superintendents.

2. All six participant superintendents (100%) provided stark evidence that illustrated how their work lives were demanding and all-encompassing; their work lives dominated and, at times, made having personal and family lives outside the role challenging to say the least.

3. All six participant superintendents (100%) provided personal and compelling evidence that the all-consuming 24/7 nature of the role, the excessive and pervasive nature of public scrutiny, the ease of public flogging at the push of a button, the negative impact on their physical and mental health, and the high levels of work-related stress resulting from competing political agendas, numerous conflicts, and multiple diverse demands exacted the greatest personal toll.

4. The data revealed in detail that 100% of participant superintendents did not fully understand or anticipate the weight of responsibility of the superintendency, nor did they anticipate the gravity of the life-altering elements in their work lives or the extent to which these elements would impact their personal and family lives.

5. The data reveal how the changing nature of society involving the politicization of education, the me-generation's sense of entitlement, the pervasive use of social media, and the many diverse demands on the education system has translated into the superintendent's position, today, being different from what the job was only a decade ago.

6. The data revealed a significant paradox surrounding superintendents and our public education system and clearly showed how the push for reform towards standards of practice was intended to link school system leadership to student learning. Yet, the evidence also indicated how all participant superintendents recognized student success as the key work they needed to do, but they felt hindered by the divisive board politics, political interference, numerous conflicts, the 24/7 work of the superintendent, the loss of privacy, lack of resources, among others.

7. In order to more fully prepare superintendents for the unique and varied demands of the work, the data suggest that post-secondary institutions' preparation programs should incorporate a heavier focus on scenario-based learning and include key issues and questions surrounding the superintendency.

8. Both the totality of participant experience and the commonality in the advice they offered incoming superintendents is cause for concern. It appears that superintendents need help in mitigating the

serious impacts of the work life on their personal lives. Unless such help is forthcoming, the people serving in this unique leadership position will most likely continue to experience adverse personal and family life impacts.

Scholarly Significance

Parsons' (2016) study revealed that the superintendent's position is a highly demanding and complex role, which exacts a tremendous toll on superintendents' personal and family lives. The impact is so great that it conceivably calls into question the future viability of the position. Unless action is taken to clarify and support the superintendency, those in the position of superintendent will continue to be hindered in their efforts to effectively champion student learning, and the high personal cost currently exacted on superintendents and their families will continue.

REFERENCES

Antonucci, J. J. (2013). *The experience of school superintendent leadership in the 21st century: A phenomenological study* (Doctoral dissertation). Northeastern University, Boston, MA. Retrieved from ProQuest Dissertations and Theses database. (UMI 3525736)

Blumberg, A. (1985). *The school superintendent: Living with conflict.* New York, NY: Wiley.

Brandon, J., Hanna, P., Morrow, R., Rhyason, K., & Schmold, S. (2013). *The Alberta framework for school system success.* Edmonton, Alberta: College of Alberta School of Superintendents.

Creswell, J. W. (2012). *Educational research: Planning, conducting, and evaluating quantitative and qualitative research* (4th ed.). Boston, MA: Pearson.

Crowley, K., & Elster, K. (2012, December 31). Helping women shape a healthy workforce [Web log post]. *Smartblogs on Leadership.* Retrieved from http://smartblogs.com/leadership/2012/12/31/helping-women-shape-healthy-workforce

Edwards, M. (2007). The modern school superintendent: An overview of the role and responsibilities in the 21st century. Lincoln, NE: iUniverse.

Friesen, S., & Lock, J. (2010, April). *High-Performing school systems in the application of 21st century learning technologies: Review of the research.* Retrieved from http://o.b5z.net/i/u/10063916/h/Pre-Conference/cass_lit-review_final.pdf

Glass, T. E., & Franceschini, L. A. (2007). *The state of the American school superintendency: A mid-decade study.* Lanham, MD: Rowman & Littlefield.

Hodgkinson, H. L., & Montenegro, X. (1999). *The U.S. school superintendent: The invisible CEO.* Washington, DC: Institute of Educational Leadership.

Houston, P. D. (2007). *From custodian to conductor.* Alexandria, VA: The School of Superintendents Association. Retrieved from http://www.aasa.org/School-AdministratorArticle.aspx?id=7078

Jensen, A. J. (2011). Two decades as a shared superintendent. *School Administrator, 68*(4), 14–15. Retrieved from http://www.aasa.org/SchoolAdministratorAr-ticle.aspx?id=18558

Jonsson, P. (2008, March 31). Rise of the 'rock star' school superintendent. *The Christian Science Monitor.* Retreived from http://www.csmonitor.com/2008/0331/p01s03-usgn.html

Kisch, M. (2012). The balancing act. *School Administrator, 69*(10), 42–48.

Konnert, W. M., & Augenstein, J. J. (1990). The superintendency in the nineties: What superintendents and board members need to know. Lancaster, PA: Technomic.

Leithwood, K. (2008, April). *Evidence-based characteristics of high-performing school districts.* Paper presented at the Moving and Improving Symposium, College of Alberta School Superintendents, Edmonton, Alberta, Canada.

Leithwood, K. (2010). *Turning around underperforming school systems: Guidelines for district leaders.* Paper prepared for the College of Alberta School Superintendents, Edmonton, Alberta, Canada.

Leithwood, K. (2011, March). *District effectiveness framework.* Paper presented at the Annual Pre-Conference of the College of Alberta School Superintendents, Edmonton, Alberta, Canada.

Litun, B. (2015, November 3). Dennis Parsons' interview with the president of the College of Alberta School Superintendents recorded in Calgary, Alberta, Canada.

Louis, K. S., Leithwood, K., Anderson, S., & Wahlstrom, K. (2010). *Key findings: Learning from leadership: Investigating the links to improved student learning:* New York, NY: The Wallace Foundation.

Lowe, G. (2015, May 25). *Resilience in leadership project, Phase 1.* An in-house unpublished report commissioned by the College of Alberta School Superintendents and the Alberta School Employee Benefits Plan, Calgary, Alberta, Canada.

Marzano, R. J., & Walters, T. (2009). *District leadership that works: Striking the right balance.* Bloomington, IN: Solution Tree Press/McRel.

Merriam, S. (1998). Qualitative research and case study applications in education: Revised and expanded form case study research in education (2nd ed.). San Francisco, CA: Jossey-Bass.

Merriam, S. (2009). Qualitative research: A guide to design and implementation. San Francisco, CA: Jossey-Bass.

Murphy, B. J. (1994). *The superintendent of Nova Scotia: Role, effectiveness, influence and job satisfaction* (Unpublished doctoral dissertation). University of Alberta, Edmonton, Alberta, Canada.

Orr, M. T. (2006). Learning the superintendency: Socialization, negotiation, and determination. *Teachers College Record, 108*(7), 1362–1403.

Parsons, D. G. (2016). *The impact of the office of superintendent of schools on the personal lives of superintendents* (Doctoral dissertation). University of Calgary, Calgary, Alberta, Canada. Retrieved from http://theses.ucalgary.ca/jspui/handle/11023/2993

Pettigrew, B. (2000). *The work life of a superintendent of schools* (Doctoral dissertation). University of Alberta, Edmonton, Alberta, Canada. Retrieved from http://www.collectionscanada.gc.ca/obj/s4/f2/dsk1/tape3/PQDD_0011/NQ60208.pdf

Porter, M., & Nohria, N. (2010). What is leadership: The CEO's role in large, complex organizations. In N. Nohria & R. Khurana (Eds.), *Handbook of leadership theory and practice* (pp. 433–473). Boston, MA: Harvard University Press.

Schlechty, P. C. (2002). Working on the work: An action plan for teachers, principals, and superintendents. San Francisco, CA: Jossey Bass.

Sheppard, B., Brown, J., & Dibbon, D. (2009). *School district leadership matters.* LaVergne, TN: Springer Press.

Short, P. M., & Scribner, J. R. (Eds.). (2002). *Case studies of the superintendency.* Lanham, MD: Scarecrow Press.

Sovine, D. (2009). *First year: Challenges and mediating strategies for novice superintendents* (Doctoral dissertation). University of Virginia, Charlottesville, VA. Retrieved from ProQuest Dissertations and Theses database. (UMI 3353822)

Yin, R. (2009). *Case study research: Design and methods* (4th ed.). Thousand Oaks, CA: SAGE.

CHAPTER 13

EVOLVING PRACTICES FOR DEALING WITH SUPERINTENDENT STRESS

Compassion, Self-Compassion, and Mindfulness

Caryn M. Wells
Oakland University

Mindfulness provides a simple but powerful route for getting ourselves unstuck, back into touch with our own wisdom and vitality.

—Kabat-Zinn, 1994, p. 5

Jon Kabat-Zinn, the molecular biologist who brought the practice of mindfulness to the University of Massachusetts Medical School in 1979, and is credited with helping to make mindfulness mainstream in the Western world, offers a perspective in this quote to slow down and take notice of all that is happening. He is referring to practicing mindfulness while reminding us that things are always changing, much like the rushing stream of our own thoughts and our overcrowded agendas. Such is the life for the busy and often overwhelmed agendas of school superintendents. This chapter

The Contemporary Superintendent, pages 225–248
Copyright © 2019 by Information Age Publishing

is written for them, and the people who offer training and professional development targeted for their needs. The hope is for learning resilience and ways to follow the advice given on airplanes, to simply put on the oxygen mask first, before trying to do the same for others. The messages in this writing invite busy superintendents to slow down their world to: *face the storm—it is there anyway; and embrace the quiet—it is there within.* Kabat-Zinn (1994) reminded us, "You can't stop the waves but you can learn to surf" (p. 30). *This chapter is about learning to surf…*

In this chapter, I advocate for the inclusion of compassion, self-compassion, and mindfulness for school superintendents. These practices have a duality of purpose; to relieve the stress that superintendents encounter, and to arm them with characteristics that are associated with emotional intelligence, ones that relate to effective school leadership. This chapter is written to address the issues inherent in the reality of the job of superintendents that are not unnoticed, yet the interventions, programs, or training to address these challenges is strangely and woefully absent in the literature, professional organizations, or preparation programs. If we are concerned about the personal narratives of school superintendents, the attrition rates, and the reported levels of stress, we include programs that can teach them to "bounce back" or become resilient at work. As will be apparent in this chapter, the solutions are not binary with an either/or approach that either cares for the self or the people in the organization. Instead, I posit that the practices that can support superintendents are the same practices that can support the people in the school district.

BACKGROUND

It is an established fact that the stress levels of superintendents have increased substantially in recent years, with concerns for the high sense of frustration, dissatisfaction, and pressures that are compounded in a job that may feel impossible (Glass & Franceschini, 2007; Hawk & Martin, 2011; Wells, Maxfield, & Klocko, 2011). Stress can have deleterious impact on the physical and emotional life of the leader, leaving the person with a diminished resolve for handling the daily pressures of the job (Boyatzis & McKee, 2005; Heifetz & Linsky, 2002; Sorenson, 2007). Stress levels are not reserved only for the school superintendents; over one third of workers in the United States reported that their jobs ranged from often to always stressful (Murphy & Sauter, 2003). It can be understood that stress is a common complaint, with companies looking for methods to alleviate stress for workers, for job productivity, or health of the worker (Murphy, 1995; Murphy & Sauter, 2003). The stress levels of workers have become a concern for organizations; reports of illness and sick leave continue to increase in the workplace (Richardson & Rothstein, 2008). Workers complain with regularity that they are expected to have "24/7" connectivity (Fries, 2009). Stress levels often result in serious health issues that include the overproduction of cortisol, learned helplessness, depression, and other chronic diseases (Garland, 2007).

School district superintendents are expected to provide leadership and vision for the district, while being available for concerns, questions, and conflict within the community; workdays can become blurred with regard to when the workday begins and ends, with work expectations that extend into evenings and weekends. Challenges and problems that contemporary superintendents face vary by districts, with the most pressing issues of urban districts not necessarily surfacing on the list of those in rural locations (Kowalski & Brunner, 2005; Kowalski, Young, & Petersen, 2013). While the issues and stressful situations facing school superintendents may differ, there are common understandings that they are facing financial challenges, pressures in a day of accountability and high visibility, school board and special interest group pressures, expectations for improved student achievement, litigation, declining enrollment, students with increased social and emotional issues, and expectations for increased job performance (Glass & Franceschini, 2007; Harris, Lowery, Hopson, & Marshall, 2004; Hawk & Martin, 2011; Kowalski & Brunner, 2005, Orr, 2006, 2007; Trevino, Braley, Brown, & Slate, 2008). In particular, superintendents report the unrelenting pace of the job with expectations that flood the horizon throughout the day and evenings, making it difficult to prioritize and address all of the issues (Orr, 2006).

Glass and Franceschini (2007) reported findings of the highest stress levels of any previous study conducted in an American Association of School Administrators (AASA) study, with 44.3% feeling considerable stress as superintendents and 34.1% experiencing *very great stress*. Together, these figures result in almost 60% of superintendents reporting feeling considerable to very great stress, a serious issue that is reported to have worsened since these figures were released. Glass and Franceschini further reported,

> Interpersonal relations is the factor both facilitating and restricting superintendents' effectiveness. Key professional development needs identified by superintendents are interpersonal skills, strategic planning, and systemic thinking. (p. xvi)

In a study with public school superintendents in Texas, the top challenges listed by superintendents were organizational, economic, personnel, and student-centered, citing issues of how the superintendency has changed and become more stressful (Trevino et al., 2008). Rural school superintendents that encountered involuntary turnovers in their positions were related to political conflicts, financial problems, internal problems with teachers and principals, and external problems with the larger community (Tekniepe, 2015).

Concerns have surfaced over shortages for educational positions of educational leaders, including that of superintendents (Orr, 2006), based partly upon the level of stress in the position (Tekniepe, 2015; Trevino et al., 2008). Glass, Bjork, and Brunner, (2000) reported that the average tenure of superintendents is approximately 5 years. A study in California revealed that 45% of the 215 superintendents hired in 2006 left the position within 3 years (Grissom & Anderson, 2012). In addition to the stress levels of superintendents are the problems to which they may contribute, such as entering a district with a belief that they can cause change in a district that has a history and culture that is well established (Kerrins & Cushing, 2001). Despite the fact that the stress of superintendents is well documented, the physical or emotional implications are not. The research about superintendents primarily focuses on the nature of the job, nuances between leadership and management, and leadership preparation (Glass & Franceschini, 2007), while there is a dearth of information regarding the results of the levels of stress that they face. Educators who are dealing with chronic stress levels may encounter various types of physiological or psychological problems, including anxiety, boredom, or nervous breakdowns as they try to cope with the pressures from work (Sorenson, 2007). Professionals in higher status occupations experience increased job duties, where the expectations of the job reduce their availability for family obligations, with extended workdays and a sense of loss of control over the workday (Moen, Lam, Ammons, & Kelly, 2013) much like the reports of the stress levels of school superintendents. The lack of control and overwhelm of the higher level positions creates a sense of perpetual overload.

When superintendents were asked, in a research study, to describe what strategies might make a difference for them with regard to their stress, the themes that emerged were: no known strategies, getting away, assistance from the school board, mentoring efforts, wellness programs, or professional development (Hawk & Martin, 2011). In this chapter, efforts related to wellness will be explored, citing the effectiveness of programs that have made a positive difference to address stress levels in a variety of work environments. The wellness programs that will be reviewed are efforts that address stress levels and the accompanying levels of burnout that stress enhances, and the sense of disappointment, failure, and challenge that all leaders face in their careers.

DEALING WITH DISAPPOINTMENTS AND FAILURE

Superintendents, like all people, deal with life's disappointments, challenges, and failures. The stress involved with these failures can take a toll on the emotional and physical health of an educational leader (Sorenson, 2007). If the superintendent is dealing with challenges from school board members, budget reductions, or any other problems that relate to conflicts or legislative mandates, it matters how they work with the failures. If the superintendents fall into what Boyatzis and McKee (2005) refer to as the sacrifice syndrome from chronic or acute stress where they have given too much of themselves, falling into emotional exhaustion, they are at risk for burnout. Failure and disappointments do not have to be the end of the personal narratives of superintendents.

Failures can offer incredible insights as to what happened, with learning from what did and did not work. If leaders look objectively at the failure, powerful learning examples can emerge (Weinzimmer & McConoughey, 2013). Mindfulness and self-compassion offer inroads to an acceptance of reality that allows for introspection and analysis. Because people are led to believe that failures are negative, it is easy to understand why leaders can get caught up in defensive posturing, denial, or blame, as opposed to building learning cultures that gravitate toward understanding what occurred for the purpose of forward growth (Edmondson, 2011). Weinzimmer and McConoughey (2013) related, "Mistakes are part of taking healthy risks" (p. 8). It takes courage to take the risks to be with the problems, disappointments, and failures (Frost, 2004); leaders who practice self-compassion see the common humanity in errors and they develop resilience for forward movement.

DeLong and DeLong (2011) advocated for leaders to learn to put the past behind in favor of learning, allowing oneself to become vulnerable to the reality of the situation and accepting support and guidance from a network worthy of that trust. Mindful acceptance assists in seeing the reality of the situation without developing a storyline as to what occurred, who did what to whom, and who is to blame. Unfortunately, many leaders do not learn from failure or success; failures may be brushed aside or denied, and successes carry another weight of disregard. Leaders may be involved with errors in thinking where they believe that the success of the organization is a result of their efforts without looking to the larger system, they may be overconfident in previous success, and they might not fully analyze the why behind that success (Gino & Pisano, 2011). It is easy to see how distraction and preoccupation might interfere with being fully present for observing a current situation or in reflecting or responding to a precious one. Being overwhelmed and exhausted are understandable; they are also symptomatic of a word that has been as obsequious as stress-burnout.

THE NATURE OF JOB BURNOUT

Burnout is a pervasive symptom of working too hard and giving too much. The characteristics of burnout include hopelessness, cynicism, and feelings of inefficiency (Maslach & Leiter, 2008). When people experience burnout they fall under the categories of an erosion of engagement with the job, an erosion of emotions, and an experience of lack of fit between the person and the job (Maslach & Leiter, 1997, p. 23). With burnout, the level at which a person begins a job begins to slip to the level of erosion where that person no longer feels the sense of enthusiasm or connection with the actual work or the people in the organization.

Burnout involves a type of emotional exhaustion noted within helping professions such as social work, medical professions, police work, legal professions, or psychotherapy (Schaufeli, Leiter, & Maslach, 2009). The original model of burnout was noted in being overextended on the job, as researched in either human services or educational occupations (Leiter & Maslach, 2004). With demands for increased service, or extending service of care, burnout tendencies rose for people in a broad base of occupations (Schaufeli et al., 2009). The Maslach burnout inventory (MBI) scale lists exhaustion, cynicism, and inefficiency as the indicators, beyond the first label of exhaustion that is a common complaint of contemporary workers (MBI; Maslach & Jackson, 1981).

Cynicism and exhaustion are present with work overload and social conflict, and the feelings of inefficiency are related to either the lack of resources to complete the job as defined, or the resources that are needed to do the same (Maslach, 2003). The level of superintendent burnout is a statistic that is not reported in the literature; therefore, research from the research about occupational burnout is reviewed, and noted for its application to the job demands of superintendents. The research involving superintendents clearly outlines the overload of the job, the conflicts endemic to the job, stressful relationships with school board members, or the diminishing resources available for the job (Kowalski, 2005). The characteristics of burnout such as cynicism, emotional exhaustion, and a sense of inefficiency are aligned with the conditions inherent in the superintendency, and they appear in the literature where the nature of the superintendents' jobs are described by the high levels of stress and demands they encounter.

Interventions for individuals experiencing burnout have often focused on either removing the person from the position or providing training for the person to change behaviors associated with the job or fortify the internal resources needed to complete the job (Maslach, 2003). The primary interventions to counter workplace stress include jobs that are redesigned or risk factors reduced; secondary interventions are the teaching about coping skills, about the symptoms of the stress before illness are manifested; tertiary programs offer clinical approaches such as employee assistance programs of mental health therapy (Murphy, 1995). New programs are emerging to deal with stress and burnout in other occupations; one such program is the one that has been designed for physicians by physicians

(Krasner et al., 2009). This particular program was designed for physicians who have experienced stress and burnout at concerning rates.

The burnout rate for physicians is listed as one out of three at any given time within their career (Shanafelt, Sloan, & Haberman, 2003) where doctors begin to experience the sense of exhaustion and sense of inefficiency; depersonalization may be another byproduct of burnout. Physician burnout has been listed as a major concern for the physicians who practice, with subsequent concerns for their well-being (Dyrbye & Shanafelt, 2011; Spickard, Gabbe, & Christenson, 2002; West, Shanafelt, & Kolars, 2011). Although widely understood and accepted that physicians experience high levels of stress, few studies have been conducted to evaluate interventions that may be applied to reduce that stress (Shanafelt, 2009). Krasner et al. (2009) developed a curriculum program in mindfulness and self-awareness that positively impacts physician mood, burnout, and empathy. The physicians reported changes in which their levels of attention in mindfulness were increased, and the resulting changes in a reduction in their own levels of distress.

The majority of research reports on mindfulness in the workplace have focused on occupations within health, well-being, or psychology, as opposed to issues of management. In education, mindfulness research has focused on teachers and students (Flook, Goldberg, Pinger, & Davidson, 2015; Flook, Goldberg, Pinger, Bonus, & Davidson, 2013).

A program in mindfulness that was offered for 113 teachers resulted in greater mindfulness, focused attention, and self-compassion associated with work, with lowered stress levels for the teachers (Roeser et al., 2013). *How might a program of mindfulness work for school superintendents relative to stress or burnout reduction, and specifically, how might mindfulness or mindful self-compassion play a role in the same?*

CONCEPTUAL UNDERPINNINGS: MINDFULNESS, COMPASSION, AND SELF-COMPASSION

Mindfulness, compassion, and self-compassion are explored in this chapter for the numerous health benefits they offer, and to the opportunities that they might present for the workplace. They are also examined for the contributions that they may make to the school superintendent for stress reduction, and for the alignment they have with leadership effectiveness. Components of mindfulness, compassion, and self-compassion are aligned with empathy, where understanding and non-judgment are part of the core. Empathy is foundational to emotional intelligence, a key variable in the effectiveness of leaders (Goleman, 2000).

The workload pressures of superintendents provide a portal into understanding the relentless pace of their jobs and the reasons for the attrition

232 • C. M. WELLS

rates of that position. Stress reduction practices such as mindfulness practice are aligned with leadership effectiveness, a distinct advantage for both relieving stress, and providing support for staying with the job. Mindfulness practice also adds qualities that can enhance relationships with employees. Mindfulness, compassion, and self-compassion practices embody caring, kindness, and empathy, all "soft skills" that are important for school superintendents. The soft skills such as interpersonal skills of listening, communicating, and caring has been the subject of management training programs, designed to increase the effectiveness of managers, expanding the concerns for developing a work culture that is responsive as well as productive. Emotional intelligence and resilience were correlated with leadership success for school administrators (Maulding, Peters, Roberts, Leonard, & Sparkman, 2012). Empathy is an important element in patient care (Reiss, 2010), in military leadership (Garner, 2009; Pagonis, 2001), and the corporate world (Goleman, 2000). Louis, Murphy, and Smylie (2016) referred to the importance of caring in school leadership to support student learning, and the well-being of students and teachers in the schools.

Goleman presented the "hard case for soft skills" in which leaders would be emotionally aware and responsive to the needs of the workers (2000, p. 31; 2013, p. 235). The recent criticisms of leadership have led to calls for increased sensitivity of these soft skills (Marques, 2013). Superintendents who display foundational attributes of mindfulness such as listening, compassion, patience, letting go, and being in the moment (Kabat-Zinn, 2009) are exhibiting components of emotional and social intelligence. Emotional intelligence includes factors such as self-regulation, self-awareness, social awareness, and relationship management (Goleman, Boyatzis, & McKee, 2002). Social intelligence factors include empathy, attunement, influence, the development of others, inspiration, and teamwork (Goleman & Boyatzis, 2008). Mindfulness, compassion, and self-compassion are reviewed in this chapter for the duality of purpose they provide, one in which serves both the superintendent and the school district.

Mindfulness

Mindfulness involves being in the present moment without judgment or criticism. Jon Kabat-Zinn (2005) offered, "Mindfulness can be thought of as moment-to-moment nonjudgmental awareness, cultivated by paying attention in a specific way that is, in the present moment, and as non-reactively, as non-judgmentally, and as openheartedly as possible" (p. 108). Mindfulness is a practice that involves quieting the mind to witness what is there to be observed, usually paying attention to one of the following: hearing, breathing, body sensations, or thoughts that enter and leave the mind. It is a practice that has origins in ancient Eastern traditions, and it has found its place in Western society with both interest in, and research of mindfulness that has reached exponential growth (Brown, Ryan, & Creswell, 2007; Dane & Brummel, 2014). Mindfulness can include a practice of meditation where the focus is on the thoughts, feelings, sounds, or body sensations, or it can be simply the art of paying attention to the present moment (Kabat-Zinn, 2009).

Mindfulness practice has numerous benefits. Participants who underwent an 8-week program in mindfulness known as mindfulness-based stress reduction (MBSR) demonstrated changes in the brain associated with learning and memory processes, emotion regulation, perspective taking, and self-referential processing (Carmody & Baer, 2008; Hölzel et al., 2010). Mindfulness practice is associated with reduction in anxiety, distraction, and rumination of thought (Jain et al., 2007). Mindfulness practice also shows promise to be able to overcome mind wandering, to develop multiple perspectives, and gain optimism (Niemiec, Rashid, & Spinella, 2012).

Mindfulness is positively correlated with conscientiousness and agreeableness, and negatively correlated with being neurotic (Thompson & Waltz, 2007). Depressive symptoms, stress, and medical symptoms have all been reduced through mindfulness practice (Dobkin & Zhao, 2011). Mindfulness-based stress reduction (MBSR) is taught in medical schools to help medical students deal more effectively with the tremendous stress they encounter. The MBSR training produced reduced levels of anxiety, depression, and increased levels of empathy and spiritual experiences for medical students (Shapiro, Schwartz, & Bonner, 1998).

Mindfulness practice has direct application to the workplace, stress reduction, and leadership (Dane, 2011). Mindfulness meditation decreases anxiety and increases positive affect and immune function (Davidson et al., 2003) and is correlated with psychological and physical well-being as well as intention to stay in the workplace as opposed to leaving it (Andrews, Kacmar, & Kacmar, 2014; Dane & Brummel, 2014). Psychologists and physicians have used mindfulness practice therapeutically to help patients deal with anxiety, depression, and chronic pain (Baer, 2003). Numerous professional fields have embraced practices such as mindfulness to provide emotional support, encourage emotional intelligence qualities such as self-regulation, or relaxation that can lead to renewal and resilience in the job of leading (Gelles, 2015; Tan, Goleman, & Kabat-Zinn, 2012). Mindfulness practice has a positive influence on a number of work-related outcomes, such as resilience, innovation, and job productivity (Chaskalson, 2011).

Mindful leadership has been conceptualized and includes the constructs in Table 13.1 (Wells, 2015, p. 17). The mindfulness constructs translate to and are affiliated with emotional intelligence factors, such as empathy, self-regulation, and self-management (Goleman, 2000). This chart offers a view of leadership that addresses the affective, emotional, and relational aspects

TABLE 13.1 Mindful Leadership Is		
Instead of	Mindful Leadership Approaches	Instead of acting
Unaware; not seeing the reality of the situation	← Acceptance →	Blaming others
Preoccupied or distracted	← Awareness →	Refusing to accept reality
Regretting the past	← Being Fully Present →	Worrying about tomorrow
Not caring or listening to someone in need	← Compassion →	Judging + criticism
Not caring enough to be interested	← Letting Go →	Holding on
Disregarding	← Listening →	Interrupting or telling your story
Not observing or being aware of a situation not on the "radar screen"	← Patience →	Lashing out
Denying; avoiding	← Responding →	Angry outburst; reacting
Disbelief; disregard	← Trust →	Duplicity; Not doing what you say

Source: Wells (2015, p. 17)

that effective leaders demonstrate (Goleman, 2000). The qualities that are listed in the chart are adapted from the attitudinal foundation of mindfulness as defined by Jon Kabat-Zinn (2009). These qualities are dependent on the foundation of intention, as witnessed in the intention to be fully present for what is occurring with self or others.

Mindful leaders are fully present for all that happens in the school district, being aware and emotionally available for the people and the issues, as represented in Figure 13.1.

As depicted, it is possible for a superintendent to demonstrate a range of empathy for others as well as attention to their particular situations. A superintendent may be concerned and interested about others, but simply so distracted and preoccupied that he or she is not attending to their needs or concerns. Likewise, a superintendent could observe or notice what is happening but lack interest or empathy for the situation, particularly with the rate of burnout. Situations of low attention and empathy would result in a loss of relationship building with others. When superintendents practice high degrees of empathy and interest in others, there is a tendency to be mindfully aware and responsive to the concerns and needs of others; this is a description of mindful leaders.

As with other occupations, when people are besieged by requests for personal attention or compassion, their responses can be mediated by the pace and level of intensity or stress that they experience (Maslach & Leiter, 2008). Mindfulness and mindful self-compassion interrupt the cycle of

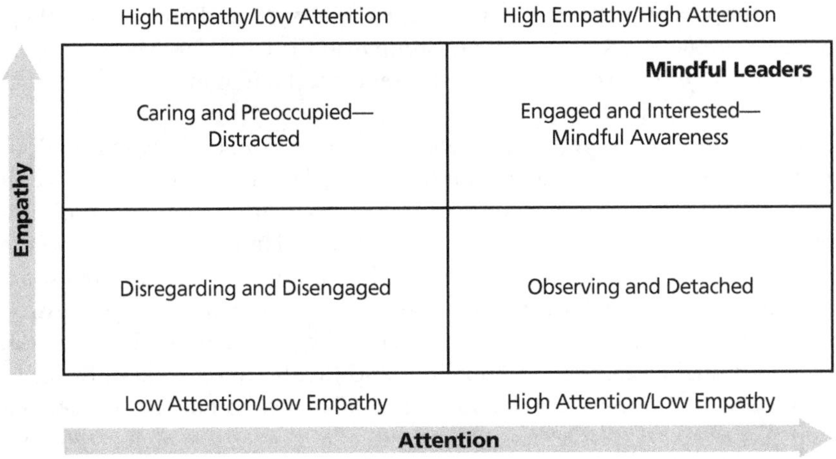

High Empathy/Low Attention   High Empathy/High Attention

	Mindful Leaders
Caring and Preoccupied— Distracted	Engaged and Interested— Mindful Awareness
Disregarding and Disengaged	Observing and Detached

Low Attention/Low Empathy   High Attention/Low Empathy

Attention

Empathy

Figure 13.1   Mindful leaders. *Source:* Wells, 2016, p. 8.

this pace and offer an alternative, one that includes the qualities that can soothe or support the leader, while attending to the requests and needs of the people in the organization.

It is the *intentional being present* for what happens in the organization that is distinguished from what otherwise might be the preoccupied or distracted leader with divided attention. Mindfulness practice reinforces the focus on the present moment without criticism or judgment, offering, instead, an empathic listening and interest in what is occurring.

Mindfulness practice is offered and promoted in diverse industries such as Target, Aetna, Ford Motor Company, Eileen Fisher, Audacity, Facebook, Google, and Twitter (Gelles, 2015; Hunter, 2013). Mindfulness is also practiced in medical schools, hospital settings, and the military and for non-civilian roles such as police officers (Gable, 2014; Gelles, 2015; Hunter, 2013; Kabat-Zinn, 2005). In this chapter, mindfulness is presented for its application for superintendents.

Compassion

Compassion has been referred to as choosing to do something for someone in distress, or going beyond empathy for another person, to choose to act upon those feelings (Davenport, 2015; Frost, 2011). As such, compassion involves energy and action and it is directed outward to others in need. Compassion is part of the fabric of social connection, an area that sociological research indicates is decreasing with speed that concerns researchers because of the importance of connection with emotional well-being; as such, compassion is viewed as a means to increase social connection (Seppala, Rossomando, & Doty, 2013). Compassion is part of a dynamic, along with empathy, altruism, and sympathy, seen crucial to human development and survival (Radey & Figley, 2007).

Compassion, often referred to as empathy in action, relates to the various acts of kindness and caring for the students and workers in the districts that superintendents can foster. Compassion relates to areas such as modeling a responsive approach for people in need, adding elements of concern to the workplace, encouraging the culture, and exhibiting affective, humanistic, and emotional ties with the students and faculty of the district. Compassion relates to social and emotional intelligence factors, such as self-awareness, organizational awareness, influencing, and flexibility (Goleman, Boyatzis, & McKee, 2002). These are the qualities that are evident in effective leadership (George, 2012; Goleman, 2000; Goleman, Boyatzis, & McKee, 2002).

The role of compassion is considered for its relation to the role of the leader. Some leaders display compassion with ease; their compassion is a feeling that permeates the culture of the organization (Goleman, 2000). Tragedies, disequilibrium, or problems within an organization often result in a collective response of compassion (Madden, Duchon, Madden, & Plowman, 2012). Compassion is linked with various types of leadership and examined by occupations where it is related to part of the function of the particular job.

Compassion and vision are considered important elements of physician leadership where the physicians mediate the problems that emerge within the hospital (Quinn, 2015). Additionally, empathic physicians have patients with stronger immune systems, shorter post-surgery stays, and stronger placebo response (Reiss, 2010). Compassion in healthcare occupations is often reviewed for its value to the profession (Kneafsey, Brown, Sein, Chamley, & Parsons; 2015). Compassionate listening is a form of active listening in which one person shifts away from thought of self to that of another, extolled for its benefits to the healthcare profession (Kimble, 2103).

Compassion, within an organization, is viewed for its ability to inspire action like what happens when a compassionate person influences people in the workplace to act similarly to promote harmony and growth in others (Dutton & Workman, 2011). Compassion, as a verb implying action, is thus able to inspire a forward movement of more action, generating kindness and concern. Leadership models, such as servant leadership, have a foundation of compassion and caring at its core (Davenport, 2015; van Dierendonck & Patterson, 2015). The display of compassion at work is associated with commitment to the workplace and emotions that are strongly positive (Lilius et al., 2008).

The generative force of compassion that is evident in healthcare or corporate organizations is important in education, where the suffering of anyone in the school or school district can be attended to with kindness and understanding by the leader of the district—the superintendent. A question emerges: Can compassionate superintendents also have compassion for themselves, and if so, how is it demonstrated?

Self-Compassion

Simply stated, self-compassion is kindness directed inward. Neff (2003) conceptualized self-compassion to include three qualities of being open to one's own suffering and offering kindness instead of criticism, seeing the common humanity of life's disappointments and failures, and being mindful of them by not overreacting to or dismissing those problems. Self-compassion is not reacting in self-indulgence; instead it is clearly seeing the problems one has and providing a type of emotional security where the feelings can be experienced without the harsh criticism of anger or belittlement (Neff, 2004).

Self-compassion has been associated with numerous positive benefits. Among them include a sense of optimism and emotional intelligence, working against the sense of anxiety associated with self-evaluation, and an increased sense of well-being (Neff, Kirkpatrick, & Rude, 2007). Self-compassion is negatively correlated with anxiety and depression (Barnard & Curry, 2011). People who practice self-compassion are associated with increased risk or perspective taking, because of the tendency to display kindness toward the self; therefore the option of taking a risk is less threatening (Neff & Pommier, 2012). Instead of denying, projecting, or blaming for life's problems, self-compassion actually helps to face the problems and to do so with kindness and understanding that life problems exist for all people. The sense of well-being is important for people; those exhibiting self-compassion felt less emotional turmoil and a greater sense of well-being (Yarnell & Neff, 2012).

Interest and research in self-compassion has grown dramatically with over 200 dissertations and journal articles written about the topic since 2003 (Germer & Neff, 2013), when Neff conceptualized self-compassion and suggested measurements to study the components (2003). Neff's subscales measure self-kindness versus self-judgment; a sense of common humanity versus isolation; and a mindful approach where one does not avoid or ruminate in the thoughts concerning failures or disappointments. Because the issues of self-compassion are directed inward, there is no association or measurement in comparison with others (Neff & Germer, 2012).

Two different groups of participants that went through an 8-week program in self-compassion demonstrated gains in self-compassion, well-being, and mindfulness (Neff & Germer, 2012). Like emotional intelligence, self-compassion can be learned. Important to superintendents and their longevity on the job, is the cultivation of resilience, something that self-compassion enhances (Neff & McGehee, 2010). A meta-analysis in the relationship of self-compassion and well-being revealed the strength of psychological and cognitive well-being with self-compassion (Zessin, Dickhäuser, & Garbade, 2015). The measurements that have gained traction in education have centered primarily on student achievement and standardized tests. *What would measures of well-being look like for the superintendents who are the leaders for this nation's schools, and how important might they be for the resilience of these leaders?*

WELL-BEING AND SELF-CARE

What are the measures of well-being or wellness that can assist superintendents to stay the course in their respective positions, without bowing to the depths of frustration or despair that can be apparent in the world of work they encounter. The thought of well-being might be elusive to the overwhelm and distraction that are part of the superintendents' world. They may question exactly what wellness is, given the responsibilities and demands of the job, and how to pursue it, encourage or create it. And, it may be one thing to conceptualize mindfulness for self and entirely another for the superintendent to consider the self for well-being. *Even if superintendents know the basics of self-care, would they know what to do next to begin the process?* Probably not, given the world in which they reside with the superintendency. Well-being or wellness has not been part of the superintendents' lexicon; the literature that describes superintendents' work is often other-centered or results-driven, for students, faculty, staff, school boards, and the community, as opposed to descriptions that deal with the self. Unfortunately, programs designed for superintendent stress is absent in the literature; wellness programs are designed for student health, or employee assistance programs.

In school districts, wellness policies often deal with nutrition and fitness to counteract childhood obesity (Smith, Capogrossi, & Estabrooks, 2012) and the implementation of school wellness programs are designed to address the hunger that many school age children encounter (Budd, Schwartz, Yount, & Haire-Joshu, 2012). Despite the increased and positive attention to wellness for school children, the alarming stress levels of school administrators raise questions as to why there is a lack of information and focus on the health and wellness of school leaders (Beisser, Peters, & Thacker, 2014). Because of the dearth of information related to superintendent stress reduction, wellness, well-being, or self-care, models from health, business, or medicine are reviewed for their application and potential for administrative support.

Well-being in the workplace is associated with all levels of the organization, from management to external variables, as well as situations or people below the level of management (Biggio & Cortese, 2013). The factors that influence people in the organization are the stressors that can mount to a place of impact, resulting in emotional, psychological, or physical problems (Greeson, 2009). Various occupations and professions offer training in mindfulness to combat these stressors and teach the employees how to practice a form of self-care. A course in mind-body medicine and the art of self-care was developed to teach mindfulness and self-care to counseling students; this course resulted in positive changes in their emotional, physical, and mental conditions along with a positive impact in their counseling skills (Newsome, Christopher, Dahlen, & Christopher, 2006).

Physicians have a variety of mindfulness-based programs to reduce stress and offer teaching in self-care. As programs gain attention in mindfulness-related programs to combat the stress of physicians, research reports specifically call for the need for programs teaching and promoting, self-care for oncologists, whose stressors resulted in burnout, and psychiatric distress (Guest et al., 2011). Medical students learning mindfulness practice, related benefits of self-care that included exercise, social support, and sleep (Greeson, Toohey, & Pearce, 2015).

Mental health workers experience stress in providing care for people with serious mental health issues. Therapists learning self-care who were exposed to programs in mindfulness reported important increases in positive affect and self-compassion as well as significant declines in rumination of ideas, stress, and negative affect (Shapiro, Brown, & Biegel, 2007; Wise, Hersh, & Gibson, 2012). Students in a social work program who were being trained to work with trauma patients, completed training in journaling and mindfulness-based stress reduction and reported challenges in developing self-care practices, yet they demonstrated the ability to integrate self-care in their professional practice characteristics (Shannon, Simmelink-McCleary, Im, Becher, & Crook-Lyon, 2014). These social work students learned physical strategies that included walking, running, dance, or yoga; relational strategies such as cultivating friends or colleagues; and cognitive strategies such as mindfulness practices to calm the rumination and enter into the present moment.

Mindfulness training is gaining expansion into the business world with numerous examples of programs embedded in major corporations, including Facebook, Target, Aetna, General Mills, Google, Audacity, Twitter (Gelles, 2013; Hyland, Lee, & Mills, 2015; Tan, Goleman, & Kabat-Zinn, 2012). The reports from corporations include improvements in the cognitive, psychological, and physical domains (Hyland, et al., 2015). Because mindfulness improves human functioning and relates to workplace effectiveness, analysts have reported the application of these characteristics to the work environment (Good et al., 2016).

All of these examples of mindfulness training and practice have common denominators, despite the variety of workplace expression of job functions from where they are expressed, and that commonality is stress reduction, self-care, and compassion. Research on mindfulness practices is depicting the impact on physiology, emotion, thinking, and behaviors; the variables that can impact work environment productivity, outcomes, well-being, and workplace relationships (Good et al., 2016). Where does the topic of self-care, stress reduction, compassion, or self-compassion appear in the various educational leadership programs, or offerings within professional organizations?

The ELCC Standards (Educational Leadership Constituent Council) that guide educational leadership preparation includes information to inspire the development of aspiring and practicing school administrators to include awareness, understanding, and application to guide the leadership of schools to focus on successful student achievement, and safe and nurturing school cultures that engage parents and the community. These standards specify ethical leadership and the creation of a vision for shared leadership. The standards do not include information about self-care for educational leaders. The affective aspects of the job have supreme importance because they augment the technical skills and lead with a different type of authority, that of emotional and social intelligence (Goleman, Boyatzis, & McKee, 2002).

In addition to preparing superintendents to handle the technical aspects of the job, such as dealing with management issues, budget and finance, data analysis, and educational law, superintendents in 23 focus group interviews identified numerous areas that would help them to deal with the daily issues that surfaced, such as dealing with interpersonal relations, political encounters, gaining consensus, and working with other leaders who could provide consultation and support (Orr, 2006). The socialization factors of these superintendents was seen as critical for them to deal with the reality of the position that could help them to cope and not take issues so seriously, areas that would support concepts of affective, emotional, or humanistic elements of the job. Emotional training and affective areas are enhanced by mindfulness, compassion, and self-compassion.

THE EVOLVING VISION FOR SELF-CARE AND WELLNESS

An evolving vision for the introduction of self-care of superintendents could include the evidence-based practices that are outlined in this chapter, with adaptations that fit the world that school superintendents inhabit. Self-care for superintendents would include learning elements of mindfulness, compassion, and self-compassion and an advocacy for the importance of learning what it means to take care of oneself, an elusive thought for one that is otherwise preoccupied and distracted. The training could be part of educational leadership preparation programs taught at universities; it could also be offered by professional organizations in workshops, seminars, or retreats. The training would focus on what these elements include, how they are practiced, and how they benefit the individual as well as the organization. The conceptual elements are best understood through experience, or practice where the concepts are embodied and felt.

The qualities of mindfulness, compassion, and self-compassion are interrelated. The essence of mindful leadership is one that offers descriptions inherent in self-care with issues of compassion and self-compassion, where patience, listening, responding, acceptance, and letting go are practiced and cultivated. Compassion, as presented in this chapter deals with empathy in action. Self-compassion offers the same understanding and kindness that one would offer a friend in a similar situation. Caring and kindness are part of the fabric of a helping profession like education, qualities that can be suppressed when burnout or stress is activated or experienced in a chronic state.

Mindfulness, and compassion training can yield a variety of benefits to the person involved with the practice or learning. Superintendents who practice mindfulness may experience the benefit of a sense of calm, and characteristics directly related to their leadership, where empathy and compassion comprise elements of emotional intelligence that are associated with leader effectiveness (Goleman, 2000; Goleman, Boyatzis, & McKee, 2002).

Because self-compassion is the expression of kindness and caring directed inward, the resilience that is possible with this practice is one that can contribute to superintendents staying with the position, instead of leaving it, through retirement or choosing another career. Superintendents who are self-compassionate find a way to offer understanding and soothing for the problems, conflicts, challenges, and stressors that have been articulated in this chapter. Instead, of harshly criticizing or feeling isolated by what the superintendent has experienced, there is an understanding of the common humanity that all superintendents may feel, and a mindful awareness of the current situation or reality without overly ruminating or dismissing what has happened. Superintendents can learn self-compassion qualities that can interrupt the darkest days of their tenure, signaling a pause from the relentless pace and struggle, with instead, a respite that offers solace and resilience.

Self-care is associated with characteristics of mindfulness, compassion, and self-compassion. It is part of a larger vision of working to increase the affective, emotional, and humanistic elements of leadership in an intentional way, where concern and caring for the leader is extended to the people in the school district. This training could be offered to school superintendents as it is for physicians or business leaders. A leadership retreat focusing on the soft-skills of the position could generate qualities that support the technical aspects of the job. Mindfulness training programs for physicians resulted in doctors reporting a greater sense of calm as well as concern for patients (Krasner et al, 2009).

As we promote technical skill development for the leaders of our nation's schools, it is apparent that the affective dimensions of their work matters greatly for the well-being of the superintendents and the districts in which they are modeling a sense of caring and kindness. We can offer a vision of compassionate leadership for the superintendents that can serve them and the districts they serve. An evolving vision such as compassionate leadership is one that places prime importance on human agency and is one that deserves further scholarship, research, and training for aspiring and practicing superintendents.

REFERENCES

Andrews, M. C., Kacmar, K. M., & Kacmar, C. (2014). The meditational effect of regulatory focus on the relationships between mindfulness and job satisfaction and turnover intentions. *Career Development International, 19*(5), 494–507. doi:10.1108CDI-02-2014-0018

Baer, R. A. (2003). Mindfulness training as a clinical intervention: A conceptual and empirical review. *Clinical Psychology: Science and Practice, 10,* 125–143.

Barnard, L. K., & Curry, J. F., (2011). Self-compassion: Conceptualization, correlates, & interventions. *Review of General Psychology, 15*(4), 289–303. doi:10.1037/a0025754

Beisser, S. R., Peters, R. E., & Thacker, V. M. (2014). Balancing passion and priorities: An investigation of health and wellness practices of secondary school principals. *NASSP Bulletin, 98*(3), 237–255.

Biggio, G., & Cortese, Cl. G. (2013). Well-being in the workplace through interaction between individual characteristics and organizational context. *International Journal of Qualitative Studies of Health and Well-Being, 8,* 1–13.

Boyatzis, R., & McKee, A. (2005). *Resonant leadership.* Boston, MA: Harvard Business School Press.

Brown, K. W., Ryan, R. M., & Creswell, J. D. (2007). Mindfulness: Theoretical foundations and evidence for its salutary effects. *Psychological Inquiry, 18*(4), 211–237.

Budd, E. L., Schwartz, C., Yount, B. W., & Haire-Joshu, D., (2012). Factors influencing the implementation of school wellness policies in the United States, 2009. *Centers for Disease Control and Prevention: Preventing Chronic Disease, 9,* 1–9.

Carmody, J., & Baer, R. A. (2008). Relationships between mindfulness practice and levels of mindfulness, medical and psychological symptoms and well-being in a mindfulness-based stress reduction program. *Journal of Behavioral Medicine, 31,* 23–33. doi:10.1007/s10865-007-9130-7

Chaskalson, M. (2011). *The mindful workplace: Developing resilient individuals and resonant organizations with MBSR.* Oxford, England: Wiley.

Dane, E. (2011). Paying attention and its effects on task performance in the workplace. *Journal of Management, 37*(4), 997–1018. doi:10.1177/0149206310367948

Dane, E., & Brummel, B. J. (2014). Examining workplace mindfulness and its relations to job performance and turnover intention. *Human Relations, 67*(1), 105–128. doi:10.1177/0018726713487753

Davenport, B. (2015). Compassion, suffering and servant-leadership: Combining compassion and servant-leadership to respond to suffering. *Leadership, 11*(3), 300–315. doi:10.1177/1742715014532481

Davidson, R. J., Kabat-Zinn, J., Schumacher, J., Rosenkranz, M., Muller, D., Santorelli, S. F., . . . Sheridan, J. F. (2003). Alterations in brain and immune function produced by mindfulness. *Psychosomatic Medicine, 65*, 564–570.

DeLong, T. J., & DeLong, S. (2011, June). The paradox of excellence. *Harvard Business Review, 89*(6), 119–123.

Dobkin, P. L., & Zhao, Q., (2011). Increased mindfulness—The active component of the mindfulness-based stress reduction program? *Complementary Therapies in Clinical Practice, 17*, 22–27.

Dutton, J. E., & Workman, K. M. (2011). Commentary on "Why Compassion Counts": Compassion as a generative force. *Journal of Management Inquiry, 20*(4), 402–406. doi:10.1177/1056492961142107

Dyrbye, L. N., & Shanafelt, T. D. (2011). Physician burnout: A potential threat to successful health care reform. *Journal of the American Medical Association, 305*(19), 2009–2010.

Edmonson, A. (2011, April). Strategies for learning from failure. *Harvard Business Review, 89*(4), 48–55.

Flook, L., Goldberg, S. B., Pinger, L., & Davidson, R. J. (2015). Promoting prosocial behavior and self-regulatory skills in preschool children through a mindfulness-based kindness curriculum. *Developmental Psychology, 51*(1), 48–51. doi:10.1037/a0038256

Flook, L., Goldberg, S. B., Pinger, L., Bonus, K., & Davidson, R. J. (2013). Mindfulness for teachers: A pilot study to assess effects on stress, burnout, and teaching efficacy. *Mind, Brain, and Education Society, 7*(3), 182–195.

Fries, M. (2009, July). Mindfulness based stress reduction for the changing work environment. *Journal of Academic and Business Ethics, 2*, 1–10.

Frost, P. J. (2011). Why compassion counts! *Journal of Management Inquiry, 20*(4), 395–401.

Frost, P. J. (2004). Handling toxic emotions: New challenges for leaders and their organizations. *Organizational Dynamics, 33*(2), 111–127. doi:10.1016/j.orgdyn.2004.01.001

Gable, M. (2014, October). The doctor is not well. *Mindful Magazine*, 53–57.

Garland, E. L. (2007). The meaning of mindfulness: A second-order cybernetics of stress, metacognition, and coping. *Complementary Health Practice Review, 12*(1), 15–30. doi:10.1177/1533210107301740

Garner, H. C. (2009, November–December). Empathy: A true leader skill. *Military Review, 89*(6), 84–88.

Gelles, D. (2015). *Mindful work: How meditation is changing business from the inside out.* New York, NY: Houghton Mifflin.

George, B. (2012, Winter). True north groups: A big idea for developing leaders. *Leader to Leader*, 32–37.

Germer, C. K., & Neff, K. D. (2013). Self-compassion in clinical practice. *Journal of clinical psychology, 69*(8), 856–867.

Gino, F., & Pisano, G. P (2011, April). Why leaders don't learn from success. *Harvard Business Review*, 68–74.

Glass, T., & Franceschini, L. (2007). *The State of the American School Superintendency: A mid-decade study.* American Association of School Administrators. Arlington, VA: Rowman & Littlefield.

Glass, T., Bjork, L., & Brunner, C. C. (2000). *The 2000 study of the American school Superintendency: A look at the superintendent of education in the new millennium.* Arlington, VA: American Association of School Administrators.

Goleman D. (2000). *Working with emotional intelligence.* New York, NY: Bantam Books.

Goleman, D. (2013). *Focus: The hidden drive of excellence.* New York, NY: Harper Collins.

Goleman, D., & Boyatzis, R. (2008, September). Social intelligence and the biology of leadership. *Harvard Business Review*, 74–81.

Goleman, D., Boyatzis, R., & McKee, A. (2002). *Primal leadership: Realizing the power of emotional intelligence.* Boston, MA: Harvard Business School.

Good, D. J., Lyddy, C. J., Glomb, T. M., Bono, J. E., Brown, K. W., Duffy, M. K., . . . Lazar, S. W. (2016). Contemplating mindfulness at work: An integrative review. *Journal of Management, 42*(1), 114–142. doi:10.1177/0149206315617003

Greeson, J. M. (2009). Mindfulness research update: 2008. *Complementary Health Practice Review, 11*, 10–18.

Greeson, J. M., Toohey, M. J., & Pearce, M. J. (2015, May/June). An adapted, four-week mind-body skills group for medical students: Reducing stress, increasing mindfulness, and enhancing self-care. *Explore, 11*(3), 186–190. doi:10.1016/j. explore.2015.02.003

Grissom, J. A., & Andersen, S. (2012, December). Why superintendents turn over. *American Educational Research Journal, 49*(6), 1146–1180. doi:10.3102/0002831212462622

Guest, R. S., Baser, R., Li, Y., Scardino, P. T., Brown, A. E., & Kissane, D. W. (2011). Cancer surgeons' distress and well-being, I: The tension between a culture of productivity and the need for self-care. *Society of Surgical Oncology, 18*, 1229–1235. doi:10.1245/s10434-011:1622-6

Harris, S., Lowery, S., Hopson, M., & Marshall, R. (2004). 'Superintendents perceptions of motivators and inhibitors for the superintendency,' *Planning and Changing, 35*(1/2), 108–137.

Hawk, N., & Martin, B. (2011). Understanding and reducing stress in the superintendency. *Educational Management Administration and Leadership, 39*(3), 364–389. doi:10.1177/17411432039400

Heifetz, R. A., & Linsky, M. (2002). *Leadership on the line: Staying alive through the dangers of leading.* Boston, MA: Harvard Business Review Press.

Hölzel, B., Carmody, J., Vangal, M., Congleton, C., Yerramsetti, S. M., Gard, T., & Lazar, S. W. (2010). Mindfulness practice leads to increases in regional brain gray matter density. *Psychiatry Research: Neuroimaging, 191*, 36–43.

Hunter, J. (2013, April). Is mindfulness good for business? *Mindful Magazine*, 52–59.

Hyland, P., Lee, R., & Mills, M. (2015, December). Mindfulness at work: A new approach to improving individual and organizational performance. *Industrial and Organizational Psychology, 8*(4), 576–602.

Jain, S., Shapiro, S. L., Swanick, W., Roesch, S. C., Milles, P. J., Bell, I., & Swartz G. E. R. (2007). A randomized controlled trial of mindfulness meditation versus relaxation training: Effects on distress, positive states of mind, rumination, and distraction. *Annals of Behavioral Medicine, 33*(1), 11–21.

Kabat-Zinn, J. (2009). *Full catastrophe living: Using the wisdom of your body and mind to face stress, pain, and illness.* New York, NY: Bantam House.

Kabat-Zinn, J. (2005). *Coming to our senses: Healing ourselves and the world through mindfulness.* New York, NY: Hyperion.

Kabat-Zinn, J. (1994). *Wherever you go there you are: Mindfulness meditation in daily life.* New York, NY: Hyperion.

Kerrins, J. A., & Cushing, K. S. (2001, Feb.) The classic mistakes of new superintendents. *School Administrator, 58*(2), 38–41.

Kimble, P. (2013, December). The journey of discovering compassionate listening. *Journal of Holistic Nursing, 31*(4), 285–290. doi:10.1177/0898010113489376

Kneafsey, R., Brown, S., Sein, K., Chamley, C., & Parsons, J. (2015). A qualitative study of key stakeholders' perspectives on compassion in healthcare and the development of a framework for compassionate interpersonal relations. *Journal of Clinical Nursing, 25,* 70–79. doi:10.1111/jocn.12964

Krasner, M. S., Epstein, R. M., Beckman, H., Suchman, A. L., Chapman, B., Mooney, C. J., & Quill, T. E. (2009). Association of an educational program in mindful communication with burnout, empathy, and attitudes among primary care physicians. *Journal of the American Medical Association, 302*(12), 1284–1293.

Kowalski, T. J., & Brunner, C. C. (2005). The school superintendent: Roles, challenges and issues. In F. W. English (Ed.). *The SAGE Handbook of Educational Leadership: Advances in Theory, Research, and Practice* (pp.142–167). Thousand Oaks, CA: SAGE.

Kowalski, T. J., Young, P., & Petersen, G. J. (2013, Summer). Examining variability in superintendent community involvement. *AASA Journal of Scholarship & Practice, 10*(2), 3–11.

Krasner, M. S., Epstein, R. M., Beckman, H., Suchman A. L., Chapman, B., Mooney, C. J., & Quill, T. E. (2009). Association of an educational program in mindful communication with burnout, empathy, and attitudes among primary care physicians, *JAMA, Journal of American Medical Association, 302*(12), 1284–1293.

Leiter, M. P., & Maslach, C. (2004). Areas of worklife: A structured approach to organizational predictors of job burnout. In P. L. Perrewe & D. C. Ganster (Eds.), *Emotional and physiological processes and positive intervention strategies research in occupational stress and well being* (Vol. 3, pp. 91–134). Boston, MA: Emerald Group.

Lilius, J. M., Worline, M. C., Maitlis, S., Kanov, J., Dutton, J. E., & Frost, P. (2008). The contours and consequences of compassion at work. *Journal of Organizational Behavior, 29,* 193–218. doi:10.1002/job.508

Louis, K. S., Murphy, J., & Smylie, M. (2016, April). Caring leadership in schools: Findings from exploratory analyses. *Educational Administration Quarterly, 52*(2), 310–348. doi: 10.1177/001316X1562758

Madden, L. T., Duchon, D., Madden, T. M., & Plowman, D. A. (2012). Emergent organizational capacity for compassion. *Academy of Management Review, 37*(4), 689–708.

Marques, J. (2013). Understanding the strength of gentleness: Soft-skilled leadership on the rise. *Journal of Business Ethics, 116,* 163–171.

Maslach, C. (2003). Job burnout: New directions in research and intervention. *Current Directions in Psychological Science, 12*(5), 189–192.

Maslach, C., & Jackson, S. E. (1981). "The measurement of experienced burnout." *Journal of Occupational Behavior, 2,* 99–113.

Maslach, C., & Leiter, M. P. (2008). Early predictors of job burnout and engagement. *Journal of Applied Psychology, 93,* 493–512.

Maslach, C., & Leiter, M. P. (1997). *The truth about burnout: How organizations cause personal stress and what to do about it.* San Francisco, CA: Jossey-Bass.

Maulding, W. S., Peters, G. B., Roberts, J., Leonard, E., & Sparkman, L. (2012). Emotional intelligence and resilience as predictors of leadership in school administrators. *Journal of Leadership Studies, 5*(4), 20–29.

Moen, P., Lam, J., Ammons, A., & Kelly, E. L. (2013). Time work by overworked professionals: Strategies in response to the stress of higher status. *Work and Occupations, 40*(2), 79–114. doi:10.1177/0730888413481482

Murphy, L. R. (1995). Managing job stress: An employee assistance/human resource management partnership. *Personnel Review, 24*(1), 41–50.

Murphy, L. R., & Sauter, S. L. (2003, July). The USA perspective: Current issues and trends in the management of work stress. *Australian Psychologist, 38*(2), 151–157.

National Policy Board for Educational Administration. (2011). *Educational Leadership Constituent Council (ELCC) Standards.* Retrieved from http://npbea.org/wp-content/uploads/2018/01/ELCC-Building-Level-Standards-2011.pdf

Neff, K. (2004). Self-Compassion and psychological well-being. *Constructivism, in the Human Sciences, 9*(2), 27–37.

Neff, K. (2003). Self-compassion: An alternative conceptualization of a healthy attitude toward oneself. *Self and Identity, 2,* 85–101. doi:10.1080/15298860390129863

Neff, K. D., & Germer, C. K. (2012). A pilot study and randomized controlled trial of the mindful self-compassion program. *Journal of Clinical Psychology, 69*(1), 28–44. doi:10.1002/jclp. 21923

Neff, K. D., & McGehee, P. (2010). Self-compassion and psychological resilience among adolescents and young adults. *Self and Identity, 9,* 225–240.

Neff, K. D., & Pommier, E. (2012). The relationship between self-compassion and other-focused concern among college undergraduates, community adults, and practicing meditators. *Self and Identity, 12,* 160–176.

Neff, K. D., Kirkpatrick, K. L., & Rude, S. S. (2007). Self-compassion and adaptive psychological functioning. *Journal of Research in Personality, 41,* 139–154.

Newsome, S., Christopher, J. C., Dahlen, P., & Christopher, S. (2006, September). Teaching counselors self-care through mindfulness practices. *Teachers College Record, 108*(9), 1881–1900.

Niemiec, R. M., Rashid, T., & Spinella, M. (2012, July). Strong mindfulness: Integrating mindfulness and character strengths. *Journal of Mental Health Counseling, 34*(3), 240–253.

Orr, M. T. (2007). Learning advanced leadership: Findings from a leadership development programme for new superintendents. *Educational Management Administration & Leadership, 35*(3), 327–347. doi:10.1177/1741143207078178

Orr, M. T. (2006, July). Learning the Superintendency: Socialization, negotiation, and determination. *Teachers College Record, 108*(7), 1362–1403.

Pagonis, W. G. (2001, December). Leadership in a combat zone. *Harvard Business Review,* 107–116.

Quinn, J. F. (2015). The affect of vision and compassion upon role factors in physician leadership. *Frontiers in Psychology, 6*(442), 1–14. doi:10.3389/fpsyg .2015.00442

Radey, M., & Figley, C. R. (2007). The social psychology of compassion. *Clinical Social Work, 35,* 207–214. doi:10.1007/s10615-007-0087-3

Reiss, H. (2010, October). Empathy is medicine—A neurobiological perspective. *Journal of the American Medical Association, 304*(14), 1604–1605.

Richardson, K. M., & Rothstein, H. R. (2008). Effects of occupational stress management intervention program: A meta-analysis. *Journal of Occupational Health Psychology, 13*(1), 69–93.

Roeser, R. W., Schonert-Reichl, K. A., Jha, A., Cullen, M., Wallace, L., Wilensky, L., . . . Harrison, J. (2013). Mindfulness training and reductions in teacher stress and burnout: Results from two randomized, wait-list-control field trials. *Journal of Educational Psychology, 105*(3), 767–804.

Schaufeli, W. B., Leiter, M. P., Maslach, C. (2009). Burnout: 35 years of research and practice. *Career Development International, 14*(5), 204–220. doi:10.1108/ 13620430910966406

Seppala, E., Rossomando, T., & Doty, J. R. (2013). Social connection and compassion: Important predictors of health and well-being. *Social Research, 80*(2), 411–430.

Shanafelt, T. D. (2009). Enhancing meaning in work: A prescription for preventing physician burnout and promoting patient-centered care. *Journal of the American Medical Association, 302*(12), 1338–1340.

Shanafelt, T., Sloan, J., & Haberman, T. (2003).The well-being of physicians. *American Journal of Medicine, 1146*(6), 513–517.

Shannon, P. J., Simmelink-McCleary, J., Im, H., Becher, E., & Crook-Lyon, R. E. (2014). Developing self-care practices in a trauma treatment course. *Journal of Social Work Education, 50,* 440–453. doi:10.1080/10437797.2014.917932

Shapiro, S. L., Brown, K. W., & Biegel, G. M. (2007). Teaching self-care to caregivers: Effects of mindfulness-based stress reduction on the mental health of therapists in training. *Training and Education in Professional Psychology, 1*(2), 105–115. doi:10.1037/1931-3918.1.2.105

Shapiro, S. L., Schwartz, G. E., & Bonner, G. (1998). Effects of mindfulness-based stress reduction on medical and premedical students. *Journal of Behavioral Medicine, 21*(6), 581–599.

Smith, E. M., Capogrossi, K. L., & Estabrooks, P. A. (2012). School wellness policies: Effects of using standard templates. *American Journal of Preventive Medicine, 43*(3), 304–308.

Sorenson, R. D. (2007). Stress management in education: Warning signs and coping mechanisms. *Management in Education, 21*(3), 10–13.

Spickard, A., Gabbe, S. G., & Christensen, J. F. (2002). Mid-career burnout in generalist and specialist physicians. *Journal of the American Medical Association*, *288*(12), 1447–1450.

Tan, C-M., Goleman, D., & Kabat-Zinn, J. (2012). *Search inside yourself: The unexpected path to achieving success, happiness (and world peace)*. New York, NY: Harper One.

Tekniepe, R. J. (2015). Identifying the factors that contribute to involuntary departures of school superintendents in rural America. *Journal of Research in Rural Education*, *30*(1), 1–13.

Thompson, B. L., & Waltz, J. (2007). Everyday mindfulness and mindfulness meditation: Overlapping constructs or not? *Personality and Individual Differences*, *43*, 1875–1885.

Trevino, D., Braley, R. T., Brown, M. S., & Slate, J. R. (2008, Spring). Challenges of the public school superintendency: Differences by tenure and district location. *Florida Journal of Educational Administration & Policy*, *1*(2), 98–109.

Van Dierendonck, D., & Patterson, K. (2015). Compassionate love as a cornerstone of servant leadership: An integration of previous theorizing and research. *Journal of Business Ethics*, *128*, 110–131. doi:10.1007/s10551-014-2085-z

Weinzimmer, L. G., & Zimmer, J. (2013). *The wisdom of failure: How to learn the tough leadership lessons without paying the price*. San Francisco, CA: Jossey-Bass.

Wells, C. M. (2016) *Mindfulness: How school leaders can reduce stress and thrive on the job*. Lanham, MD: Rowman & Littlefield.

Wells, C. M. (2015). Conceptualizing mindful leadership: How the practice of mindfulness informs the practice of leading. *Educational Leadership Review Doctoral Research*, *21*(1), 1–23.

Wells, C. M., Maxfield, C. R., & Klocko, B. A. (2011). Complexities inherent in the workloads of principals: Implications for teacher leadership. In B. J. Alford, G. Perrerault, L. Zellner, & J. W. Ballenger (Eds.), *2011 NCPEA yearbook: Blazing trails: Preparing leaders to improve access and equity in today's schools* (pp. 29–46). Lancaster, PA: DEStech.

West, C. P., Shanafelt, T. D., & Kolars, J. C. (2011). Quality of life, burnout, educational debt, and medical knowledge among internal medicine residents. *Journal of the American Medical Association*, *306*(9), 952–960.

Wise, E. H., Hersh, M. A., & Gibson, C. M. (2012). Ethics, self-care and well-being for psychologists: Reenvisioning the stress-distress continuum. *Professional Psychology*, *43*(5), 487–494. doi:10.1037/a0029446

Yarnell, L. M., & Neff, K. D. (2012). Self-compassion, interpersonal conflict resolutions, and well-being. *Self and Identity*, *12*, 146–159. doi:10.1080/15298868.2011.649545

Zessin, U., Dickhäuser, O., Garbade, S. (2015). The relationship between self-compassion and well-being: A meta-analysis. *Applied Psychology: Health and Well-Being*, *7*(3), 360–364.

ABOUT THE EDITORS

Meredith Mountford, PhD, is an associate professor at Florida Atlantic University in the Department of Educational Leadership and Research Methodology. She is also the director of the UCEA Joint Center for Research on District Governance as well as past president of AERA's Research on the Superintendency. Dr. Mountford researches school boards, superintendents, educational policy, and gender. She has multiple publications in these areas as well as research on educational leadership preparation programs. Meredith consults with school board/superintendent teams all over the country on how to flatten team hierarchies and lessen the burden and of power and ego around superintendent/school board decision making dynamics. She spent over 15 years in school districts in Wisconsin as a teacher, principal, and ultimately, a district superintendent. She earned her PhD in 2001 at the University of Wisconsin-Madison and took her first assistant professor job at the University of Missouri-Columbia in 2001. Meredith moved to Florida Atlantic University in 2005 and is currently a tenured associate professor who teaches ethics and policy alternatives, organizational analysis, and advanced qualitative methods to PhD candidates. She has chaired over 20 dissertations; several of which have won awards at AERA or UCEA. She continues to be heavily involved in governance and leadership at FAU by serving as the faculty assembly president for the College of Education multiple times, she serves as a member of the steering committee for the university faculty senate and as a member of the UFF-FAU's grievance and bargaining committees and is past president of UFF-FAU. Her zeal to remain involved in university governance and to assume leadership positions is to continually

The Contemporary Superintendent, pages 249–250
Copyright © 2019 by Information Age Publishing
All rights of reproduction in any form reserved.

improve her leadership skills in practice in an effort to continually improve her research on leadership and governance.

Leigh E. Wallace is a clinical assistant professor and program coordinator in the Department of Administrative Leadership at the University of Wisconsin-Milwaukee. Dr. Wallace's research focuses on leadership in K–12 educational settings. A former high school English teacher and building administrator, she is particularly interested in exploring the role of the high school principal and assistant principal, with a focus on both early-stage administrators and assistant principals. Recent work is focused on district level leadership structures and questions related to equity, access, and reducing the achievement gap. Dr. Wallace also studies family–school engagement, full-service community school initiatives, and collaborative qualitative research.

Dr. Wallace's primary teaching responsibilities currently include courses related to organizational theory, school culture and climate, organizational change and team leadership, and instructional/curriculum leadership. She is also a vocal advocate of public education, professional teacher and leadership preparation, and teacher leadership and autonomy. As a former high school English teacher and associate principal she strives to connect theory and research to practice. Dr. Wallace currently serves as an elected member of her local school board.

ABOUT THE CONTRIBUTORS

Jesus "Chuey" Abrego is an associate professor at the University of Texas Rio Grande Valley (UTRGV). He has also served as an assistant principal for a recognized National Blue Ribbon urban inner-city high school and as a suburban middle school principal. His research and teaching interests focus on teacher leadership, professional development, organizational change, and schools and districts as professional learning communities—specifically, the role of the superintendent in creating, implementing, and sustaining professional learning communities. Dr. Abrego and coauthor Dr. Anita M. Pankake recently published *Lead With Me: A Principal's Guide to Teacher Leadership* (2nd ed.). The book was released the summer of 2017.

Terry Bennett is executive headteacher of the Federation of St. John's Bethnal Green and St. Paul's Whitechapel CE primary schools in the London Borough of Tower Hamlets (LBTH), one of England's most deprived communities. Appointed headteacher (Principal) of St. Paul's School in May 2001, which was deemed to have "serious weaknesses" by Ofsted, England's national inspection agency, he improved the school to being graded "outstanding." In 2012 he was asked to lead St John's School which had been classed as "inadequate" by Ofsted and improved that school so that it is now classed as "good." Last year he completed a postgraduate diploma in social science research methods at University College London's Institute of Education and is currently studying for an education doctorate at the same institution, focusing on preschool children's speech, language, and communication needs. He is a member of the LBTH Schools Forum and the Diocesan Headteachers' Consultative Council.

The Contemporary Superintendent, pages 251–260
Copyright © 2019 by Information Age Publishing

Jim Brandon is the associate dean of Professional and Community Engagement at the Werklund School of Education at the University of Calgary, Alberta, Canada. Dr. Brandon's research, workshops, and publications focus on (a) quality teaching; (b) overall instructional leadership; (c) school district leadership; and (d) supervision and evaluation of teachers, principals, and superintendents. Current teaching focuses on graduate leadership courses at the doctoral and master's levels. Jim is a past president of the College of Alberta School Superintendents (CASS) and served as its director of leadership capacity building from 2009 through 2011. Dr. Brandon served 23 years in the superintendency in two school districts, worked as a principal for 9 years, a vice-principal for four, and began his career as a secondary social studies teacher.

Kevin Brooks is a PhD candidate in education leadership and policy at the University of Colorado, Colorado Springs.

Wendi Clouse is a research scientist in the field of institutional research and evaluation at the University of Colorado, Colorado Springs. She has produced numerous publications on educational policy, educator evaluation practices in public education, leadership theory and practice, direct democracy in educational policy, and the effects of student engagement in the arena of higher education, which has been recognized by the Institute of Educational Sciences. In 2009, she was awarded a selective research fellowship from the Association for Institutional Research. Since then, she has served as a consultant on several large projects that have explored the current state of educational leadership in the rapidly changing policy environment in the State of Colorado for the Colorado Association of School Executives.

William Dallas has served as an educational leader and principal at both the elementary and secondary level in Colorado. In these roles, he has supported the growth and development of schools requiring innovation and multiyear strategic leadership plans in order to improve services provided to students. In 2016, he was recognized by the Colorado Association of Elementary School Principals as the Reba Ferguson Memorial Rookie Principal of the Year, and has served on state and local education advocacy and advisory groups supporting educational improvements and advancements within Colorado. Dr. Dallas' primary research interests include school leadership, school policy and governance, school finance, and the position of the superintendent.

Mark Deschaine is an associate professor in the Department of Educational Leadership within the College of Education and Human Services at Central Michigan University. He has extensive local, state, and national experience in the training and development of P-20 faculty. Dr. Deschaine received his PhD in educational leadership from Western Michigan University, his MEd in educational leadership from Grand Valley State University, his MAT in education from Oakland University, and his BS in education from Central Michigan University. Dr. Deschaine holds Michigan certification and endorsements in both general and special education. He is credentialed to serve as a teacher, consultant, supervisor, principal, and central office administrator. He is a member of the graduate faculty at Central Michigan University and teaches students at the master, specialist and doctoral levels. Dr. Deschaine's research agenda focuses on the ways that theory, policy, and processes support and impact effective differentiated programs and instruction.

J. K. Donlevy is an associate professor and former associate dean (interim) of the Graduate Division of Educational Research in the Faculty of Education (as it then was) at the University of Calgary. He is the chair of the research ethics appeal board and the grievance advisor for the faculty association at that university. He teaches ethics and law.

Denver J. Fowler is currently the EdD Program Chair and and Professor of PK–12 Leadership at Franklin University in Columbus, OH. A strong supporter of education and policy reform, Dr. Fowler has spoken on Capitol Hill in order to advocate for educators and school leaders nationwide. Dr. Fowler is the author of numerous publications on educational leadership and he has presented his research or served as a keynote speaker both nationally and internationally, including presentations in China, Italy, Greece, Cuba, Africa, and Puerto Rico. His research interests include ethics, leadership, educational leadership, and research on the superintendency and principalship.

Ray Francis is a tenured professor, and member of the graduate faculty, in the Department of Teacher Education and Professional Development (TEPD) at Central Michigan University (CMU). Dr. Francis currently teaches courses in evaluation and measurement, research methods, and research capstone seminars at the MA level. In addition, Dr. Francis teaches doctoral level courses in the doctorate in educational technology (DET) program. His current research interests include aspects of student motivation in blended and online learning, concept mapping, prior learning assessment, assessment, and global experiences in teacher preparation. He is an ongoing advocate of prior learning assessment process in higher education. In addition, Dr. Francis has served as a lead auditor with the National Council for Accreditation of Teacher Education (NCATE), the Teacher Education Accreditation Council (TEAC), the Council for Accreditation of Educator Preparation, and is a member of the Peer Review Corps of the Higher Learning Commission.

Sharon Friesen is the vice dean of the Werklund School of Education at the University of Calgary. She is also the president of the Galileo Educational Network. Her research interests include the ways in which K–12 educational structures, curriculum, and learning need to be reinvented for a knowledge/learning society. She draws upon the learning sciences to study: (a) the promotion of deep intellectual engagement; (b) learning environments that promote innovative pedagogies requiring sustained work with powerful ideas; (c) the pervasiveness of networked digital technologies that open up new ways of knowing, leading, teaching, working, and living in the world; and (d) the ways in which leadership practices and orientations need to change for a learning society. She has coauthored four books. Sharon has received numerous awards for her research and teaching practice.

J. R. Falor Green is superintendent of the Fairfield County School District in Winnsboro, SC and was recently appointed to the state board of education for a 4-year term by the Fairfield, Chester, and Lancaster State Legislative Delegation. This 17-member Board is responsible for regulating the state's public school system. Dr. Green's experience spans successful tenures as an assistant superintendent for curriculum and instruction at the Chesterfield County School District, as well as serving as a high school principal, assistant high school principal, and teacher with various districts in the state of South Carolina. As an innovator in the field of education, he is responsible for initiating bow tie clubs across the state and effectively continues to develop school-community alliances.

Patricia Green is a university supervisor and lecturer for preservice teachers in the Teacher Education Licensing Program at the University of Colorado, Colorado Springs. Dr. Green also serves as an adjunct professor at Argosy University. She has served in public school K–12 education for over 30 years. Her interests include teacher education, student achievement, culturally relevant pedagogy, and race dialogue.

Paulette Hanna is vice-president academic at Red Deer College. Dr. Hanna's experience includes 14 years in the superintendency, a former CASS president, and director of leadership learning for CASS. The focus of her doctoral studies was instructional leadership.

Judy Halbert and Linda Kaser lead the Transformative Educational Leadership Program at the University of British Columbia (telp.educ.ubc.ca); the Networks of Inquiry and Innovation (noii.ca); and the Aboriginal Enhancement Schools Network (noii.ca/aesn). They are deeply committed to achieving equity and quality for all learners—and to networking for innovation and improvement across systems. To that end, they served as Canadian representatives to the OECD international research program on innovative learning environments. They are pleased to support inquiry networks in British Columbia, the Yukon, England, Catalonia, Sweden, New South Wales, and Queensland. Linda and Judy have served as principals, district leaders, and policy advisors with British Columbia's Ministry of Education. They are the coauthors of *The Spiral Playbook* (2017), *System Transformation for Equity and Quality* (2016), *Spirals of Inquiry* (2013), *Leadership Mindsets: Innovation and Learning in the Transformation of Schools* (2009), and with Helen Timperley, *A Framework for Transforming Learning in Schools: Innovation and the Spiral of Inquiry* (2014).

Aimee Howley, professor emerita, Ohio University, studies social justice issues from a variety of perspectives within the field of education: inclusive practice, rural schools and communities, school leadership, educational policy, and gifted education. Currently, as president of WordFarmers Associates, she provides evaluation services to several sponsored projects in Ohio and other states. Her most recent collaborative book projects include *Dynamics of Social Class: Race, and Place in Rural Education* (2014), *Out of Our Minds: Turning the Tide of Anti-Intellectualism in American Schools,* (2nd ed.) (2018), and *Inclusive Education: A Systematic Perspective* (In press).

Michele Jacobsen is the associate dean, graduate programs in the Werklund School of Education, University of Calgary. As associate dean, Michele provides academic leadership for research and professional graduate programs in educational research and educational psychology. As a professor in the learning sciences and educational technology, Michele studies technology-enabled learning and teaching in classrooms and post-secondary education using case study and design-based research methodologies. Michele examines designs for learning that shift instruction from standardized delivery and testing to participatory pedagogies in technology enabled learning environments that sponsor knowledge building, intellectual engagement, and assessment for learning.

Rhonda Baynes Jeffries is program coordinator and associate professor for the Curriculum Studies Program at the University of South Carolina. Dr. Jeffries teaches curriculum and diversity in education, staff development, and qualitative research methods. Her research explores school desegregation and *de-tracking*, equity pedagogies, and performance theory in education. She is editor of "Diversity, Equity, and Inclusivity" in *Contemporary Higher Education* (IGI Global, In Press), editor of *Queen Mothers: Articulating the Spirit of Black Women Teacher-Leaders* (Information Age Publishing, forthcoming), senior co-editor of the *National Network for Educational Renewal*

(NNER) *Journal, Education in a Democracy,* and has published over 50 scholarly articles and chapters in her capacity of study.

Jaime Lopez is a native of south Texas. He is married to Jessica (bilingual elementary teacher) and has three loving children; Jaime (18), Alicia (13), and little Antonio (6). His hobbies include; fishing at South Padre Island, hunting, barbecuing, and going to the movies. Currently, Jaime is a lecturer with bilingual and literacy studies at the University of Texas Rio Grande Valley. He earned a doctorate in curriculum and instruction with an emphasis in educational leadership from the University of Texas at Brownsville. He also has a master's in reading and bachelor's in interdisciplinary studies with a minor in bilingual education. His research interests include professional learning communities (PLCs), change in education, teacher leadership, and teacher preparation. He has presented at national conferences. He has 12 years of public school administrative experience, which includes central office and the principalship at the elementary, middle, and high school levels along the Texas-Mexico border.

Catherine McGregor is associate professor in leadership studies and associate dean in the faculty of education at the University of Victoria, BC, Canada. She is particularly interested in investigating the role leaders can play in schools and communities that enable socially just and transformational change. She has held several research grants investigating initial teacher education in nonschool settings, and is an experienced program evaluator; assessing and documenting the effectiveness of professional learning programs in various settings. She is currently the lead researcher investigating how inquiry enables success for Aboriginal students as well as how professional inquiry enhances teacher learning and accelerates innovation in 15 diverse school authorities in the province of BC, the subject of the book chapter in this collection.

Meredith Mountford is an associate professor at Florida Atlantic University in the Department of Educational Leadership and Research Methodology. She is also the director of the UCEA Joint Center for Research on District Governance as well as past president of AERA's Research on the Superintendency. Dr. Mountford researches school boards, superintendents, educational policy, and gender. She has multiple publications in these areas as well as research on educational leadership preparation programs. Meredith consults with school board/superintendent teams all over the country on how to flatten team hierarchies and lessen the burden and of power and ego around superintendent/school board decision making dynamics. She spent over 15 years in school districts in Wisconsin as a teacher, principal, and ultimately, a district superintendent. She earned her PhD in 2001 at the University of Wisconsin-Madison and took her first assistant professor job at the University of Missouri-Columbia in 2001. Meredith moved to Florida Atlantic University in 2005 and is currently a tenured associate professor who teaches ethics and policy alternatives, organizational analysis, and advanced qualitative methods to PhD candidates. She has chaired over 20 dissertations; several of which have won awards at AERA or UCEA. She continues to be heavily involved in governance and leadership at FAU by serving as the Faculty Assembly President for the College of Education multiple times, she serves as a member of the steering committee for the University Faculty Senate and as a member of the UFF-FAU's grievance and bargaining committees and is past president of UFF-FAU. Her zeal to remain involved in university governance and to assume leadership positions is to continually improve her leadership skills in practice in an effort to continually improve her research on leadership and governance.

Dennis G. Parsons is currently an assistant professor and academic program coordinator, instructional leadership for graduate programs in education (GPE) at the Werklund School of Education, University of Calgary, Alberta, Canada. Dr. Parsons's research, publications, and presentations revolve around the life world of the superintendent of schools/CEO. Specifically, his focus involves elements inclusive of systems leadership, policy and school board governance, school district leadership, instructional leadership, and the supervision and evaluation of teachers, principals and superintendents. Current teaching involves courses at the undergraduate and graduate level that help prepare and strengthen teachers and educational leaders. Dennis has worked extensively in the K–12 education system as a teacher, principal and 20 years in the superintendency, of which 18 were in the position of superintendent/CEO for different school boards across Canada. Dennis is driven by the need to make a positive difference for others.

Robin Precey began working in higher education in 2004 having previously taught in secondary schools for 32 years including 13 years as a headteacher. He was a senior consultant with the National College for School Leadership. He is interested in the development of leaders for now and the future. He has written extensively on the challenges of leadership and how leaders may be developed for the C21. He has developed a keen interest in international collaboration based on Masters' programmes and international study visits for leaders and has been part of a team developing an international school self-evaluation online tool. At CCCU he founded a MBA in education and teaches on the Masters Teach First (similar to Teach for America) transformational leadership program as well as being the pathway leader for the doctorate in leadership. He is chair of two charities—Human Scale Education and Mindful Music and of a Federation of Primary Schools in Tower Hamlets.

Barbara Qualls is the coordinator of the MEd—leadership/advanced certification programs at Stephen F. Austin State University in Nacogdoches, Texas. The combined principal and superintendent programs at SFA have an enrollment of approximately 400 students. She has served as superintendent in three widely differing school districts, as well as high school principal, junior high school principal, curriculum director, and band director. Her scholarship activity and teaching concentration are in school law, with emphasis on discrimination and first amendment issues. She is a frequent contributor to the *Education Law Reporter,* reviewing higher education and K–12 cases from federal decisions. A frequent speaker at national school leadership and school law/governance conferences, Dr. Qualls brings both scholarship and firsthand experience to her presentations. Recent research activity includes the nature of ethics, legal literacy and "free speech" in the era of Trump.

Patrick Radigan is a visiting assistant professor of management at the Malik and Seeme Hasan School of Business at Colorado State University in Pueblo, Colorado. He researches job quality in multiple industries and teaches courses in organizational behavior. He obtained his BA and MBA from the University of Colorado at Colorado Springs and is currently pursuing a PhD in educational leadership, research, and policy.

Al Ramirez is an education policy and finance consultant and is professor emeritus in the Department of Leadership, Research, and Foundations at the University of Colorado, Colorado Springs. His transition to university level teaching follows an extensive career in PK–14 education. Al's experience includes positions as a teacher, counselor, principal, central office administrator and superintendent of schools. He has also held key education policy positions in the Nevada and Illinois state departments of education and served as chief state school officer in Iowa. His book, *Financing schools and educational programs: Policy, politics, and practice,* is published by Rowman and Littlefield. Dr. Ramirez has also served appointments to several national education advisory boards and commissions. Al's consulting work is international in scope and has a client list that includes corporations, foundations, governments, school reform organizations, and education entities.

Dallas Strawn has served in the public school system for 43 years, serving as a high school educator, alternative school director, assistant high school principal, high school principal, curriculum director, assistant superintendent, and superintendent. Additionally, he has been an assistant professor at Murray State University, an adjunct faculty member at University of Colorado Colorado Springs, Regis, University of Northern Colorado, University of Northern Colorado, University of Denver, and Point Loma Nazarene University. Dallas has worked as a consultant in the area of stress management and has presented and consulted on various topics in school districts throughout Colorado. He is currently the president and founder of "Educational Leadership Search Associates, Inc." which assists school districts who need assistance in finding and hiring the "right" superintendent for district leadership.

Deborah M. Telfer is director and research associate with the University of Cincinnati College of Education, Criminal Justice, and Human Services (UC CECH) where she oversees the Columbus-based UC Systems Development & Improvement Center and serves as director of a number of state and federally funded projects, including the Ohio Deans Compact and the National Center on Educational Outcomes (NCEO) technical assistance and dissemination initiative Moving Your Numbers. Prior to joining higher education—first at the University of Dayton beginning in 2011 and later at UC—she served as executive director of the Ohio Department of Education's (ODE) Center for School Improvement where she was responsible for the development and growth of Ohio's statewide system of support, including development of the Ohio Improvement Process and the Ohio Leadership Advisory Council leadership development framework and, before that, as associate and interim director of ODE's Office for Exceptional Children.

Martha Thurlow is director of the National Center on Educational Outcomes and senior research associate at the University of Minnesota. During her career, Dr. Thurlow's work has emphasized the need to ensure accessible curricula and assessments for students with disabilities, English learners, and English learners with disabilities, with the ultimate goal being to enable these students to leave school ready for success in college or a career. She has worked toward this end by addressing the implications of U.S. education policy for these students, striving to improve inclusion and access to appropriate assessments for all students, and collaborating with others on standards-based educational systems and inclusion for these students. Dr. Thurlow has a long history of contributing to the professional literature through peer reviewed journal articles and chapters, as well as through numerous publicly available reports.

Leigh Ellen Wallace is a clinical assistant professor and program coordinator in the Department of Administrative Leadership at the University of Wisconsin-Milwaukee. Dr. Wallace's research focuses on leadership in K–12 educational settings. A former high school English teacher and building administrator, she is particularly interested in exploring the role of the high school principal and assistant principal, with a focus on both early-stage administrators and assistant principals. Recent work is focused on district level leadership structures and questions related to equity, access, and reducing the achievement gap. Dr. Wallace also studies family–school engagement, full-service community school initiatives, and collaborative qualitative research. Dr. Wallace's primary teaching responsibilities currently include courses related to organizational theory, school culture and climate, organizational change and team leadership, and instructional/curriculum leadership. She is also a vocal advocate of public education, professional teacher and leadership preparation, and teacher leadership and autonomy. As a former high school English teacher and associate principal she strives to connect theory and research to practice. Dr. Wallace currently serves as an elected member of her local school board.

Caryn M. Wells is an associate professor in the Department of Organizational Leadership at Oakland University in Rochester, MI. Her research interests include mindfulness, stress reduction and resilience for educational leaders, and mindful and compassionate leadership. She teaches mindfulness practice to graduate and doctoral students and has taught introductions of mindfulness to medical students. She is the author of *Mindfulness: How school leaders can reduce stress and thrive on the job.*

CPSIA information can be obtained
at www.ICGtesting.com
Printed in the USA
BVHW040557040120
568494BV00005B/16/P

9 781641 135245